POSITIVELY FALSE
FLOYD LANDIS
WITH LOREN MOONEY

THE REAL STORY OF HOW I WON
THE TOUR DE FRANCE

SIMON SPOTLIGHT ENTERTAINMENT
New York London Toronto Sydney

NOTE TO READERS

This book is a memoir. It reflects my present recollections of my experiences over a period of years, as well as information from interviews and other research performed by Loren Mooney. Conversations and events have been recounted to evoke one or more participants' recollections of what was said or what occurred, but are not intended to be a perfect representation.

SIMON SPOTLIGHT ENTERTAINMENT
An imprint of Simon & Schuster
1230 Avenue of the Americas, New York, New York 10020
Copyright © 2007 by Floyd Landis

SIMON SPOTLIGHT ENTERTAINMENT and related logo are trademarks of Simon & Schuster, Inc.
Designed by Ann Zeak
Manufactured in the United States of America
First Edition 10 9 8 7 6 5 4 3 2 1
Library of Congress Cataloging-in-Publication Data
Landis, Floyd.
Positively false : the real story of how I won the Tour de France / by Floyd Landis with Loren Mooney. — 1st ed.
p. cm.
ISBN-13: 978-1-4169-5023-3 (alk. paper)
ISBN-10: 1-4169-5023-0 (alk. paper)
1. Tour de France (Bicycle race) (2006). 2. Landis, Floyd. 3. Cyclists—United States. 4. Cyclists—Drug use. I. Mooney, Loren. II. Title.
GV1049.2.T68L356 2007
796.6'2092—dc22
[B]
2007014777

CONTENTS

I dedicate this book, first and foremost, to my family:

To my wife, Amber, whose patience makes up for my lack thereof.

To my daughter, Ryan, who has taught me
what it means to be a father.

To my mother and father, Arlene and Paul Landis,
who gave me life, love, and discipline,
and taught me how important each is.

And to the memory of David Witt. We will always miss you.

ACKNOWLEDGMENTS

I'd like to acknowledge the following people for their hard work in making this book happen.

All the fine people at the William Morris Agency and Simon Spotlight Entertainment, including Mel Berger, Tricia Boczkowski, Jennifer Robinson, and Katherine Devendorf.

Amber Landis, Loren Mooney, Will Geoghegan, Brent Kay, Arnie Baker, Maurice Suh, Howard Jacobs, Paul Scott, Brian Rafferty, and Michael Henson.

I'd also especially like to thank all the cyclists out there who share the same passion for riding that I have. It is a beautiful sport filled with inspiring stories. I hope you enjoyed mine.

PROLOGUE

To accomplish much
you must first lose everything.
—Che Guevara

My fuse is short and it's lit.
—Kid Rock

"I'm going to attack today," I told Dave Zabriskie. "At the base of the first climb. Don't know if you heard."

We were standing over our bikes in the tiny Alpine village of Saint-Jean-de-Maurienne before the seventeenth stage of the 2006 Tour de France. Thousands of fans pressed against the metal barricades that kept them off the narrow streets and gave the 143 riders still in the race room to sign in, grab a final energy bar, and prepare for another day in hell.

Before noon, the temperature was already near 90 degrees Fahrenheit, and we had 125 miles to cover, with five major mountain climbs before a final descent into the town of

Morzine. Onlookers were already using copies of *L'Equipe*, a French sports newspaper, to fan themselves. There was my picture on the paper, with the headline *"Landis a Craqué"*— "Landis Cracks." I could feel the people looking at me, pitying me after my performance the day before.

I had blown my chance of winning the Tour. It was humiliating. In Stage 16, I had been in the leader's yellow jersey, worn by the rider with the shortest cumulative time, but early on the last mountain climb of the day I had nothing left. My legs were just empty, and the other contenders sensed my weakness and attacked as hard as they could. It was like I was pedaling backward. I went from leading the race to ranking eleventh overall.

There were only four stages left until we reached the finish in Paris—and only the seventeenth offered me much chance of making up time. The best time to attack is when the terrain is hardest, and only the strongest riders can go. Still, a rider having the best day of his career can only make up maybe three minutes on a rival in a mountain stage. I was more than eight minutes behind.

To the riders, the team directors, the media—to everyone, really—making up an eight-minute gap was unthinkable. It had never been done. It was a joke.

"Oh, man, that's gonna hurt," Zabriskie said with a nervous laugh. "Do you think it will work?"

I told him I had no idea, but at that point I didn't really care. I wasn't going to just give up. Winning the Tour had been my dream for more than ten years, and I had worked hard for it. I was going to try the only thing that would still give me a chance: Attacking early. "I don't want to get eleventh," I told him. "I want to win. And if I don't, I don't care if I end up eightieth."

Zabriskie just laughed. He was on team CSC, and he had been one of my best friends since we raced together on the U.S. Postal Service team with Lance Armstrong four years before. In a way, he was right to laugh. Chances were good that I'd end up getting caught by the peloton, as the main pack of riders is known, well before the stage ended. If I were a betting man, I wouldn't have bet on myself. A group of cyclists is far more efficient than one—those in the draft have to churn out only 50 to 60 percent of the power of those at the front of the pack breaking the wind. It was almost certain that I'd shoot off from the front of the pack, ride alone for a while, and then be swallowed up as the group sped to chase me. I'd look like an idiot for even trying.

Fortunately, I've never let the possibility of looking like an idiot keep me from trying anything in life. By my way of thinking, I'd either be spectacular or fail spectacularly— either way I'd make my mark on the 2006 Tour de France.

Word spreads fast in the peloton. As we rolled out of town to cheers of the crowd and reached the open road, all the riders knew exactly what my tactic was going to be. During the first few miles, as we all warmed up, I pedaled around to anyone I could find and started trash talking like it was a joke. They already thought my plan wasn't going to work, but I figured it would be even better if they thought I wasn't taking it that seriously.

"First climb, I'm going," I said to George Hincapie, another old friend from my days on Lance's team. "As hard as I can."

George shook his head. "Aw man, come on," he said. "Please don't do it." George knew that when I went, his day would become miserable. We had already ridden more than 1,700 miles around France in just over two weeks, with the last two days in the Alps covering more than 100 miles per day and taking us up some of the tallest, steepest mountain roads in the country. Many riders were so tired that they weren't sure they were going to make it to Paris—thirty-three had dropped out of the race already. If I attacked early, instead of just another painful day in the mountains, the peloton would have to chase me for five brutal hours.

George's teammate José Azevedo, a Portuguese climbing specialist who had been my roommate on Lance's team in 2004, tried to talk me out of it. "Look, why don't you just wait until the last climb?" That was what riders typically did when they launched an attack. He said that if I attacked on the last climb of the day, on the legendary Joux Plane, a seven-mile climb so steep that in the mountain difficulty rating system of five categories, race organizers ranked it in the hardest, *hors categorie*, or beyond classification, I'd win the stage.

"Nah," I said in a joking way, "that's not good enough."

Thirty miles in, when the road began to turn upward on the slopes of the Col des Saisies, all eight of my Phonak teammates were at the front of the peloton, ready to attack. I gave the signal, and every one of them lined up in front of me, each taking a turn pulling the rest of us through.

First Miguel Ángel Perdiguero set a ridiculously high tempo, and then Alex Moos, Bert Grabsch, Nicolas Jalabert, and Axel Merckx followed, one after another. The peloton was chaos. Teams didn't have time to mobilize against us. Robbie Hunter took over at absolutely full speed, then Koos Moerenhout, and finally Victor Hugo Peña. I glanced back and saw that the peloton was shattered. Riders were popping off the back of the group. One by one, my guys pulled out of line and faded back, having given everything they had. They had done their job, launching me like a big booster rocket.

The rest was up to me. I took another long look behind me to see if anyone from another team was strong enough to come with me. Oscar Pereiro, who was in the yellow jersey, was already fifteen seconds back and fading fast. There were only four of us left, including Andreas Klöden of T-Mobile, sitting in third place overall, with a good chance to catch Pereiro. "If you want to win the Tour, come with me now," I told him. "We can work together."

Deal making is a classic cycling strategy. I knew we stood a better chance of staying away from the others if we were together than if I went solo. But Klöden said no way, it was too far, it would never work. So I stood out of the saddle and sprinted. That was it. I was alone.

By the time I reached the top, I was three minutes ahead of Pereiro. Soon after I started the downhill, my team director, John Lelangue, drove the Phonak team car past the straggling chasers and pulled in behind me. "Good, Floyd. Come on, Floyd," I heard John say into the earpiece of my two-way radio. "Keep going, keep going." I sped down the hill at more than 50 miles per hour.

As I pushed hard up the next climb, Bruce Springsteen's "Badlands" started playing over and over in my head: *I don't give a damn for the same old played out scene, I don't give a damn for just the in betweens.*

John kept giving me updates on my lead. By the start of the third climb of the day, the Col de la Colombiere, he said, "Six minutes. Six minutes. Go. Go. Go." And by the top, "Seven forty-five! Go, Floyd. Come on, Floyd." I was actually climbing faster than the chasers. At the bottom of the descent, John said, "Eight forty-five! Eight forty-five, Floyd!" I could hear in his voice that he almost couldn't believe it. At one point, my lead was nine minutes, which even I thought was absurd. They should have been chasing harder, I thought, but everyone was too tired and disorganized. Or maybe they still thought I couldn't do it.

I knew I could do it. My breakaway wasn't so different from how I train at home in the mountains north of San Diego. I ride hard, alone, all day long. The key today was to stay focused, and to be sure that I wasn't going too hard too early.

Pro racers train with power meters on their bikes, little gauges that measure in watts how much force you're putting into the pedals. I'm one of the few riders who uses my power meter in races, so I kept an eye on my watts to pace myself, and dumped water over my head to stay cool.

The temperature reached 104 degrees Fahrenheit in the valleys, and 95 at the summits of the climbs. John drove up the team car next to me, and he and the team mechanic reached out the windows to hand me bottle after bottle of ice-cold water straight from the cooler. I realized early on that when I dumped a bottle of water on my head, my legs would churn out the same watts, but I felt much better.

When you're stuck in the peloton, the team car has to ride far behind and it's hard to take more than ten or fifteen bottles during a stage. But because my lead was so big, the Phonak car was able to follow right behind me. In all, I used eighty-two bottles, only about fifteen of them for drinking. The rest went straight over my head.

In the long valley stretch before the Joux Plane, I leaned forward to put my elbows on my handlebar to mimic the aerodynamic position I use on my time trial bike. I was trying to squeeze every bit of speed I could out of my body. But I didn't have much left.

It's not just that my legs hurt or that my lungs seared with the effort. Those are givens. But when you push your body past a certain point, you enter a whole different area of pain when you can barely will yourself to go on, and it feels like the more you think about it, the less you even care about pushing.

When I got to the base of the Joux Plane, John said, "Six thirty-five, Floyd. Come on. Come on." They were catching me, but that was the last bit of information I heard. I had dumped so much water on myself over the course of the day that my radio shorted out.

I didn't care. It was the last climb, and no matter what the time gaps were, or what anyone might have said in my ear, it was time to spend everything I had left. Thousands of spectators lined the road on the climb, waving flags, screaming, and leaning in close, only to move away at the last second so I could ride through the tunnel of noise.

I got over the top, and then instead of cheering, all I could hear was the wind as I rode downhill. At that point, I knew no one was going to catch me unless I crashed. The backside of the Joux Plane is deceiving, though, with lots of turns that all look exactly the same. You can go full speed through most of them, but there are a couple that suddenly become U-turns, and you only realize once it's too late. I was just careful enough to stay upright.

As I sped in to Morzine, on some level even I didn't believe what I was doing. A few seconds from the finish I looked behind me, just to be sure I wouldn't get passed in the last second. When I saw with my own eyes that I was still all alone, it started to hit me.

I pumped my fist as I crossed the finish line. *I did it.*

After I got off my bike, I went behind the podium to check the time gap. My wife, Amber, was there. "Oh, baby, can you believe it!" she said as she gave me a big hug.

"It's not over yet," I said. I watched the others come in. Finally, seven minutes and eight seconds after I finished, Pereiro crossed the line in his yellow jersey. Not only did I win the stage, but now I was also close enough to him that three days later I would go on to win the whole Tour.

Eddy Merckx, my teammate Axel's dad, who is the most successful cyclist of all time, walked up to me behind the podium, shook my hand, and said, "Only the big champions do it like that."

I had proven everyone wrong. I stood on the podium with my baseball cap on backward and my sunglasses on my forehead. I stuck both fists into the air and smiled as the crowd screamed.

If things had ended then, my story would be just another part of cycling legend, just another amazing sports feat that people doubted could be done.

But after the podium ceremony, I went to the small trailer used for drug testing. It was the fifth sample I had given during the Tour, just another one of the more than sixty I had given in my career. I dropped my shorts and peed into the cup while the two officials watched me, as usual, and I didn't give it a second thought.

Now it's all I think about.

CHAPTER 1

Breaking Away

I have nothing to hide.

As far as I'm concerned, people can know everything about me if they want: how much money I've made, when I've been a fool or felt regret or shed tears. I don't care. There's no reason to hold anything back. I don't feel the need to be selective in order to create some image of a person who isn't me. I'm me. That's it.

I ended up making a living in a sport where a bunch of men wear spandex and shave their legs—and that's not even the funny part. The funny part is that cycling and its anti-doping program are run by people so incompetent they couldn't even run a Ralphs grocery store. I couldn't always laugh about it, because they wrecked my life. But I don't ask for sympathy. I take what I'm given in life and try to make some good out of it, always.

In the end, cycling is a beautiful sport, and it deserves better. It rewards focus, strength, and endurance, and also requires negotiation, teamwork, and a strategic mind. You have to be the best at all those things in order to win the Tour de France, and it's a long journey. Maybe the things I've done or the way I've done them will inspire disbelief, and people will think I lied or made things up. If that's the case, then the only thing I can say is, at least they got to hear the whole story.

It starts in Farmersville, Pennsylvania, in Lancaster County, the heart of Mennonite and Amish country. My family is Mennonite, a branch of the Anabaptist Protestant religion that bases its beliefs on a more literal interpretation of the Bible and encourages nonparticipation in mainstream society. It's related to Amish. Basically, the Amish split from the Mennonites centuries ago to become a more inflexible, conservative sect. The Mennonites embrace modern culture more, but not much more.

We lived on Farmersville Road, where my parents, Paul and Arlene, moved to when they got married thirty-five years ago. The road stretches for miles of white farmhouses, red barns, cornfields, and silos, with no variation except maybe when the farmhouse is red and the barn is white.

My parents' house has three bedrooms, one for them and two for the kids. First, my sister Alice filled one of the bedrooms, and then I came along and took over the other.

Over the next fifteen years, my parents added Bob, Charity, Priscilla, and Abigail. Until I was nineteen, Bob and I slept in a double bed in one room, and the girls stayed in the other in bunk beds and a double bed.

Some Mennonites are what you'd call "horse-and-buggy," but my parents are more progressive than that. We had cars, but there was no television or video games, no movies, and definitely no alcohol or swearing. We had a radio, but it stayed tuned to a gospel station, and we also played gospel records and sang along. Men wore long pants all the time, and women wore dresses or long pants and kept their hair in buns and wore head coverings— that's still how it is at my parents' house.

The Mennonite life is simple: Glory goes to God, not to the self. You go to church, you work, and you take care of the people around you. Everyone contributed to the household however they could, with work or chores, but growing up we never had any money. None of the Mennonites did. It was easy to spot a Mennonite kid at the public high school where I went, because we were the quiet ones in whatever plain clothes our parents could find for cheap—completely outside of the world of teenage fashion.

We went to church twice on Sundays and sometimes on Wednesdays, and on top of that there were prayer meetings, Bible school, and seminars with intensive Scripture study.

To support our family, Dad owned a self-serve carwash/laundry down the road. It never really made much money because almost everyone owned a washer-dryer, and if people weren't going to wash their own cars, they went to an automatic carwash. The equipment at the laundry was old, so I spent a lot of time figuring out how washing machines worked and fixing them.

For a while he made money as a real-estate agent and did other odd jobs. When my uncle was diagnosed with a brain tumor, my dad started driving my uncle's delivery truck part-time to help out, hauling stone to concrete and blacktop plants in Delaware and New Jersey. When my uncle died, Dad kept driving for two years to support my aunt. Then he bought the truck.

My mom stayed home to raise the kids. Every afternoon she practically danced around the kitchen as she made home-cooked dinner with fresh, homemade bread, and if I sat at the big family dining table while she was working, she'd talk to me in a way that sounded almost like a song. My dad always spoke so softly that sometimes you had to lean in to hear him, and he chose every word carefully. I can say with 100-percent certainty that they are the most wonderful parents I could possibly have.

Everything we had was old, so we spent a lot of time making repairs. We had crappy cars that my dad taught me how to work on, even in the middle of winter when my fingers were freezing off. I painted the house and barn, and pruned trees. We had a septic tank that would fill every few months. It had wooden boards on top and we'd have to stick shovels in through the liquid to shovel out the solid parts at the bottom, and by the time we were done my sneakers would be soaked. Dad wouldn't pay anyone to come pump it out, because he never liked to pay money for anything.

When it was time to have fun, I spent a lot of time with my cousins and my best friend, Eric Gebhard. Eric wasn't Mennonite, but his family was conservative Christian. His parents were divorced, and he lived with his father, so my mom pretty much adopted him and he was at our house all the time.

We went fishing or swimming or swinging off the rope swing in the river down the road. Some of my cousins had an aboveground pool that they stocked with catfish, and we'd fish in the pool, which I'm pretty sure means we were rednecks. If there's any doubt, my family had an aluminum fishing boat we'd take to the river, and Bob, Dad, and I sometimes hunted squirrels from the boat, and that night Mom would make squirrel pie, which doesn't taste very good.

For family vacations, we always went camping, because it was cheap. We'd load up the family van, hitch up the aluminum fishing boat, and pile everyone's bikes into the boat to haul them to the campground.

Everyone in the Mennonite community had bicycles. I once saw a guy riding with a shotgun perched across the handlebar and a rack in back that held the deer he'd just shot. On Sundays the roads were cluttered with Amish horses and buggies and Mennonites on bikes riding to church. Even today, my parents often ride their bikes to church, six miles each way.

My mom taught me how to ride just like she did all my

siblings, at the top of the rise in the driveway. I learned on Alice's yellow girl's bike, which Dad had picked out of someone's trash. Mom cheered me on while Alice ran in front of me. "Follow Alice, Floyd," she said. "Look where you're going. Don't look around. When you look around is when you wobble." It didn't take me long to figure it out.

Green Mountain Cyclery was a tiny bike shop in a yellow two-story house a few miles away owned by a couple, Jen and Mike Farrington. In the spring when I was fourteen, my dad drove me there to look at bikes. I walked right to the one I wanted. It was neon green and orange, a Marin Muirwoods fully rigid steel mountain bike. It was last year's model, on sale for three hundred dollars.

"Floyd, I'm not paying that much money for a bicycle," my dad said. If he had his way, I'd keep riding my fifty-dollar Huffy from Kmart and be happy with it. But I wanted something that would last through the beating I was going to give it. Plus, even at three hundred dollars, it wasn't anywhere near the top of the line. But we didn't buy it. We went home.

A few days later, I went to my dad to talk about the bicycle. He said I'd have to pay for it myself, and besides that, he didn't think I needed it. "You already have a nice bike," he said. "But you make that decision yourself, you're old enough to do it."

I went back to him after a few more days and told him I wanted to put a deposit on it. "I'd rather you didn't," Dad said. "But it's up to you." This was my dad's way. We never argued or even had disagreements. He never told me no. It was clear that if I was going to buy it, I'd be going against his wishes, but he believed it was important for me to think through things in life and make my own decisions. I went back to him once more, and he gave me the same answer. "I'd rather you didn't, but it's up to you."

I thought about it for another week, and then I put a deposit on the bike.

Eric and I rode everywhere, and spent entire afternoons practicing wheelies. I could ride a wheelie around the block, which was three miles. We'd find all sorts of stuff to jump off of. Our bikes broke so often that we'd bring a rope on every ride, so we could tow each other home if we had to. When we couldn't fix the bikes ourselves, we went to Green Mountain, and Mike showed us how to and let us use his tools, because we didn't have any money to pay for repairs.

Eventually, we started making pit stops at the shop even when our bikes were fine. Mike called us "shop rats." We liked hanging out, eating whatever Jen gave us, talking bikes, and meeting some of the older guys who raced for the shop's team. There were mountain bike races pretty much every weekend, and Mike also put on a training race every Wednesday night. It didn't take long for me to ask if we could come one Wednesday. Mike said, "If you get permission from your parents, then I'll drive you there."

It was in Brickerville, about 15 miles away. "No, thanks," I said. "We'll ride there." We pedaled up in sweatpants, T-shirts, and sneakers on our three-hundred-dollar bikes. Everyone else had bike shorts and jerseys, biking shoes, and three-thousand-dollar bikes. We got creamed. But we kept going back. Throughout the summer, even when it was ninety-plus degrees, I went on four-hour rides in my sweatpants with Mike and his friends. After a couple of months, I asked Mike, "What about a real race?"

My first beginner race was nine miles. Eric and I rode there, and Jen signed our permission slips. All the different age groups began one-minute apart, with the juniors going last. I started six minutes back, and still passed everyone and won the whole race. The following Monday, when I went into the shop, Mike said, "Dude, you've got to race for me." He gave me a yellow-and-blue Green Mountain Cyclery team jersey, which I wore with my orange sweatpants. After a couple of races, he bumped me up to junior expert.

Eric started racing for Mike, too, and we began to train all the time. We read in cycling magazines that to get in shape you should do intervals. If the magazine recommended eight intervals, two minutes hard, two minutes easy, then we'd do fifteen of them, five minutes hard, one minute easy. We thought rest was a waste of time. One day Eric read that pros ride 500 miles a week in the winter, so that's what we did.

The only road that was plowed well enough to ride on all winter was Route 322 to Hershey, 30 miles away. So we'd ride there and back to get the miles in, and nothing stopped us, not even single-digit temperatures with whipping wind and warnings on the radio to stay inside. We put on everything we had to stay warm: cheap long underwear, sweatshirts and sweatpants, big winter coats and gloves, two pairs of socks with plastic bags on our feet in between the layers, and five-dollar sneakers with plastic bags over those. We'd wear ski hats and pull the padding out of our helmets so they'd fit over our hats, and we'd duct tape the vents of the helmets to keep the wind out. The roads were covered in ice and slush, and often we'd finish with icicles hanging off of our bikes.

The next spring, I got a job at the Oregon Dairy market after school as a checker. The only way I could fit riding into the day was to go after work. I got off at about 8 or 9 p.m. and rode for two or three hours, sometimes more, by moonlight on Ephrata Mountain. For a while I tried taping a flashlight to my handlebar, but it kept falling off, so I stopped bothering.

"Now, here's the thing," Mike said. "With the amount you ride, you're going to hurt yourself if you keep wearing those sweatpants." He wanted me to wear padded bike shorts.

First, I wore the shorts underneath my pants, but by the end of a rainy race the sweatpants would weigh ten pounds from all the water and mud. I was sick of them.

"I don't know," I said to Eric one day. "Do you think God really cares if I wear shorts?" I didn't. There was no logical way in my mind that showing my legs during a bike ride could be seen as something self-glorifying or wrong.

"Yeah, I don't know either," he said. Eric and I had a lot of philosophical discussions about the finer points of fundamentalist religion. The beat of rock music was supposed to be a form of communication with the devil, but I found that unlikely. Also, when you're a boy and you're a teenager, there's no getting past the fact that you sometimes think about sex—but that automatically made you a sinner. I couldn't figure out how it could be true that every teenage boy was going to hell. "Well, what about me?" Eric said. "People who get divorced are supposed to be bad people." He was worried that because his parents were divorced he would somehow be bad by association, though he didn't believe his parents were bad people in the first place.

None of it seemed quite right to us, but when you've been told something since you were born, it's hard to question it simply using logic. We thought maybe we just didn't have all the information, and that we should continue to believe until we knew more. But it was difficult to believe, no matter how hard I tried.

I'm pretty sure my parents didn't realize that I was questioning these things at the time, because we never talked about it. "You're attentive with your Scripture," my dad said to me. I was good at memorizing Scripture because I was good at focusing for hours on end and blocking out everything else around me. It was a contest to me.

I made games out of everything I had to do, whether trimming the hedges, or memorizing Scripture, or working at the Dairy, where the item-scanning machine tracked the number of items scanned per minute, and I held the record. I played the trumpet in the high school marching band, and

I was good at it because once I start anything, I become obsessive about it until I master it.

But there was no mastering these questions Eric and I had, and it was driving me crazy inside. I felt guilty for even doubting, and I wanted to believe it all because I knew that would make life easier . . . but I just couldn't.

A funny thing happened when I got on my bike. It was like therapy for me. As I worked the cranks around and around, I felt like I was emptying my uncertainty through the pedals. Being on a bike was the one time in my life when everything felt unquestionably right.

I took off the sweatpants and wore shorts to ride.

Dad went to the community auction house, which is sort of like a local eBay without the Internet, and bought a Betamax video camera and player and a tiny television set—with no antenna, so it was only for watching home movies, not TV. "I paid forty dollars for the whole lot," he said when he got home, proud of his bargain. (Although in retrospect, this was in the early 1990s, and Betamax was already dead to the rest of the world so it probably wasn't even worth forty dollars.)

My father videotaped every single thing that happened in our family, especially my bike races. He got into it. On weekends he started driving Eric and me to races that were out of state. Mom would pack us a big cooler full of food and see us off. When we got to the race venue, we'd set up the family tent in the parking lot. Dad used the Coleman camp stove to prepare all our meals, and then he'd get out the Betamax and start filming. In addition to the big camera, there was a separate recorder part that fit into a big shoulder bag that Dad carried. The thing was giant. Once I saw Dad interview some guy on camera, and I asked him afterward, "Who were you talking to?"

"I don't know," he said. "But he thought I was from a TV station because my camera equipment is so big." We laughed about that one all night long.

We drove to Traverse City, Michigan, for the U.S. junior mountain biking championships when I was seventeen. I had only done maybe a dozen real races and by now I had a nicer race bike, but still wore my Green Mountain jersey. The top guys were all sponsored by bike companies, and I beat them all, including the defending world champion.

By being the best junior in the country, I earned a spot on the U.S. team going to the World Championships in Métabief, France, a tiny ski town in the Alps. I had never been on an airplane before, much less out of the country. Back home, Mom pulled the *F* volume of the encyclopedia down from the shelf, and we looked up France to find where the French Alps were on the map.

I was excited that I'd get to represent my country and hang around the pros who would be racing the same week. By that time, I was hoping to make a living riding my bike. I wanted to show the pros that I had a future in the sport. The morning of my flight, my parents drove me to the Philadelphia airport, and I boarded the plane to Geneva by myself. I'm sure I found the flight strange, but I don't remember anything in particular about it because it wasn't nearly as surreal as the rest of the trip.

Our chaperones from the mountain biking federation picked me up in a bus with a bunch of other juniors and some of the pros whose names I had only read in magazines, such as Mike King, Greg Herbold, and John Tomac. I showed up wanting to be professional like they were, but most of the other juniors weren't nearly so serious. They all seemed to be out for a good time, so they spent their time finding alcohol and drinking, because it was France, where the drinking age is sixteen.

I had never seen a bottle of alcohol in my life. Not only did I see alcohol for the first time on that trip, I'm pretty sure I saw alcoholics for the first time. Our chaperones were drunk the entire trip. One of them even had a glass of wine in his hand as he drove us from our hotel to the race course.

There was one intelligent guy there who I hung out with, Mike O'Reilly, another junior. He was a rich kid with a trust fund, but we got along. In the week before we raced, the people in charge would drive us to the course so we could ride a lap or two for practice. Then they'd set a time to pick us up and drive us back to the hotel.

Mike and I were the only ones to go one day. When we were done riding, nobody came to pick us up—they probably drank too much and forgot about us. Finally Mike said, "Screw it, let's just ride back." It was about 15 miles to where we were staying—not a big deal—so I went along. Mike had the brilliant idea of taking a shortcut over a pasture and through a field and on a dirt road for a while, and then across a big stream. "We can cross this thing, no problem," Mike assured me, but the water was cold—snowmelt from the Alps—and it looked to me like it was moving fast. He dipped his bike in to see how deep it was, and the current submerged his bike and almost pulled Mike in.

We hiked back to the road and went in a different direction. By then it was getting dark, and Mike had some money, so we stopped at a little shop that sold newspapers, magazines, fruit—and bombs.

We thought that the long sticks with the fuse at one end were roman candles. They were only thirty cents each, so, being teenage boys, we bought ten of them. By the time we got back to the hotel, it was nighttime. The team stored everyone's bikes in an old barn next to the hotel, and the mechanic slept down there so no one stole the bikes. Mike wanted to scare the guy, so we put the bomb in the dirt driveway, lit it, and ran. I thought, *Cool, the balls of fire will shoot into the air, the guy will scream, and we'll all have a good laugh.*

But they weren't roman candles. They were quarter sticks of dynamite. There was a deep boom so loud that the mechanic thought he was going to die, and it echoed against the buildings and along the narrow streets of the tiny French town. There were stones landing on the roof of the hotel as people came running out to see what happened.

"Holy shit," Mike said, and then, thinking of the trouble we might get in he said, "I didn't hear anything, did you?"

"Nope," I said, terrified. "Not a thing." We got over being scared pretty fast, and over the next few days, we set off our nine other bombs. In that time all the juniors realized they could buy them, too, so the town sounded like a war zone. I had no idea why that place sold dynamite, but every single thing about the trip was strange to me, so at the time it was just one more oddity.

Race day, it was pouring rain. The guys who did well were the ones who were best at jumping off their bikes and running when the mud got deep. My bike didn't have the right tires to race in the slick mud, and I was exhausted from being out of my element. I finished last. Not just in the last group of riders, but dead last. I started crying before I even reached the finish line. I just wanted to go home.

My flight wasn't for three more days, and all the other kids were cutting loose drinking. Not only did I not join in, but I was baffled by it and by the way the entire trip was run. That was my first experience in the world of pro cycling, and it wasn't professional at all.

When I got home I was so disappointed, I didn't ride for a couple of months. School was starting, and it was the beginning of my senior year, and I just didn't care.

Of course, that didn't last long. I needed riding to stay sane. I thought so much about the Bible and how the literal interpretation didn't seem possible, and the more I analyzed it the more confused I got. It was a long process for me to go from Mennonite to whatever I am now. When you're taught something for seventeen years, it's not like you just switch it off. At that point the one thing I knew for sure was that the more I traveled away from Farmersville, the smaller it seemed and the more I wanted to see other places.

I never rebelled in the typical American teenage sense, but I began to embrace culture. I went to a movie in a theater for the first time in 1994 and saw *The Lion King*, and found it quite good. I bought a portable tape player and headphones, and started listening to country music, and later to AC/DC—though I wouldn't tell anyone what it was because I didn't want my parents to find out.

My parents could tell I was changing and didn't know what to make of me. We never discussed it, though. They didn't try to change me, and I didn't try to change them. The rest of the world could learn a lot from the way my parents live and care about other people. There are many wonderful things about their way of life. But when we didn't understand things about one another, we did what most families do: We didn't talk about it.

And I rode.

I got a sponsorship from GT bikes, and started doing expert class races.

"Floyd, you got a phone call," my dad said. It was Will Geoghegan, a pro rider who was a few years older than I was. I had met him at a race once or twice.

"Man, what's up with your dad?" he said to me. "Is he always so quiet? Hey, listen, I need you on my team." Will was organizing a crew for a twenty-four-hour race in West

Virginia. Nobody had ever wanted me to be on their team for anything, so I said yes.

Will had sponsors and extra bikes, and he loved to organize things, so he put the whole team together. Our name was Willy and the Poor Boys, and it was Will, me, and two pros, John Stamstad and a guy from Indiana named Art Keith. We had our own team mechanic and stayed in a condo. Will stocked the cupboards with food. I felt like a king with the deluxe setup. "I've never gone to a race and not camped before," I said, and Will looked at me funny.

That night, while the guys were watching TV and making last-minute adjustments to their bikes, I was practicing riding wheelies in the parking lot. "Dude, you gotta come in," Will yelled out to me. "You need to rest. We're going to ride for twenty-four hours straight."

"I don't care," I said. "That's fine with me." I didn't want to stop, so the guys took my bike from me and locked it in a closet. I sat down in front of the TV with them, but because I wasn't used to it, I got bored fast. I fidgeted for a few minutes and then got up.

"Where's Floyd?" Will asked a few minutes later, and then noticed that his bike was gone. I was out in the parking lot doing wheelies on it. He took it away from me.

The next day, Will was preparing for his first lap. "You want an espresso?" he offered. I didn't know what he meant. I had never heard of espresso and had never had anything with caffeine in it. "Man, you're like some kind of unfrozen caveman," he said, fixing me my first brew. It wasn't just a shot of espresso. It was a full mug of espresso, which I followed with a Mountain Dew, the first in my life.

I set out on my lap moving in fast motion compared to the rest of the world. The rush was something I had never come close to experiencing; it felt like I had superpowers. I was convinced I was going to ride the world's fastest lap. The first downhill was a narrow singletrack, and the leaders were in my way, riding too slowly. So I rode off to the side into the tall weeds to try to pass. It was actually working until I hit a stump and flew over my handlebar, pinwheeling down the hill with my bike. When I finally came to a stop, I got up to keep riding but the front wheel was bent into a U-shape. I needed to change the wheel as quickly as possible and keep going, so I rode a wheelie down the hill back to the condo. The mechanic gave me Will's wheel, and I went back out to do my lap.

I felt terrible about getting the team behind, so throughout the night Will kept giving me coffee and I kept riding faster and faster trying to make up time. We ended up in second place, only about three minutes behind the leaders.

The next couple of summers, Eric and I drove around the country looking for expert races with prize money. We drove Eric's pickup with our bikes in the back, and slept wherever we could find that didn't cost money—parking lots, cornfields, golf courses. Churchyards are a good place to sleep, because they're quiet and usually no one bothers you. Baseball fields are good too, as long as they don't have automatic sprinklers that come on at 2 a.m. We learned that one the hard way.

Typically, we won just enough in prize money to pay for gas and food to keep the trip going. But that second summer, Eric bowed out in California, so I had to find a ride on my own. I was at Mammoth Mountain and needed to get to Spokane, Washington.

One of my buddies from the France trip was there and hooked me up with these guys he had been smoking pot with, who owned an upstart mountain bike clothing company called Show 'Em You're Nuts. I thought the company didn't stand a chance with that name, but this was during mountain biking's heyday, when people bought anything related to the sport as long as it seemed "edgy" or was purple.

I hopped in their truck and we headed out. It never occurred to me that they might at some point pull out their marijuana. I had heard about pot as one of the evil things in society, but I had never considered that I might someday encounter it. Sure enough, halfway through the desert, these guys pulled over on the side of the road for a smoke. One asked me, "You want some?"

"No," I said, stiffening. I walked behind the truck and paced. They sat on the hood and got stupid, saying "deep" things about the stars and the universe. That night, I learned that when people are getting stoned, they become complete idiots to someone who is sober. Then, the Nuts guys got back in the truck. I was scared because I didn't have any idea how they were going to drive after getting stoned. But I didn't really even know how to protest, and I had no idea how I would get to Spokane if I didn't ride with them. So I thought, *Oh well, if I die, I die,* and climbed in the back of the truck and fell asleep while they drove.

We stayed in downtown Spokane and the race was about 40 miles away at a ski resort. The guys drove me up the mountain the day before the race so they could put up their Show 'Em You're Nuts booth in the expo area, and I could ride around the course. Once they were finished, they left, saying they'd come pick me up later. I pedaled a couple of more laps around the course. When I got back, they weren't there, but I didn't think much of it because there were still all kinds of people milling around, so I hung out and chatted with other riders.

By dusk, everyone else had left, and it started getting cold. I was still in my cycling shorts and jersey. A couple of more hours passed, and still no one came to get me. There was one road down the mountain, and I thought about riding, but I had no idea where to go, and I didn't have any lights for my bike to help me see in the pitch-black night. There were a few condos at the top, but I didn't have any money and didn't know anyone staying in them. By 10 p.m. I hadn't eaten anything, and I was tired. I figured I'd take a nap until they came to get me, because surely they were coming.

To keep warm, I took down a PowerBar banner and put it underneath me, and rolled myself up in another banner. I tried not to shiver, but the cold kept me from really sleeping. That, and fear. It was so dark, and the woods were thick—I had no idea what else was out there. I had images of a wild animal coming to attack me.

I must have eventually dozed a little, because I woke up to, "Dude, what are you doing?" It was one of the Nuts guys, who showed up at 6 a.m. to finish setting up the expo area and found me rolled up like a burrito.

"What am *I* doing?" I asked. "You guys were supposed to come get me." Then he remembered and said, "Oh, man," a lot, and offered to let me take a nap in the back of the truck until the race. I slept for two hours, and then got third in the race.

Afterward, I saw Will. "I am so mad," I said. "I should have won that race." I told him the whole story, about how I hadn't slept or eaten, and how all my stuff was still in the hotel in Spokane, so I had no money or clothes to change into.

"You're kidding me," Will said, laughing. "You slept in your bike shorts? That is *rough*. I'm staying in a condo a couple hundred yards from here. You could have crashed there." He invited me there to clean up.

I took a hot shower while Will turned on the TV and flipped around the channels until he found a bike race. It was the Tour de France. I had never seen it or even heard of it. "The thing is absolutely brutal," Will said. It covers more than 2,000 miles over three weeks, he explained, and goes over some of the steepest, harshest roads in the Alps and Pyrenees. The whole race is a traveling circus that starts and finishes in a different city each day, making a different loop around the country each year. The rider who does it the fastest wins the yellow jersey, and is considered to be the best cyclist in the world.

On the screen, we saw this pack of about twelve guys flying, handlebar-to-handlebar. The road started going up, and this one rider in a blue-and-red Motorola jersey took off like he was possessed. By the top of the climb, he was all alone. "That guy's crushing everyone," I said. The announcers explained that three days before, a Motorola rider named Fabio Casartelli had died when he crashed on a high-speed descent in the Pyrenees. The possessed Motorola rider, whose name was Lance Armstrong, had been close friends with Casartelli. Coming down the final stretch to the finish line, Armstrong pointed to the sky and blew a kiss upward toward heaven in remembrance of his teammate. Then he won a stage of the Tour de France.

I decided right then that if the winner of that race was the best in the world, then that was the race I wanted to win. Of course, at the time I was just a decent mountain biker, not even a pro. And I didn't have a plan for how to achieve my new goal, or even a clue where to start. The Tour was a long, long way from sleeping wrapped up in sponsor banners at a ski slope outside Spokane. But there it was. There was my dream.

CHAPTER 2
A Bunch of Screwups

"Mother, I'm moving to California," I said. "Tomorrow."

A bunch of guys were picking me up in their motor home to drive to Moab, Utah, for a race. From there, I'd go to California, for good. My poor mother. I was so worried that my parents would be disappointed in me for leaving that I didn't tell them until I absolutely had to. A mountain bike parts company, TWP, which stands for Two Wheel Performance, made me an offer to turn pro. They would pay my way to races, and the owners also invited me to live with them in Irvine in their spare bedroom, so I had year-round warm weather for training. It was my ticket out. There was no way I'd turn it down.

"Oh, really?" my mother said. She didn't know what to

say. I'm sure the timing was a shock, but beyond that the idea of it seemed odd to her. My goals and interests were simply beyond her understanding. I could tell that my parents were very concerned because they became quiet.

"You're nineteen, so it's up to you," my father said, finally. I asked Dad if I owed any money for bills or anything. "No, Floyd," he said. "I think we're even."

The next day I threw a few duffle bags into the motor home. My parents stood outside to see me off, but didn't say anything. The silence was awkward. "Don't worry," I said. "I'll make you proud." They waved to us as we pulled away, and that was it.

By that point, I had been traveling around the country for a couple of years and meeting all kinds of people who were very different from those I grew up around, so California wasn't strange to me. Life continued pretty much like it had been, except once I was done racing I went back to a little room instead of back home. In a way I finally felt free, but there were also times when I really missed Farmersville.

I didn't have a car, so I hitched rides with other guys to races. Or I'd use my bike to get around. The morning of a race, I'd wake up early, ride 15 miles to Peet's for coffee, then ride back, race, and ride some more. "You don't know what you're doing," a mountain bike racer, Brian Wester, said to me after only a couple of months. "You need a coach." His dad knew a coach, Arnie Baker, in San Diego, whom he thought I might get along with.

Arnie was a medical doctor who had become so interested

in cycling that he scaled back his family practice to coach local riders. He gained respect over time, and had recently written the training manual for USA Cycling and started working with Tinker Juarez, an older pro who at the time was a three-time national mountain bike champion, Olympian, and World Championship silver medalist.

I went to Arnie's house, a converted old dance studio with a spacious living room, and could tell right away he was eccentric. Tandems and other bicycles lined the walls. Arnie brought out a plate of cookies, all different kinds. "My wife, Gero, makes them just about every day," he said. "Would you like a glass of milk?" We settled down to talk. Arnie stood five-foot-seven with glasses that overwhelmed his face, and he didn't swear or drink alcohol. He was meticulous even in the way he described the cookies, and was one of those people you can sense is intelligent the instant you meet them.

"I don't care if you're any good or not," he started. "I'll only work with you if I like you as a person." Arnie was more like a counselor than a traditional coach who tries to motivate by yelling or bossing you around. That kind of attitude belongs in football, not cycling. I had always been motivated more than enough on my own. I just needed someone with expertise to help me steer my energy in the right direction.

"So, what would you like to do?" Arnie asked. "What's your ultimate goal?" Arnie was big on goals. If you don't have an objective, he figured, what's the point?

"I saw the Tour de France on TV," I said. "I'd like to win that one day."

Arnie didn't laugh at me or call me crazy, and I guess he liked me because he became my coach. I started going to San Diego for Wednesday-night and weekend rides. One day he suggested I try riding up Mount Palomar, a climb about 60 miles from San Diego. Up the south grade from the main road turnoff, the road gains 2,300 feet in 6.8 miles. I had already been on a long, hard ride, but I went up as hard as I could, saving nothing. At the top, Arnie looked at his stopwatch. "Twenty-nine minutes," he said, and then looked up at me through his glasses. "You know, Rominger just did it in thirty-one." Swiss pro Tony Rominger had been a favorite to win the Tour de France that year, before he crashed out in an early stage. He had won the Tour of Spain three times, and the Tour of Italy once. "Hm, twenty-nine," Arnie said again.

A few weeks later, when I was fresh, I did the climb in twenty-seven minutes and change. "That's about as fast as anyone in the world can climb," Arnie said. He was very matter-of-fact. He used a math equation to determine how much power my legs were producing to get myself up the hill at that speed. "You're putting out about six watts per kilogram of body weight," he said. "That's right up there with the best that's ever been recorded."

"Why can't it be more?" I asked. I didn't like the idea that I might not be able to get any better.

Just about anyone else would have thought that this was a ridiculous question from someone who has just been told he has world-class potential, but Arnie liked how I questioned everything. "Well, I don't know," he said. "Maybe it can be." Then he thought for a minute. "If your goal is to win the Tour de France, perhaps instead of trying to make it more, you should work on being able to do it more often, since the race is three weeks long."

Arnie did more calculations from there. He estimated that my VO2 max, or capacity for processing oxygen, a key factor for athletes, was ninety ml/kg/min, which is also close to the best that's ever been recorded. Across the board, I had big numbers, which was great, Arnie said, "but they're only numbers." If I were in a numbers contest, I'd win. But this was bike racing. "Tinker doesn't have numbers like yours," Arnie said. But Tinker could beat me on any trail because he was more efficient on his bike and had decades of experience on me.

To even be capable of doing a race like the Tour de France, I needed to build serious endurance. Arnie took a paper and pencil and wrote out a basic training plan. The way he figured, it would take me eight years to be ready. The first year I was supposed to ride 16,000 miles, which was close to what I was doing at the time. The peak year, I was supposed to ride 25,000 miles, an insane volume that no one in the pro peloton even comes close to doing, though I didn't realize that at the time. "If winning the Tour is your ultimate goal," Arnie said, "then this is what's required."

I rode all the time. Even though I was still racing mountain bikes, I had a road bike and did most of my miles on the road. I went to Arnie's twice a week for workouts, and most of the time ended up sleeping on his couch because Irvine was too far from San Diego. About two years after I moved to California, Arnie suggested I move in with a forty-five-and-up masters racer he coached, David Witt. David owned a popular restaurant in town, and he typically rode during the day before going to work in the afternoon. "David just ended a bad marriage, and he's a little bit lost right now," Arnie said. "I think he'd like the company." It sounded good to me, so I moved in to David's condo.

David handed me an envelope that came in the mail with my mother's handwriting on it. Inside was a three-page letter. "Dear Floyd," it started. "I'm writing to you because I'm in pain." Someone had given her an article from a mountain biking magazine that quoted me talking about a race, saying, "I rode like hell to pass him." My mother was so upset that I had used profanity that, within two hours of reading the article, she started to have flulike symptoms. For a whole week, she ached all over. She wanted to let me know that she had figured out the root of her pain. It was me. "I don't know why I've let this make me so discouraged," she wrote. "Please realize what an awesome privilege you have in your life to be a good example to others. I want you to always be a man of integrity." She mailed the letter.

My brother, Bob, had been hunting snow geese all season, but hadn't shot one yet. Right after Mom mailed the letter, my dad called to tell Bob there were snow geese in a nearby town where he was making a store delivery. Mom had been praying to God, hoping that I'd hear her message. When my father mentioned snow geese, she thought, "Floyd flies in airplanes a lot, so a bird would be a perfect sign that he's heard me." She prayed again, and asked, "Lord, could I have that bird?"

That day, Bob finally got his bird, and to my mother that was stone-cold proof that God was granting her wish. She sat down and wrote me another letter the next day explaining the whole story. "God is in charge of your life," she wrote. "And nothing will happen to you that is meant for evil. Everything will be to make you a better man." Bob had the goose stuffed, and my mother insisted on mounting it in the front living room as a reminder.

I don't think I even read her first letter all the way through because I couldn't stand the idea of causing her pain. While I was relieved to get the second letter saying that she felt better, I didn't comprehend how it was possible that my brother killing a bird was in any way related to me or how I lived my life. God doesn't sit around waiting to hear prayers for snow geese as signs. To me, that doesn't make any sense.

By then I was growing certain that I did not believe what my parents believed. As for my language, it's true that by my mother's standards I had slipped. Not only did I say much worse than "hell"—and do so quite often in my daily life—but I also enjoyed beer, though not until after I turned twenty-one. I liked to watch Chargers games on TV, and I had a growing obsession with popular music and memorizing lyrics. My collection of CDs—none of them gospel—included artists like Kid Rock, Weezer, Creedence Clearwater Revival, and Guns N' Roses. To me, these things are surface matters. Even though my parents and I don't see things the same, I believe that our ways of thinking are far more similar than they are different. We both believe in honesty, fairness, kindness, and hard work. Those are the important things, and I wanted my mother to know that I understood that.

David never charged me a penny in rent, and pretty much let me bum everything off him. He bought bread, and it was gone the next day. He bought coffee, and a couple of days later it was gone. He bought beer and we'd drink it that night. David never minded. In fact, he was happier than he had been in a long time, and stopped taking the antidepressant medication he had gone on when times were bad. David and I rode together every day and talked about our dreams, his of opening a bigger, nicer restaurant and mine of winning the Tour. "You have to follow your dream, no matter what," he said. "It's the only way to live."

We had a similar curiosity and willingness to try things. David was up for anything, even when I wanted to bring a ten-foot City of San Diego water pipe into his home.

After reading a bunch of scientific research about altitude and performance, Arnie bought an early-model high-altitude sleeping chamber. The theory is that spending time at high altitude, where there is less oxygen in the air, forces your body to produce more red blood cells and make other changes to be able to process oxygen more efficiently. I didn't get into the research, but I knew that when I trained or raced at altitude, I was able to ride stronger a couple of weeks later. I slept in Arnie's chamber, and I could feel the difference. The contraption looked like something from a tanning salon. It was a gigantic cylinder, with domes on each end, and you were supposed to sleep in the tube while a vacuum pump sucked air out of it to reduce the density of the air.

"I want one of those," I told David. But I could never afford it. Arnie's cost about twelve thousand dollars. "Maybe I can make one. They're pretty simple if you think about it." We didn't talk about it after that, but a few weeks later I got a call from David while he was out on a ride.

"I think I found your chamber," he said. He was at a construction site where the workers were laying water pipes. The thickness and diameter of the pipe was identical to the one used in Arnie's chamber. The difference was that it was made of some type of heavy resin, weighed hundreds of pounds, and took four people to move. "You have to see it," David said. I rode over to meet him and ended up buying a ten-foot segment from one of the workers—who I'm pretty sure wasn't authorized to sell it—for two hundred dollars. Later, David and I borrowed a truck to haul it back to his place.

For weeks it sat out front, taking up a parking space, until I figured out how to cap the ends with material strong enough that it wouldn't be sucked in by the pressure. I ended up using thick, bulletproof Lexan to cover the ends. Then I ordered the same electric vacuum pump that was in Arnie's chamber, figured out a safety-release system, and put a cheap mechanical altimeter inside as a monitor. The whole thing cost me about eight hundred dollars.

I tried sleeping in it, and at first it was unsettling because, even though the Lexan is really strong, you can see it flexing when the vacuum pump is going. But after a while, I really liked it. Because of the difference in pressure, you couldn't hear anything from the outside. It was peaceful. I still have it in my house, and still use it.

A year or so later, Will Geoghegan talked his way into a sponsorship from Chevy Trucks and started his own mountain biking team. He hired me, and moved in to David's condo not long after. There was another Chevy teammate, Matt Smith, who lived there for a while too, making it a true flophouse. We lived on coffee, steel-cut oats, wheat bread, bananas, nonfat milk, ice cream, and beer. David didn't charge them any rent either.

While David focused more on his restaurant, Will and I trained like we were possessed. I was riding twice a day and taking naps in between. I usually slept on the living-room floor wearing earplugs. As long as I had earplugs, I could sleep through anything.

Will and I went to mountain bike races, but my results were never that great. For a change of pace, we decided to race the U.S. road nationals in Cincinnati. The day was blistering hot, in the high 90s with 90-percent humidity. A group broke away and I didn't know any better, so chased after them by myself. I never caught them, but the pack behind me didn't catch me, either. "Man, you were out there flapping in the wind on your own," Will said afterward. "I just kept thinking, 'God, Floyd, slow up a little, so we can work together to run up that gap.'"

I didn't know anything about race tactics. In mountain biking, you go all out from the gun, but a road race often plays out like a game of chess. The peloton rides along in sync with subtle moves that the untrained eye wouldn't even notice. The strategy is designed to conserve energy and set up an attack later in the race, so that a rider can get away and put time on the competition. I didn't have the first clue how to play. I'd put my head down and charge forward to try to force things on my own instead of using pack dynamics to my advantage.

My other problem was that every lap when I rode past the aid station, I took two ice-cold bottles of Mountain Dew— and the race was fifteen laps long. Still, I finished seventh.

Back in San Diego, I told Arnie about the race. He brought out his tandem bicycle, and on the next group ride he began to teach me tactics, with me on the back of the tandem. "Look," Arnie said as we pedaled along. "You can create situations just by where you position yourself in a pack." We let gaps open up, and then watched people react to bridge the distance. In a four-person group, you can put everyone exactly where you want them. "You shuffle the deck," he said. "If possible, you want the biggest person in front of you to break the wind, and the weakest person behind you. And you want the strongest sprinter in back, so he has to go past more people." We shifted in the group, and others reacted to us by falling into line as Arnie planned. The key for races, he told me, was to not get shuffled too far back in the pack. You always want to be in position to respond to attacks.

That fall, at a time of the year when most pro cyclists are resting from the long season, I averaged forty-six hours per week on my bike, and in the month of December I climbed a total of 168,000 feet. I didn't quite reach the 25,000 miles Arnie prescribed, but I did ride 24,000. Not only is riding that much probably unhealthy, but it doesn't make you better right away. I was laying a big foundation for later, but in the meantime, I wasn't racing well.

Losing discouraged me. "This is just stupid," I told Will. "I think I'm ready to quit." On top of the losing, Chevy was dropping its sponsorship of Will's team, and the entire sport of mountain biking was losing popularity. Quitting seemed like the right thing, even though I didn't know what I'd do for a living if I didn't race my bike.

"You can't quit," Will said. "Hey, let's do more road races. We'll wreak havoc in every race we can find." That was his way of job hunting. We'd enter the races as individuals, and then torment everyone by going hard from the very beginning. Eventually, by his logic, teams would hire us just to make us stop.

Will had uniforms made that said "Lords of Dirt." I wore argyle socks pulled halfway up my calves. Instead of sleek road helmets, we used mountain bike helmets with visors on them. In our first race, Will shot to the front, sprinting all out in the first few seconds. The race was 70 miles long.

"What the hell is going on?" one pro from a sponsored team yelled.

"Huh? We're just mountain bikers," Will said. "We're here for training."

The problem was, there were just two of us, and everyone else had a whole team, such as Mercury, Saturn, and the Navigators. Without a bunch of teammates to support us, we had to do way too much work throughout the race to be able to take the lead at the end. No matter how early I broke away or how hard I rode, there was always a good sprinter on one of those big teams who could draft on my wheel and then pass me at the finish. I got second place a lot, which was frustrating. But part of Will's plan was working: We were getting noticed and making everyone miserable.

We did our best to make the pain mental as well as physical. When Will and I were in a breakaway with everyone struggling to keep up, gasping and wondering why on earth we were pushing the pace so hard so early in the race, Will and I would start fake-arguing. "It's my turn to go," he'd say.

"No, I want to attack," I'd respond. "It's my turn." I'd sprint for five minutes, then sit up and pedal easy. Will would attack the same way a few seconds later.

Other times I'd spout quotes from my favorite satirist of all time, Jack Handey. There's nothing more effective than being annoying to break the spirits of riders around you.

Trying to keep up in a pack that's going all out is like being in a contest to see who can hold his hand above a lit candle the longest. It starts to hurt, it starts to burn, and the person who is best at not caring that any of it is happening usually wins the battle. "I hope life isn't a big joke, because I don't get it," I would say as we pedaled furiously, wheel-to-wheel. Or, "It takes a big man to cry, but it takes an even bigger man to laugh at that man." Then I'd smile as if I didn't have a care in the world.

On the surface we were a couple of fools. But I came to realize a few months later that the reputation you create for yourself in the peloton has an impact on the race. I was in a three-man breakaway with two Mercury guys, David Clinger and Scott Moninger. They were sitting on my wheel as I pulled them along, and they wouldn't take the lead to do their share of the work. "Come on," I said. "You need to help me."

"No way," Clinger said. "Screw it."

"Okay," I said, starting to slow down. "Then I guess we'll just get caught."

They wanted to win, but they were afraid that if we worked together, I'd pull a stunt at the end to mess it up for them. Clinger offered to make a deal. "We'll all take turns pulling," he said. "But you have to let one of us win, and you can take second."

I had no problem making a deal, but that one was stupid. It didn't have any upside for me: If I agreed, I'd be guaranteed to lose. If I kept going on my own, at least I had a shot of winning. "I'm riding," I said. "You guys just get on my wheel." I led the two of them to the finish, doing all the work up front to set the pace and block the wind, and I still got second.

Mercury's team director, John Wordin, called me a few days later. "We like that attitude," he said. "We don't sell races." Wordin hired me and paid me five hundred dollars per month to start. I was a pro racer. My job was to attack and break apart the field in the last few miles of a race to pave the way for our top sprinter, Gord Fraser, to win stages.

I was pretty good at it, but that first year I crashed a lot. Once I crashed three times in one race, and by the end I had no skin left on my fingertips because when I fell, I'd try to stop myself by clawing the road like a cartoon character. In a mountain bike race, if you don't like what's happening on the trail, you jump or fall off your bike, and then you get back on and try again. That first year I raced that way on the road.

My team thought I was crazy. Really, I was just raw, with more energy than I knew how to control. No one in the pack wanted to ride near me, because they knew I could go down at any moment. The funny thing is, the fact that I wasn't afraid of crashing ultimately made me a better bike handler than just about anyone in the peloton. Without fear, I stayed relaxed and focused. Once I got used to the road, I almost never crashed.

Will didn't find a job on a road team, so he started working at a software company, moved out of David's, and got a real life. David did too, when he started dating a teacher from the preschool across the street. Her name was Rose Basile, but everyone called her by the name her students used, Ms. Rose. She first noticed David because of the giant pipe taking up a parking spot outside, and the sounds of whirring indoor trainers and laughter that would come out of his apartment on rainy days when we'd all ride indoors.

Ms. Rose had five children, two girls and three boys. The oldest was Amber, who had a three-year-old daughter, Ryan, and lived with Ms. Rose. Amber taught at the preschool as well, and was also a flight attendant. After a while, Ms. Rose suggested that Amber and I meet. Whenever Ms. Rose saw me, I was lying on the couch in a T-shirt, boxers, and white socks, resting after a ride. Whenever Amber was home from flying, she'd be home with Ryan. "You're both always just sitting around," she said. "You should sit around together."

I said fine, but Amber was a tougher sell. "I want you to meet Floyd," Ms. Rose said to her. "He's a bike racer who lives with David, and he's really nice."

"I don't know," she said.

"He's also a Mennonite," Ms. Rose pointed out.

"Oh, even better, Mom," she said. "A Mennonite named Floyd."

A big group of us went to dinner at David's restaurant, Fifth and Hawthorn, one night, and I didn't even speak to Amber. I couldn't. I just stared at her. I had always been way more interested in bikes than in girls, but something clicked right away, and I think it scared me.

The next day, David and Ms. Rose were out riding their tandem bicycle, and Ms. Rose found a cell phone in the gutter. "Let me see it," I said when she brought it back to David's. I grabbed it from her and tried to find out who it belonged to, but I jammed it up.

Amber walked in a few minutes later. "What's that?" she asked, and I explained that Ms. Rose had found it, but that it was jammed. "Let me see it," she said, and grabbed it from me.

"What are you going to do with it?" I said. "You can't fix it." She fixed it.

"Oh, I'm the woman," she said. "And I can do anything I want." I loved that she didn't take any crap from anyone, and she spoke her mind no matter what she wanted to say or who she was talking to. She was strong and independent, and it was pretty much a done deal from the beginning. Whenever we were both in town, which wasn't often since I was racing and she was flying, I'd ride my bike over to her place and we'd hang out. When we were apart, we'd talk all the time.

Instantly, the four of us became a family. We would sit in David's condo going around the table with the long list of money worries, work troubles, and huge areas of uncertainty in each of our lives. "Look at us," Ms. Rose said one night. "What a bunch of screwups." And we laughed.

"Maybe so," David said. "But I wonder if other people are lucky enough to find what we have." David was right.

Things happened really fast between Amber and me. Three months after we started dating, Amber was working, and Ryan had a really bad fever. Amber was really upset when I talked to her on the phone. "Mom had to take her to the emergency room," she told me. "And I'm stuck in Dallas. This isn't working."

"So, quit," I told her.

"I can't quit," she said. The concept didn't exist to her. She was a single mom with two jobs, and she had to do everything she could to provide for her daughter.

"Quit, and I'll take care of you," I said. I didn't have much money, but by that time Mercury was paying me thirty thousand dollars per year, and I told her we'd figure it out. Over the next couple of months, we got a joint checking account and bought a car together, because neither of us had one. We made plans to move Ms. Rose in with David, so that I could live with Amber and Ryan.

About a year after Amber and I met, I went to visit Ms. Rose. I was nervous, but I came out with it: "Ms. Rose, I'd really like to marry your daughter."

She knew it was coming. "Do you realize what you're getting into?" she asked.

"Yes," I said.

"She can't cook," Ms. Rose said.

"I know."

"She can be a bitch on wheels."

"I know," I said. "But I love her." I wasn't exactly a prize for Amber either. I traveled for months on end, and had only that year gotten my first one-year contract with a salary. All I did was ride and sleep. And often, I'd want to sleep in my altitude chamber, so I'd lie with her until she fell asleep, then go to the chamber and come back in the morning before she woke up. The way I figured, we'd have to tolerate each other.

I proposed to Amber over shrimp cocktail while she, Ryan, and I were having dinner at David's restaurant. Amber had been hounding me the whole day, "You better be proposing to me tonight." I did, and David proposed to Ms. Rose the next day. He was going to become my father-in-law.

Amber wanted a wedding, we both wanted a house, and in reality we could afford neither. We went to the justice of the peace and got married, with David and Ms. Rose serving as our wedding party. Two days later, I left for Europe to race for three and a half months.

The world of European racing was different from what I had experienced before, and sometimes truly bizarre. The races themselves were much more intense than domestic races. It was like the big leagues versus the minors. You had to pay attention every second, and bad things could happen to you if you were in the wrong place at the wrong time. Mostly it was typical crashes and pileups, but I also saw some unbelievable stuff that happened to riders—and they had the will to keep going, like their bodies were on autopilot and wouldn't stop trying to win no matter what was happening to them. I once saw a guy get road rash without even falling down. In Milan-San Remo, an Italian race that winds from Milan to the Italian Rivera along a coastal road carved into a cliff, the pack of riders was so tight that this guy got jammed as we rounded a corner, and he was dragged along, scraping against the rocks. He kept racing to the finish, but he looked as if he'd been beaten by a belt sander.

In addition to the racing, the European riders were different. They had traditions and superstitions that seemed strange to me. During every race, they ate pasta at every meal, even breakfast, which seemed asinine to me. Of course you need carbohydrates to fuel for the ride, but why pasta? There was one guy who obviously thought that showering during a multi-day race would somehow bring him harm. Poor, crazy guy. And it was widely believed that air-conditioning causes colds, which I never believed. I'd blast the AC whenever my hotel room had it, which wasn't often.

My results in Europe the first two years with Mercury were good—with a few top-ten finishes, good enough that I received a couple of calls from Tailwind Sports in San Francisco, which ran the U.S. Postal Service team. Lance Armstrong had just come back from battling cancer and had won the Tour de France twice in a row. They were interested in talking to me about riding with the team. It was exciting to have them call, but things seemed to be going well with Mercury, so I stayed.

I felt like a real professional, since I had just re-signed with Mercury for sixty thousand dollars. David and Ms. Rose loaned Amber and me money for a down payment on a house an hour north of San Diego, in a booming little valley town called Murrieta. The location was perfect for training. In every direction from the valley were steep ridges with mile after mile of hilly pavement and few cars, and it was much closer to Palomar and other mountains. David, Mrs. Rose, and Amber's brothers helped her and Ryan move into the house while I was racing in Europe.

When you turn pro, you sign an athlete's contract with the International Cycling Union (UCI). There is no rider's union. The UCI is supposed to be an advocate for the sport of cycling and ensure fair competition. Part of the contract outlines a rider's obligations, including drug testing. Anti-doping in cycling is overseen by the World Anti-Doping Agency (WADA). WADA was created in 1999 by the International Olympic Committee to systematically combat doping in Olympic sports by adopting standardized testing practices and a uniform list of banned substances.

Through WADA, the UCI does drug tests at races, and also outside of competitions, anytime and anywhere they want. Every quarter, athletes are required to send a fax or e-mail to the athlete's national anti-doping agency's office to notify them of their whereabouts. I started sending faxes, the same way I would do for the rest of my career, listing where I planned to be every single day throughout the quarter: home, training in Europe, racing, on vacation— everywhere. If a urine-sample collector showed up at the location where you said you'd be and you weren't there, you'd receive what they call a "missed test." A missed test is like a strike. Three strikes in eighteen months is the same as a positive test. You receive an automatic two-year ban, as if you'd been caught with something illegal in your system.

The first anti-doping urine collector came to our house in Murrieta shortly after I returned home from Europe. I was out on a training ride, so he waited for me in his car. When I rolled into the driveway, he shouted, "Mr. Landis, don't try to run! You're on video camera!"

I laughed at him. "Why would I run?" He continued to be an overly serious and presumptive jerk. We went inside, into my bathroom, and closed the door behind us. I then washed my hands and peed into the cup while he watched— the idea is that he has to see the entire process so I don't try to slip anything into my sample. Then, according to their process, I watched as he poured the urine into two containers, an A sample and a B sample. I signed a bunch of forms stating that I understood what was going on.

That was just the first of dozens of home visits to collect my urine. I asked one of the collectors once how much he got paid to pick up my urine as an independent contractor and he told me the job paid one hundred dollars per sample.

Over the years, dozens of different people have seen me with my pants down, though oftentimes I'd encounter the same collectors. There's one guy who regularly came to my house in California, and I grew to like him. He lives just down the street, his wife is a schoolteacher, and they have kids. (There's plenty of time for conversation while they're waiting for you to have the urge.) But many times, the collectors were disrespectful or drunk with authority in a way that showed they obviously presumed all professional athletes are dopers.

◆ ◆ ◆

I stopped getting paid in May 2001. The bottom line is that John Wordin ran out of money for Mercury. When a team registers with the UCI, it is required to set up a bank guarantee to ensure that employees get paid if the team runs dry. After thirty days of not being paid, an athlete can request in writing to be paid from the guarantee. So when a month passed, I wrote the letter. The UCI asked me to wait a little longer to give Wordin a chance to try to save the team. According to the rules, once the UCI draws on the bank guarantee, they have to suspend the team. I thought that was fair enough. I could understand wanting to do everything possible to accomplish something you're passionate about. I also didn't want to hurt the team or my teammates by provoking sanctions. I was willing to give Wordin a chance to pull it together.

But I saw the writing on the wall. We had more or less stopped racing because the team didn't have any money to travel. I called back the guys at Tailwind and said, "If Postal is still interested, I need a team." I had a one-year deal signed a couple of weeks later.

Wordin didn't come up with the money, of course. Toward the end of the summer, I was piling up credit-card debt trying to support my new family, so I again made the request to be paid. The UCI again stalled, saying they wanted to give Wordin just a little more time.

By fall the team had basically folded, and I had a lawyer send a letter to the UCI saying that I needed to pursue whatever other options for getting paid that were open to me, including legal options, because the bank guarantee didn't seem to be working, and my family needed the money that I was owed under my contract. In response, he got a letter signed by the head of the UCI at the time, Hein Verbruggen, saying he believed the UCI hadn't violated its rules. He then added, "Such an aggressive approach might perhaps work in the U.S.A. but it does not in Europe and most definitely not with me. . . . I have given order to our legal department to take the tone of your approach into account when it comes to following up on your request."

Verbruggen never returned my subsequent phone calls, so I never figured out exactly what he meant by his statements, or how we were being aggressive, or why he wasn't willing to protect riders from mismanagement. I didn't press the issue at the time because, really, I didn't care. I was going to race for the best team in the world.

CHAPTER 3

Life with Lance

Lance Armstrong wasn't just a bike racer, he was a celebrity. By the time I joined the U.S. Postal Service team for the 2002 season, Lance was thirty years old and had gone from cancer-surviving underdog to three-time Tour de France champion. Among many other things, he had met the president, become buddies with Robin Williams and Arnold Schwarzenegger, played golf with Kevin Costner, and hung out in the New York Yankees' dugout. He had made tens of millions of dollars in endorsement deals. He had a staff of assistants, lawyers, advisers, and public relations people circulating around him to manage his image.

During the spring and summer, Lance was based out of Girona, Spain, a small city about an hour up the coast from

Barcelona, for training and easy access to European racing. Girona is quiet, with quick access to excellent riding and the Pyrenees Mountains to the northwest. Lance had a huge apartment in a renovated palace off of one of the main plazas in the old, historic part of town. He buzzed in and out of town on a private jet between appearances and races.

Over the years, Girona had become a training hub for Americans on the Postal team. I went there the spring after I joined the team. I was twenty-six years old and owed sixty thousand dollars on my credit cards. Supporting my family gave me plenty to worry about. Still, compared to Lance's life, mine was simple, and that's the way I liked it. Most pro cyclists don't make nearly as much as people think: My salary was sixty thousand dollars that year. After the Mercury mess, I was happy to have a deal at all, and felt lucky to be working for Lance.

I had, and still have, a good deal of respect for him. I was pretty new to European racing, so I saw him as a mentor— but it may sound surprising that I never saw him as a hero. Obviously, there are millions of people who consider him a big inspiration, and if he helps others fight their own battles harder or achieve greater things for themselves, that's great. I've never had any heroes in cycling, though. For me, it's always been more of an individual challenge. My hammering away on my bicycle hour after hour has never been so that I could be like anyone else. It has been so that I could be me, only faster.

In Girona, I stayed in a cramped apartment that belonged

to a teammate, Tony Cruz, with another young rider, Dave Zabriskie. Tony's place was across the railroad tracks from the historic part of town where Lance's place was, which meant we were literally on the other side of the tracks. Tony liked to sleep late, so Zabriskie and I hung out a lot. Zabriskie was from Salt Lake City, Utah, and wasn't Mormon, so growing up he never felt like he fit in. I could relate to that.

There were twenty-five riders on our team, but only nine were on a Tour de France team, so for early-season races we'd split up and send different riders to different races. Not everyone lived in Girona, and even though we were a team, it's not like we trained together every day. Sometimes guys rode in groups, but I found this annoying. Half the time you'd end up riding behind other guys in their draft, and the ride would be too easy. Most days I trained alone or with Zabriskie, or with Lance when he was in town, which wasn't often. We didn't have any control over our racing schedules, so we went to the races that team director Johan Bruyneel, a wily Belgian ex-pro who decided the strategy in races and drove the team car, picked for us. The rest of the time Zabriskie and I trained and tried to entertain ourselves.

We didn't have a car, so Tony would loan us his Vespa to cruise downtown to a café or chocolate shop. "You drive a little crazy for me," Zabriskie said after our first trip, so from then on he drove and I rode in back. There was only one motorcycle helmet, so Dave wore it, and I used my bicycle helmet.

"Hey, it's Dumb and Dumber," Lance said when he saw

us. He also began calling us Beavis and Butthead because of the way we goofed off together.

Zabriskie and I had all sorts of escapades on the Vespa, like the time we bought four hundred dollars' worth of tires. At a race I had asked the team mechanic for new tires for training because mine were shot. "Go buy them at the bike shop," he said. "Even Lance buys his own tires on this team." It didn't make any sense to me that the team wouldn't provide tires, but I didn't know any better.

The next time I was riding with Lance in Girona, I asked him if he bought his own tires. "What?" he said. "That's ridiculous." Then I asked him the last time he'd even been to a bike shop, and he looked at me like I was crazy.

Back at Tony's, I told Zabriskie the whole story. He wasn't surprised. "That's the way it is on this team," he said. It was an attitude that I found strange: If you're not Lance, you don't get what you ask for, and you're not supposed to question anything.

"That's not how it is anymore," I said. "We're going to get everything we need." Zabriskie and I puttered on the Vespa to Decathlon, a big sporting goods store and bike shop in town. "We need tires," I said to the guy behind the counter. He asked how many. "All of them," I said, and he looked surprised. "Every single one."

Zabriskie got an indoor trainer and some protein powder for Tony. "And that giant dartboard too, please," he said, unable to resist. The total bill was four hundred dollars.

To haul everything on the Vespa, Zabriskie wedged the

trainer into the place where you put your feet, and I crammed everything else into a backpack and two shopping bags, one in each hand. Back at the apartment, while Zabriskie hung the dartboard, I said, "Now it's time to get paid." I wrote on the receipt that the race mechanic had instructed me to buy training tires and that I needed reimbursement. Then I mailed it to Tailwind Sports.

A few weeks later, I received a check for the full amount. The bill was written in Catalan so they couldn't read what it said—they'd even paid for the dartboard.

I will say this about Lance's lifestyle: It is very nice to have a private jet. When Lance and I did the same races, he'd invite me to fly with him. It was a huge advantage. By avoiding major airports, ticket lines, and security, we'd be back in Girona six or seven hours before everyone else. Lance had more pressure from outside commitments than anyone else, but he could also afford advantages no one else had.

With his teammates, Lance didn't flaunt his wealth, and he was generous in taking me along on his flights. But he did like to tease Johan. Once when we were driving home from the tiny Girona airport, he called Johan. "Hey, Johan, where are you?" he asked. All I heard was Johan's booming voice through the phone. Lance just smiled. "Okay, bye Johan." Then, turning to me, he said, "He's still at the ticket counter in Brussels."

Other than a few rides on the jet, I never really paid attention to all that other stuff Lance had going on. To me and the other guys on the team, he was just a bike racer—an obsessed bike racer. Every single part of the man's life was focused on winning. He scrutinized everything about his training and did whatever he could to gain an edge, from keeping careful track of what he ate to sleeping in an altitude tent to training with a power meter that you could mount on your bike to record your wattage, which at the time was a fairly new invention.

Lance always had to have the most cutting-edge equipment, set up precisely to his liking. Before every ride he'd go over his bike meticulously, and still he'd stop and change his seat height three times during a single ride. I understood his interest in technology and training methods, but the bike fiddling seemed excessive to me. I could go an entire ride with my seat height a half-inch off and fix it later. To me, it wasn't even worth worrying about. But Lance was Lance. "There, that's much better," he'd say after moving it one millimeter.

Our whole team was set up around Lance. What people saw on TV was him riding away from everyone else at the end of the race. What they didn't necessarily notice were the eight other guys doing absolutely everything they could to ensure that Lance was as fresh as possible once he got to that takeoff point. A rider who works for a team leader is known as a *domestique*, which in French means "servant." We *domestique*s shielded Lance from the wind, drifted back to the team car to pick up food and fresh bottles of water for him, and covered moves in the peloton so that he never had to exert himself by accelerating to keep up.

We were known as the Blue Train, or *le Train Bleu*, for the efficient way we delivered Lance to the end of a stage. Once our jobs were done, we'd fade back to rest, not caring about our own finishing places. All that mattered was that Lance either had the yellow jersey or was in a good position to claim it.

Lance had his own way of being a jerk in the peloton to get what he wanted. He intimidated other riders with a yell or a small shove. It was never anything illegal, just simple gestures to be sure people knew: You don't mess with Lance. He never yielded, so other riders stayed out of his way because that was easier than spending the energy fighting him. The result was that Lance was the boss of the peloton. For Lance it was basically a war. And sometimes it wasn't even a war to win—it was a war to inflict suffering. If a group of riders tried to launch a breakaway when he didn't want them to, we'd break out "the hurt stick," as we called it, by sending Postal riders forward to pick up the pace until the breakaway riders begged for mercy. The result was that everyone gave Lance control, because they were afraid of the consequences if they didn't.

The thing about Lance was that his domineering attitude wasn't just directed at the competition; it was embedded deep in his personality, even when he was off the bike. When Lance felt in control he was happy, and when he didn't it drove him crazy. Everyone on the team followed his lead, because things were just easier that way. The entire team could be sitting at dinner during a race, telling jokes and goofing off, but once Lance came into the room the whole tone changed. It was as if you couldn't laugh unless he laughed first.

It was a rainy day in Girona, and Zabriskie and I didn't want to ride. We ended up at a café ordering cappuccinos. Coffees are smaller in Europe than in America, so when ours were finished we ordered another, and then another. The waitress thought this was so funny that she brought us each yet another one, which we drank. And then she kept bringing them and giggling. We sat there for hours, and in the end Zabriskie and I had thirteen cappuccinos—each. My head hurt like hell.

Lance didn't like it one bit. On a ride a couple of days later, he confronted me. "You can't do it this way," he said. "You have to focus more." Zabriskie and I were a couple of fools who liked to waste time together, it was true. But Lance had this idea that we shouldn't goof off at all because it meant we weren't being obsessive enough about training and winning. I believed that I could train hard and still have fun when I was off the bike.

"No, it doesn't work like that," he said, insisting that part of my problem was living in Tony's apartment. He said it was distracting. "You need your own place." When I explained that I didn't have any money, he said I should forget about that and do it anyway. If I rode well and made the Tour team, I might get bonuses that would make it worthwhile.

It was a huge financial strain to rent a place, but I did it, partly because Lance was the boss, and I listened to him. But having my own place also meant that I could pile a couple more European plane tickets on the credit card so that Amber and Ryan could come stay with me. I missed them.

The two-bedroom apartment on the outskirts of town had all the character of a dorm room. There was one regular bedroom and one tiny bedroom for Ryan that pretty much fit the bed and nothing else. The showerhead dribbled, we had no phone hooked up, and only a single fan that we moved from room to room.

Amber and Ryan flew to Spain for a three-week visit, and we rented a car and drove to the Ikea in Barcelona to buy furniture. "We don't have the money for this," Amber said.

"Well, what are we going to do," I said, "sit on the floor?"

"I mean it," she said.

"I know," I said. "But don't worry, babe. It's going to work out."

We bought everything—a couch, a table, sheets, towels, plates, silverware—and blew about two grand. Every square inch of that rental car was crammed with stuff on the trip back to Girona, with poor Ryan wedged into a corner of the backseat with some pillows.

On Postal, the married riders transplanted their families to Girona during the racing season, though it quickly became apparent that mine wasn't happy that way. A few of the riders had kids; but at five years, only mine was old enough to care that she was being uprooted. Amber didn't like it much either, since she didn't know anyone.

That first year when I was away racing, Amber had to use a pay phone to call me. "It's so hot here," she'd say. "We have to take baths because that shower sucks so much." I didn't like what I was putting them through. They were used to being independent, and now it was like they were putting their lives completely on hold to wait around for me. Finally, the next year, I couldn't take it anymore.

"We were watching the playground today," Amber told me over the phone while I was away. There was a playground across the street, but Ryan didn't know any of the kids and didn't speak Spanish, so they just watched. "So, I said to Rye, 'I miss Daddy,' and you know what she said to me?"

"No, what?"

"She said, 'Mommy, you should pretend that he's here. That's what I do with my friends.'"

"What?" I said. "All right, that sucks. That is not okay." We made some new ground rules: No more pretending. They would come overseas for something really big, like the end of the Tour. Otherwise, they'd stay in California where they had their lives. I'd fly home more so we wouldn't go more than two or three months without seeing each other, and we'd figure out how to make it work being apart. Mostly, that meant a lot of talking on the phone, sometimes four or five times a day.

My first season with Postal, I focused hard on training and racing—not because Lance or anyone else told me to, but because that's how I did things anyway. In the six weeks before the Tour, I went with Lance to St. Moritz, Switzerland, to train at high altitude and scope out some of the Alps mountain stages of the Tour, which were across the border in France. It was only the two of us. None of the other riders volunteered to go.

"You better be careful," Dirk Demol, one of the team directors, warned me. "Other guys have gone with him before, and they've never been the same since." Lance's famous pre-Tour training sessions consisted of hard rides every day, six hours a day. I suppose Dirk's point was that riders pushed themselves so hard trying to keep up that they'd use up their legs and be unable to recover. I wasn't worried.

"That won't happen to me," I told him. "But if he kills me, he kills me. At least then I'd know that I don't have what it takes to win the Tour and I can stop wasting my time." Dirk probably thought I was just being a cocky kid.

That first year, I couldn't quite do everything that Lance did, but it certainly wasn't easy for him to get rid of me either, no matter how long or hard the climb, or how many times we rode up it. What I learned was that, when it came to desire and work ethic, Lance and I are a lot alike. We set a goal and then we do absolutely whatever it takes to figure out how to achieve it. Neither of us liked to lose—at all. His approach was how I expected a Tour de France winner to train.

But, we didn't train exactly the same. There were times when I actually rode more than he did. When I told Lance and his training adviser that I had once ridden 24,000 miles in one year, they didn't believe me. Still, I was happy to be in Switzerland with Lance, if only to see that I could ride with him when he was training all out. He was glad to have me there too. For one, I pushed him, but he also liked being able to watch over me to be sure I was ready.

I was definitely ready. In the middle of our Switzerland boot camp was the Critérium du Dauphiné Libéré, a week-long race in France that many riders use as their final tune-up before the Tour. Lance had spoken to Johan about how I had been proving myself in St. Moritz. The two of them saw eye-to-eye on everything. Lance trusted Johan's opinions and tactical decisions. Johan knew that as long as Lance was happy, he would win races. They were so in sync that sometimes it was as if they were the same person.

"Okay," Johan said to me. "Let's see what you can do." I had stayed within about a minute of Lance in the first two stages, but then he crushed me in the individual time trial, in which racers ride one at a time against the clock. I finished nearly three minutes behind him. Clearly, I had work to do on my time trialing if I was ever going to keep up with him.

Lance's time trial was good enough to give him the race's leader's jersey. The next day, I got into an early breakaway and, instead of defending Lance's lead, my teammates let me go enough so that I could gain enough time to move up in the ranks but not pass Lance. At the end of the day, Lance was still in yellow and I had made up more than three minutes. I was in second place overall, just sixteen seconds behind

Lance. "Very good," Johan said. "Now, you protect Lance's wheel."

For the next stage, while my teammates worked hard on the front, I rode directly behind Lance to be sure no one got near him. I spent the whole day sitting in the draft, enjoying the ride. "Johan, I like this spot," I said on the team radio, and he laughed at me.

Stage 6, the final mountain stage, had a brutal climb up the Joux Plane before a big descent to finish in Morzine. The Joux Plane had been in Lance's head ever since he cracked on it in the 2000 Tour and lost precious time to his rivals. The plan was for me to stick on his wheel again, but if the team faltered or Lance got into trouble, I'd sacrifice my second-place spot to help Lance. The team defended Lance's lead perfectly to the base of the Joux Plane. "Nothing crazy here, guys," Johan said. "Respect this climb."

Lance was loose and relaxed, and he began pulling away from everyone. He blasted up the end of the climb and descended into Morzine to win the stage. I finished eighth, which was good enough to stay in second place overall. After the final stage, Lance and I stood together on the podium, him in first and me in second. From there, we went to a nearby airfield and jumped in a helicopter Lance had chartered from Grenoble, France, back to St. Moritz. It's a six-hour drive, but we were back at our apartments two hours after the race ended.

On a ride about a week later, Lance asked me who I

thought should be selected to ride for the Tour de France team. "Obviously, I'm going to say me," I said.

He went through a list of seven top guys whom he wanted before saying, "And obviously you." I felt like I had won the lottery. I was going to the big one.

You don't really understand the magnitude of the Tour de France until you see it in person. It is bigger, faster, and harder than any other bike race in the world. It's so long that they give you a thick course book that riders call the "race bible" so you can study each day's route before you set out. We had already scouted many of the Tour's toughest stages in training camp, but it's impossible to know the entire course before you start.

Spectators come from all over the world to watch, typically about fifteen million of them. The start and finish areas are packed with fans hanging over the barricades waving at you, wanting a water bottle or team cap or autograph. It was a mob scene like I had never experienced, and some things felt so strange. No one had ever wanted my signature before.

During the race, fans are within an arm's reach much of the time, with nothing between them and the riders. It's a small miracle that fans rarely interfere with the race. In some stages, for more than 100 miles people stand five deep along the side of the road. They are like walls of sound on either side, and sometimes you can't even hear the guy next to you. If it's hot and the crowds are big, you can smell the beer wafting through the air.

The first week of the race usually rolls through flat parts of France or neighboring countries, and because everyone can sustain the pace, the peloton stays tight until the very end, when a sprinter cranks it up to eke out a high-speed win. Crashes happen all the time, and can take out half the peloton.

Lance's main focus was to stay out of trouble, which meant staying toward the front of the pack. Every day, I went to the front with teammates while Lance tucked safely in our draft. This meant that for Lance, the first week was almost a recovery period, while I worked like a dog. After the first few stages, I was cooked.

"Is the whole thing this hard?" I asked George Hincapie, a soft-spoken teammate from Queens, New York, who had ridden with Lance for each of his wins, and who is one of the nicest people you'll ever meet. That day we had finished a flat, fast 120 miles through the wind in Normandy. Even though the pack had finished all together, George and I had jumped into an early breakaway to be sure that no one escaped from ONCE, the team of Joseba Beloki, Lance's biggest rival that year. The pack regrouped, but still we rode on the front to keep Lance out of trouble.

"No, not the whole thing," he said quietly, and then smiled. "It gets harder."

Knowing that there's a guy on your team who can win the whole race is a blessing because it provides crucial motivation. There are dozens of guys who bust their asses for 2,000 miles with no hope of ultimate individual or team success—I have no idea how they do it. Of course, the flip side of having a chance to win is that there is also way more stress. Every day we had to watch for breakaways from ONCE. We could never let our guard down.

In the middle of the Tour, a reporter from a cycling website asked me about my old team, Mercury, and the status of the riders being paid. I told him the truth: I had tried to follow the UCI's rules to be paid by the bank guarantee, and still I had never received my money. Within a few hours of the interview being posted on the site, I got an e-mail from a UCI official that copied Lance, Johan, and various members of the U.S. Postal team management, stating that if I didn't retract my comments within forty-eight hours, I would be suspended indefinitely.

My phone started ringing. It was Johan, telling me to retract the statements, now. "No," I told him. "Not until I understand why. I didn't do anything wrong here. I'm the one who didn't get paid."

Lance called too, and I told him the same thing. "It doesn't matter if you're right," he said. "You can't say things like that about the UCI. You're going to have to deal with them in the future, and you don't want them to be against you."

Someone from Postal management even found a rule that says riders aren't supposed to comment on actions by the UCI. If he hadn't found that rule, I probably wouldn't have backed down. Instead, I retracted what I said and called Hein Verbruggen to apologize.

I didn't like the way the UCI system worked, but after that

I tried to keep my mouth shut because my team wanted me to play the game. In the end, I finally did get my money—nearly three years after the fact.

For all the difficulty of the flats, the race doesn't really start until you hit the mountains. Stage 12 went through the Pyrenees and finished going up the Tourmalet, a nine-mile monster with an average grade of 7 percent. Even though we had a whole arsenal of world-class climbing specialists on the team, such as Colombian Victor Hugo Peña and Spaniards José Luis "Chechu" Rubiera and Roberto Heras, Johan picked me to be the final rider to lead Lance up the Tourmalet.

From the very beginning of the stage, my legs felt like lead weights. I tried to figure out why I felt so bad, but I couldn't come up with a reason. I had slept enough and eaten well. When the first climb came, I fell off the pace and got left in the dust. The team had asked me to perform, and no matter how much I wanted to go, I just couldn't. I felt terrible about it.

There were still 60 miles to go in the stage, though, and there were seven other guys who could look after Lance, so it wasn't a crisis. In the end, Chechu paced Lance up the Tourmalet. Lance took off at the end to win the stage and gained enough time in the general classification to take over the yellow jersey. Heras ended up third in the stage. Despite my poor performance, the result for the team couldn't have been much better.

That night, Lance came by my hotel room. He told me that everyone has a bad day at the Tour. Over the years I would learn that he was right. Some days are miserable, and the only thing you can do is hope that, on the day you feel bad, the stage is flat enough that you might be able to fake it and reach the finish without cracking. The only consolation of feeling that bad is that typically it doesn't last more than one stage. In fact, often the next day the body bounces back to have a good day. But Lance didn't tell me any of this. Instead, he became demanding. "You have to be better tomorrow," he said with complete conviction. "It can't happen like that." Afterward, Johan came in and said, "This is unacceptable."

Their attitude made me mad, because I already felt bad enough about how things had gone. "You think I'd humiliate myself like that on purpose?" I said to Johan. "It's not like I was being lazy. Of course I'll give one hundred percent tomorrow and try not to let it happen again, but you can't make it happen simply by ordering me."

Ultimately, I think Lance and Johan said those things more for themselves than for me, to make them feel better, like they were doing something to control the situation. To me, it was a pretty clear example of our different ways of thinking. If it had been me with an underperforming young rider, I would have said, "Look, we have to avoid bad days, but you can't change it now. Don't be depressed about it. This is how it goes at the Tour: You have a bad day, and then the next day is often your best."

And, in fact, the next day was my best of the whole race. I started out angry, and Johan even had to tell me three or four times on the team radio to slow down. After that I settled in and, on the last climb of the day, I looked around and saw there were only twelve of us left in the group, and four of us were from Postal. Lance won the stage again, and this time Heras was second. At this point in the race we were dominating so much that Lance's biggest challengers were his teammates.

But just because Lance and the team were killing everyone else doesn't mean the race was easy. By the third week of the Tour, everyone was thinner from burning more calories than they could possibly take in. We ate pasta for breakfast and dinner every day, and I desperately wanted a beer, a big bowl of chips and guacamole, and ice cream. I felt worn and haggard. If there was no reason to speak or move, I didn't. Every bit of energy went into riding. There was nothing to spare for anything else.

In the end, Lance beat ONCE's Beloki by seven minutes, practically a landslide. I finished sixty-first and I was a wreck. That I even finished was a big accomplishment— many riders don't finish their first Tour. Lance didn't finish until his third try. I couldn't believe where I was—taking a victory lap around the Champs-Élyseés with the winning team—compared to where I had been less than a year ago, not racing and not being paid. I did manage to find the energy to pop a wheelie and ride it for a while as Lance carried the American flag. He and the guys laughed.

After the race, I called my parents, and they were pretty proud. "I watched you every day," my mother said. Their neighbors, the Martins, have a television set, so they gave their house keys to my mom, and she'd go watch the race live during the day. If she caught a glimpse of me in the peloton, or if I had been mentioned in the broadcast, she'd tell my dad and he'd go watch the rerun after work.

Amber met me in Paris. I hadn't seen her in more than two months. "You look terrible," she said. "Your shoulders are like a coat hanger with your skin hanging off." I'm five feet ten inches tall and I went into the Tour at about 152 pounds. In three weeks, while eating as much as I possibly could, I had lost about seven pounds. My upper arms were thinner than my forearms, and my ribs were sticking out through my skin.

The night the Tour ended, we all went to a big U.S. Postal sponsor party. Before it, though, Lance had his own private party for the riders and their wives. He sent a bunch of Mercedes around to pick us up, and we went to a special room he had rented.

As we all stood around telling stories, Lance worked the room. He had a bunch of envelopes in his hand, and eventually he made his way to me. "Here's your Lance bonus," he said.

It's a tradition for the winner to split his official prize money for winning the Tour, which is 450,000 euros, among the riders and staff on his team. And Lance also liked to give his teammates an additional bonus from his own private bank account. Lance stood to gain millions of dollars in endorsements and sponsorships for what we had helped him do, so he wanted to spread the wealth a little.

"Thanks, man," I said. "I'm so glad it worked out." I couldn't think of what else to say. I was out of it; it felt like a layer of fatigue was smothering me. I stashed the envelope in my pocket.

Later, I was so worn down that Amber and I left the sponsor party early and went back to our hotel. I took the envelope out of my pocket. "Hey, let's open it," I said, and she came over as I ripped it open. Inside was the biggest check we had ever seen.

"Holy crap," she said. "That's a lot of money." We were mesmerized just looking at it. My cut of the Tour prize money was about fifty thousand dollars, and Lance added an extra forty thousand on top of that.

In an instant, our money problems vanished. Suddenly we could pay off all our credit cards and repay the money David and Ms. Rose had loaned us for the house.

We stayed in Paris for a few extra days, and celebrated by going to McDonald's for french fries. And I slept for two days straight.

CHAPTER 4

Just Barely

Besides fast, the only other speed I do well is slow. I can sleep and lie around and do nothing all day with the best of them. The fall was a quiet time of recovery, and I loved every minute of it.

Postal had signed me on for another two years—by far the longest contract I had ever had for anything. I would make $215,000 for 2003 and $240,000 for 2004. I felt relief at having the job security and financial stability, and excitement that I was continuing to ride with the strongest team in cycling. Finally, I thought, I've made it.

My favorite part of being home was that I got to read to Ryan at night and then have breakfast with her in the morning, things I really missed doing when I was in Europe. I also went to a few of her soccer games. Watching six-year-olds play soccer isn't much of a spectacle of strategy or athleticism, but it's hard to beat in terms of cuteness. And, for the first time in years, I didn't have to worry about how I was going to come up with the money to buy her Christmas presents. In fact, we were working on moving to a nicer house in Murrieta.

We went back to Pennsylvania to visit my parents for Thanksgiving, and I stuffed myself with the big platters of food my mom had prepared. I knew that hard training would come soon enough, and I could worry about going on a diet then.

When my break was up, I was ready to get back to it. I was determined to train as hard as ever to help Lance win his fifth consecutive Tour de France in 2003, which would tie him for the record number of wins along with the other legends of cycling: Jacques Anquetil, Eddy Merckx, Bernard Hinault, and Miguel Indurain.

It was January 11, and I went to the gym in the morning to do leg presses, then went out for a two-hour ride to one of my favorite training areas in the Murrieta area: the short, steep hills of the ridge in De Luz, just a few miles from my house. When I ride there it's like a roller coaster, but fast going uphill as well as down.

That morning, halfway down one of the descents, I decided to take a right turn I almost never take. I'm not sure why I wanted to go that way, or why I waited so long to act. I made the decision a half-second too late, so I had to hit the brakes really hard. As I tried to carve the turn near the road edge, my front wheel hit some gravel and slid out from under me.

I never even saw the stones. They were smaller than BBs, and the same color as the road. If you were to reach down and skim your fingers across the asphalt in that corner, it would feel slick, like wet glass. I didn't have time to do anything to try to recover. The wheel slid sideways, and I went straight down onto my right hip.

I hit with so much downward force that I didn't even slide, and I ended up lying on my side in the middle of the intersection. My feet were still connected to the pedals.

The first thing I thought was, *What an idiot.* I know how to handle my bike—better than just about any other rider—and I had been in plenty of crashes over the years, but never when I was out alone. I had lost focus for only a moment. That's all it took.

The sharp pain and tunnel vision snapped me out of my thoughts. I clicked my left foot out of the pedal, then realized that I couldn't move my heel outward to free my right foot. I had to reach down under my bike and jerk my foot free.

It was the most painful thing I have ever experienced. I tried to get up a couple of times, but I couldn't even stand, much less walk, so I kind of dragged myself and my bike to the side of the road using my arms. Almost instantly I thought, *I must have dislocated my hip.* The pain was so bad I just had to lie down.

There's hardly any traffic up there, so I knew I couldn't count on someone driving by. And there's almost never a cell phone signal on the ridge, but when I pulled my cell phone out of my jersey pocket, I had a signal. I called Amber and said, very calmly, "I need you to come get me." I had never asked her to pick me up during a ride before, and she knows that the worse things are, the calmer I get. So she dropped everything and sped to reach me.

I perched next to a fire hydrant on the side of the road. By luck, a woman did drive by, and she stopped to ask if I was okay. I said, "Sure, I'm fine," with no more concern than if I'd had a flat tire with no way to fix it. "Thank you, though. My wife's coming."

The sun warmed me, and the same wind that blew the gravel onto the street blew the scrub grass on the desert hillside. I looked out in the distance at the mountains where I trained—Big Bear, Idyllwild, Mt. Palomar—and waited for what seemed like forever. Amber finally got there.

"You're covered in blood!" she screamed. I hadn't really thought about it, but my shoulder was exposed through my torn jersey, and covered in road rash. Blood was dripping from my knee all the way down into my shoe. She had to help me stand up, and I had to hold my right leg and lean against her while I hopped toward the car. "We're going to the hospital," she said.

"No, I think it's just dislocated," I said. "Let's go home." She argued with me, so I said, "I'll call Arnie. He'll know what to do." After we got down the ridge and had a better cell signal, I dialed.

"Hey, Arnie, it's Floyd," I said. "Hey, what does it feel like to have your hip dislocated?" I explained that it didn't seem to be sticking out at a funny angle, but that I couldn't move it at all. Arnie told me to go straight to the hospital, but still I said no, that it was probably just dislocated.

Amber wasn't thinking very clearly either, because she let me convince her to drive home. When we pulled into our garage, I couldn't get out of the car.

She brought me Aleve, but it didn't help. So after about an hour, I finally agreed to go to the hospital—but not before I changed out of my Postal clothes and into a T-shirt and pair of jeans. My leg was starting to swell, but, in my mind anyway, it was fine. It was just dislocated.

David joined us at the emergency room, and we waited for three hours. It was after dark by the time the doctors took X-rays and told me that I had fractured the neck of my femur. Looking at the X-rays, I could see a black line all the way across the top of my thighbone. Basically, I had snapped off the ball part of the ball-and-socket joint of my hip.

On a ride a couple of months before, I had met Brent Kay, a sports medicine doctor who ran a clinic in neighboring Temecula, the OUCH Medical Center. We had become friends, and I called him to explain what had happened. He came down to the ER and he never left. I was a little surprised that someone I didn't know all that well would go so far out of his way for me, but it turned out to be just the first of many times.

When Brent arrived, he was shocked that I caught a ride home and cleaned up before going to the hospital. He said that just about everyone who breaks a hip like this ends up having paramedics scrape them off the ground and put them in an ambulance. He shook his head at my pain tolerance as I sat there cracking jokes with the staff of the small trauma hospital.

They put me in a hallway to wait, and a few hours later the doctors finally explained to me that I'd need surgery, but said it could wait until tomorrow. I figured they were the experts and that they knew what they were doing, but Brent jumped in. "You don't understand," he said. "This is his career. It has to be tonight." Brent knew that even with the best care, people with fractures like the one I had are at high risk for developing a condition known as avascular necrosis (AVN), where the bone dies as a result of the injury. The most important factor in reducing the risk is having fast treatment. He called the orthopedic trauma surgeon on call that day, a personal friend of his, and I was prepped for surgery. During the operation they drilled three big titanium screws into my thighbone to hold it together. And when I got out at two in the morning, David and Brent were still there.

I went home the next day, and it started to sink in: I might never be able to race the same again. I didn't want to believe that everything I had worked for could all be taken away by a stupid accident. Then, there was money to worry about. I had the deal with Postal, but there's a UCI rule that if you're injured for three months, your team has the right to terminate your contract. Plus, I didn't want just to stay on the team; I *had* to make the Tour team in July. That was where the bonuses were.

Brent became my personal physician and helped me get dozens of medical opinions on my case. Just about everyone told me not to ride until I was completely healed. But early on I told Brent, "I'm doing the Tour de France this year." That was my objective, and nothing was going to stop me, especially not my body.

Less than two weeks after the crash, I snuck some time on a stationary bike. When no one was home, I went into the garage and dragged a bike over to my stationary trainer and set it up. But I couldn't come close to throwing a leg over the bike. For starters, I couldn't lift my right leg. Then, I couldn't put enough weight on my right foot in order to pick my left foot up off the ground. So I just sort of hung on to the handlebars and slid onto the saddle from behind, and from there I worked my way into position.

At first, I pedaled only with my left leg. But that seemed dumb, so I started using my right, too—though I still had to reach down and click my foot in and out of the pedal with my hands. The flex of my right leg came back very slowly. The first few times I tried riding, it was more like the momentum of my left leg was pushing my right leg along. Sure, it hurt. It was incredible pain, but I figured complaining about it wouldn't do any good, so I just kept my mouth shut.

I continued pedaling on the stationary trainer, and six weeks after surgery I ditched the crutches. I started riding on the road again and boosted my mileage slowly, until I finally began feeling like a bike racer again. By the time of my first race, three months after the crash, I was up to my normal training range, riding 500 miles a week.

Off the bike, getting around was pretty rough, but I just

did my best to ignore the fact that I couldn't get around all that well. At the Tour de Georgia in April 2003, a reporter noticed how badly I was limping and asked how my hip was healing. I didn't want to talk about it, but I didn't want to leave him hanging, either, so I said, "I'm not limping. This is my strut!"

No one really persisted in asking me questions because it's typical for a cyclist to avoid walking altogether, or mosey along slowly only when he absolutely has to. Of course it hurts to walk after you spend all day pedaling hard, but mostly riders avoid it because of a silly superstition: Walking wastes precious energy, and therefore could hurt cycling performance. I always thought it was a ridiculous idea. If walking is going to set you back, you've got way bigger problems than having to get somewhere on foot. But whenever I was asked about my slow gait, I'd use the "I hate walking" excuse.

The truth was, my hip had been getting better, but it was starting to hurt like hell again. And this time it wasn't just the pain of healing but a different sort of pain, an evil pain. Every time I'd lift my leg to pedal, it was like someone was stabbing me with a knife.

I went to San Diego to see Brent's friend, Dr. David Chao of Oasis Sports Medicine, an orthopedist and team doctor for the San Diego Chargers.

He found that my thighbone had compressed during healing, which was normal—but it was causing those long titanium screws to stick out of my thigh bone by about a centimeter. You could even feel the screw heads through my skin.

That explained the pain: With every pedal stroke, the screw heads were grinding against my iliotibial band, or ITB, the big tendon that runs along the outside of the leg from the hip to the knee. They had to come out. Dr. Chao said that the fracture hadn't healed completely, so he wanted to replace them with smaller screws.

The problem was that Johan was freaking out. By this time, it was early May, just two months before the Tour, and the team was in rough shape. George was just coming back after a bad respiratory infection that had kept him out of all the spring races, and some of the other guys weren't in top form. Lance's marriage was in the process of breaking up, and for the first time he didn't seem like his usual 100-percent-focused self.

There were chinks in the U.S. Postal armor. I had to get to Europe as soon as possible to train so Johan could see for himself that I was okay to ride. At one point, he insisted that I fly to Spain the same day I had surgery. But we finally talked him into letting me wait until the day after to fly.

Dr. Chao took out the old screws and replaced them with three new ones, each one three and a half inches long and a quarter of an inch wide. It was an outpatient procedure, so on the way home from Oasis, Amber and I stopped at In-N-Out Burger for lunch. By the time we got home to our new house, though, I was bleeding through my pants onto the seat. My surgical wound had opened up. I called Brent at OUCH.

We didn't have any furniture yet in the new house, so I was lying on the floor in the living room when Brent got there. He put a bath towel against my hip and leaned on me with all his weight to try to stop the bleeding. It worked.

Later, Amber wondered how we'd keep the bleeding from starting again while I slept.

"We need a way to keep pressure on it," I said. "Something heavy." After hunting around the house, we found a spare granite slab from our new kitchen counter. That night I slept on my side, and Amber pressed the slab against my hip and laid against it. We left for the airport at 4 a.m.

There was never a question of whether I'd go. Johan needed climbers to help Lance win the Tour, and he needed to see that I was okay to ride. That was all that mattered. When I arrived in Spain, I couldn't even walk up a step with my right foot, but I had left my crutches at home because I wanted it to seem like I was fine. After hardly even looking at me, Johan had me see a doctor, who said my hip was completely healed, and that he didn't even see why they bothered with the second surgery. On one hand I knew he was a quack, but on the other I was happy to have the team's go-ahead to ride.

Less than a week later I did the five-day Tour of Belgium, and my entire leg turned black. There was still swelling, and blood under the skin was going down my leg. My whole foot and calf were bruised. I'm sure the guys on my team were thinking, *What the hell's wrong with this guy?* But I acted like everything was fine, so no one mentioned it. During the race it was cold, so I wore leg warmers to cover up, and no one noticed my horribly discolored leg.

I finished the race, barely. And then it was off to a team

training camp in the Pyrenees. The funny thing was, I had lost some muscle tone from all the time off since my accident, so I weighed a little less than normal. Less body weight meant less to carry up the hill, so I was actually climbing well, considering. All the best climbers were there: Lance, me, George, Chechu, Peña, and Manuel "Triki" Beltrán, a Spaniard who Johan had hired midseason. I was about as strong as the other guys, though not as strong as I should have been, and not as strong as Lance.

Over the course of the camp, things slowly got better, and at the end I sent Brent an e-mail: "The bruise is almost gone and there is no more pain. I don't know if 550 miles in the mountains with the team helped or not, but I guess time will tell."

Of course it probably wasn't smart. Of course I probably would have healed better taking time off. Was I doing myself permanent damage that would come back to haunt me later? Who knows. Some doctors guess yes, and some guess no. One thing I've learned is that if you ask enough experts for their opinions on anything, you'll eventually find the opinion that matches the one you'd like to hear. I had doctors give advice from, "Stop everything and don't move for three months," to, "You're perfectly fine," and every shade in between.

I wanted to ride, so I listened to the doctors who said I could. In cycling you race unless you absolutely can't. That's just how it works if you're going to be good. If there is any possible way you can do it, you go. Our careers are short—for a Tour de France racer, thirty-four is over the hill. And opportunities don't come twice.

◆ ◆ ◆

Johan waited until the week before the Tour to finalize the team, just to be sure he had the strongest riders. The waiting drove me crazy, but I was eventually chosen. By then, I was walking without too much of a limp and I felt strong.

But Lance clearly didn't. It showed in the very first minutes of the race. In the prologue, the short time trial that often begins the Tour, he finished seventh instead of demolishing his rivals as he had done in years past. He was only seven seconds behind, but the prologue is where the contenders all size each other up, and he had been beaten by his archrival, Jan Ullrich of T-Mobile, and by his former *domestique*, Tyler Hamilton of CSC. Other teams used his bad day as inspiration.

From there, it seemed like there was a crisis nearly every stage. In Stage 1 there was a huge pileup of riders in the sprint with just 500 meters to go, and Lance went down in a crash for the first time since he started winning the Tour. Luckily, he wasn't hurt. In a brief break from mishap, our team rode strong in the team time trial—where we all speed on our time-trial bikes at the same time—and we won it, my first ever stage win in the Tour. But as we entered the mountain stages, Lance discovered halfway through the stage to Alpe d'Huez that his brake was rubbing (a silly mistake for someone so meticulous about his bike), and then the next day he just narrowly avoided a high-speed crash on a descent by detouring off the road and through a field.

The team played it conservatively, which was also out of

character. Instead of unleashing a furious attack in an early mountain stage to give Lance a few minutes on his rivals, we sent the strongest climbers—usually Chechu and Triki—to the front to make sure that Lance stayed near the lead and that he didn't lose any time. When we weren't on the gas, we were conserving everything we could.

In the stage to Alpe d'Huez, I helped pace Lance over the massive Col du Galibier, and then went to the front on the descent to set up a draft for him. By the time we got to the base of the Alpe, our team had been hammering all day, so we gave a final sprint and shot Lance off on his own to duke it out with the contenders. From there, George and I called it a day, with eight miles of climbing still to go. We sat up and chatted all the way to the top, finishing nineteen minutes back and saving ourselves for the mountain stages to come.

Lance would come around and have his great day—we hoped—and when he did we would be fresh and ready to help.

Then came Stage 12, a long individual time trial. Ullrich raced like a bullet, and Lance seemed affected by the heat, unable to push his big gears. He finished second in the stage, but Ullrich beat him by a minute and a half. All of a sudden Ullrich was only thirty-four seconds behind Lance overall, and the big problem was that, as they days went on, Ullrich was getting stronger. I loafed my way to seventieth place, knowing that the Pyrenees were looming and I had to be ready. But Ullrich gaining on Lance by that much? That was not good. Other teams knew it.

And our team knew it, though no one dared to admit it out loud. We all just quietly went about our business, and Lance got quiet too, in the same way he'd get when he was mad at something. He was worried and didn't want it to show.

George and I were rooming together, and the night after the time trial we started talking about it in our own way, which is to say, not really talking about it. "Man, what do you think?" he asked generically.

"Oh, man, I don't know," I said, being equally unspecific.

"Yeah," he said, shaking his head.

This went on for days. We'd go through our daily ritual of packing, racing, and then unpacking our uniforms and jeans, listening to a little gangsta rap, and then having the same conversation. "Yeah, I don't know," followed by, "No, me neither." We weren't saying anything, but the subtext was more like, "You know, sooner or later this team is going to lose this race. We still have a few big mountain stages left, and a long time trial toward the end that Ullrich could crush if he keeps riding like he has been riding. Then, there's the possibility that he'll get even stronger. Oh, man, what if Ullrich gets *stronger*? And what if this is the year that Lance can't do it? What if this is the year we can't help him do it?"

Of course we were going to fight as hard as we could no matter what happened. Lance would too. No one fought harder than Lance that year. His ability to suffer and persevere was at a level you typically only see in cheesy movies, not in real life.

He wanted it, and he went for it when it counted, even

though he had more bad luck: On the stage to Luz Ardiden in the Pyrenees, Lance was riding an inside line close to the spectators, and a fan's bag snagged his brake lever. He went down sideways, and hard, with only about eight kilometers to go. But it was like something in the fall jolted his fury loose, because when he got back up, he flew to the front of the remaining riders, and then past them to win the stage. Four days later, when Ullrich crashed in the final time trial in a rain-soaked roundabout, Lance secured Tour win number five by a minute and one second. Just barely.

I ended up finishing seventy-seventh, my worst Tour de France finish. I spent everything I had, even though at times that wasn't much, without saving anything for myself. My hip didn't really hurt when I pedaled during the race, but by the last week of the Tour, after the mountains, it became really painful to stand or walk. Fortunately, during the Tour you either race or rest, so I didn't walk much. Whenever I got on the team bus, though, I had to use both hands on the railing to pull myself up the steps.

Amber and Ryan met me after the race, and we went to the beach for three days. Amber was mad at me for how badly I was limping. She did have a point. I had to concentrate just to be sure I didn't fall down. "Come here, babe," I said, "it's good to see you," and I put my arm around her when we walked, partly because I had missed her and Ryan, but also for the stability. Still, I had no regrets, and was proud of what I did for the team to help Lance win.

CHAPTER 5

Falling Apart

I had been one of the strongest riders at Postal's winter team training camp, so I was picked to be the team leader at the five-day Tour of Algarve in Portugal. I won the race, and it felt good. Finally, my hip problems seemed to be behind me. My hip ached, but I could train as hard as I wanted. I was on a roll.

Next up was one of the toughest spring classics, the weeklong Paris–Nice, and I was going to be the team leader again. A few days into the race, the pack went up one of the early hills pretty hard. I was out of the saddle climbing, and suddenly I felt a weird, sharp pain in my hip. Deep down, I had been worried that the whole thing would just go all of a sudden, but I didn't want to believe that it would. So I just kept going, hoping that positive thinking would be enough. For the rest of the stage, I felt a strange click with every pedal stroke, but the pain was not as strong as before.

The next day, it felt a little better so I tried to put my hip out of my head. It was pretty easy to do, not only because I wanted to forget, but also because I had another issue to deal with: The U.S. Postal team's attitude was getting on my nerves.

I felt like I kept getting stronger and stronger, but I never gained any respect from the team management. We riders were like a commodity that kept the Lance machine rolling. No one cared about whether my hip was okay; it was always, "Will he be ready for the Tour?" And now I wanted to improve, but Johan wouldn't help me.

The trouble started with one bicycle. We have a special bike for time trials, an aerodynamic machine basically shaped like an airplane wing, curved and shaped to slice through the wind with maximum efficiency. Instead of a normal curled handlebar, it has a flat one, with pads for your elbows and handles straight out in front. Riders hunch low on these bikes, with their hands out front close together, like a downhill skier, to stay aerodynamic.

There was a U.S. Postal time-trial bike with my name on it, but the team mechanics kept it and maintained it, and it was for racing only. Lance had one for training, and I wanted one, too. If I could just become more familiar with the lower, more aerodynamic body position and work on my pacing, I thought, I could be much stronger in the team time trial at the Tour. In fact, I believed I could even win an individual time trial.

I had asked for a training bike last season, but it never showed up in California. So, at winter training camp, as we were gathering around the bikes and fiddling with seat height and brake adjustments to be sure they were perfect for the day's workout, I asked Johan again for a time-trial bike. I carefully laid out my case again for why I wanted one, that all I wanted was to be able to simulate the race in training— and then I dropped the nuclear bomb: "like Lance does."

Johan responded with his classic Belgian logic. "Eh, if you get one, then everyone will want one." Zabriskie was right from the beginning about the team attitude. As *domestiques*, we weren't supposed to request or question anything. The idea was that Lance won the Tour, so he got everything; we were lucky to even be riding with him, so we should shut up and be grateful for whatever scraps we got. We were always supposed to do what we were told, and nothing else.

I never understood the philosophy, and I wasn't very good at shutting up. "Well, why can't we?" I asked Johan. They had access to extra bikes, so why not help the team improve? By helping each of us improve, I argued, it would enable us to help Lance even more, right?

Johan didn't answer me, except to say, "George came in eighth in the time trial last year, and he doesn't have a training bike."

I felt my face start to turn red. "Is eighth good enough for you, Johan?" I asked. "Because it's not good enough for me." This was supposed to be the best cycling team in the world, and Lance not only had every bicycle he wanted, he had a million-dollar gear development program to ensure that he had the best bikes, wheels—you name it. Even his helmet and sunglasses were designed to fit together perfectly. That was fine with me—because of what he had done, he deserved to have everything he wanted. I didn't want all of that. What I wanted was a single bicycle.

It was typical for us *domestiques* to ride old bikes. My regular training bike in Girona was an ancient hand-me-down. Before me, it belonged to Dylan Casey, a rider who was about my height and was on the way out when I joined the team.

Back at Paris–Nice, during one of the later stages, I attacked like crazy on the last climb. I was out of contention to win the whole race, but I figured I'd at least try for a stage. The sprint came down to me and two other guys, standing out of the saddle and pedaling furiously, swinging our bikes back and forth for leverage. The torque broke the chain stay of my bike—it was the same bike I had raced on the year before, since we hadn't been given new ones yet. My chain fell off, and I pitched forward onto the asphalt. I lost. And I started feeling bitter.

After the stage, I walked onto the team bus swearing and complaining that we needed new bikes. I didn't care who heard.

My complaints got back to Lance. Everything eventually got back to Lance. For most of the spring, he gave me the cold shoulder. We still did our pre-Tour training and recon trip to

Switzerland, but things were different. Before, he had seen me as a young rider to take under his wing. Now he was beginning to see me as a rebel, which is to say, as a problem.

Just a few weeks before the Tour, at the Dauphiné, the team was having a meeting and talking about equipment when Lance said, "Then we got Floyd over here who thinks he's a world champion and deserves a jet." He was joking. But after months of not getting the bike and him not helping me, the comment pushed me too far.

"Wait a sec," I said. "I need to clear something up." I stopped the meeting. "You're the one with the jet. I asked for a bicycle." I went off about how we were a cycling *team* trying to win the Tour. "How can you possibly be accusing me of asking for too much when I'm asking for a single *bicycle?*"

Lance shrugged me off, and the meeting continued. But afterward, Johan came around to try to straighten me out. "You have to have more respect for him," he said.

"I respect him perfectly fine," I said. "What I don't accept is when nobody respects me." I refused to apologize.

By this point I had begun to think my days with the team were numbered. I had been asking the other guys for a while now if they had renewed their contracts yet. George had. Chechu had. Triki had. Almost everyone had deals for 2005, but no one from the team management had talked to me yet. I figured maybe Lance and Johan thought I was too much of a pain in the ass to keep around. I didn't blame them, because I knew I was more outspoken than they liked.

It wasn't that I was trying to start a team revolt. But,

more and more, I spoke up when I thought we deserved better. After we had won the team time trial at the Tour, I made a case to the management that a team time-trial win was the same as an individual stage win, and that we should each get the bonus offered in our contracts for winning a stage. I was turned down.

But when seven of us went to Texas to shoot a commercial for the U.S. Postal Service, I held my ground. Instead of featuring letter carriers, the commercial showed us delivering the mail on our bicycles. (I was the one doing the wheelie, and my teammate Robbie Ventura was the one jumping off a ramp into an alley.) It took three days to shoot, near Thanksgiving, and the sponsor rep from Postal said that we wouldn't be paid because the work was part of our contract. If Lance was doing it for free, I thought, then I guessed it wasn't such a big deal. But the next day at the shoot, Lance had a stunt double. I went back to the sponsor rep and explained that all the guys were working hard and had to be away from their families around the holiday, and how we really deserved to be paid. He was a reasonable man, and ultimately came around.

I talked to my teammates directly, too, asking point-blank how much money they made, because I was pretty sure we made less than riders on other teams. A typical conversation went like this:

"I make two-forty. What do you make?"

"Uh, I don't know if we're allowed to talk about that."

"Not allowed? What good does it do to keep it a secret?"

"Well, it's in my contract that I'm not supposed to say."

"What, you think you're going to get fired for telling me?"

Then I tried to explain that I wasn't just asking for my own benefit. "It's a big disadvantage to all of us not to know what everyone else makes. We should all be talking. The baseball players and the football players have unions and they share salary figures, and it helps them. How else will we know what we're worth in order to negotiate?" And then most of them told me. Some salaries were higher than mine, and in the cases of top riders, more than two times what I was making.

I'm not sure if knowing was helpful to any of the other guys, but I figured out that I was due for a raise, no matter what team I ended up on.

Tyler Hamilton had been a loyal lieutenant to U.S. Postal but had gone on to pursue his own Tour ambitions. He left the year before I arrived and, after finishing fourth in the 2003 Tour for CSC, was now leading a new team, Phonak, in their first Tour. I began talking to the team owner, Andy Rihs, about a job. Phonak is a Swiss hearing-aid company, and Andy was an executive on the board of directors who simply loved cycling and wanted to get involved as a relatively inexpensive way to gain publicity for the company. "I assure you the team is completely professional," he told me. "You'll get whatever you need to do your job." He was like an animated teddy bear, all smiles and enthusiasm, with a big gray beard and Einstein hair.

I didn't know Tyler that well, but the idea of working for him appealed to me. Even though I'd still be a *domestique*, I would have more freedom to choose my own races, and maybe even the chance to lead the team at the Tour of Italy or Tour of Spain. "Everything on this team is open for discussion," Andy told me. Tyler needed another strong climber, and Andy thought I would fit in well. Andy and I privately came to a verbal agreement that I'd sign a two-year deal for $450,000 per year, a decent salary for a top *domestique* but still not super high. We'd finalize things in writing after the Tour.

Postal still hadn't made me an offer by the start of the Tour, and I hadn't asked for one. In some regards, I was surprised that I was even picked to ride on the Tour team. But every day the first week, Johan sent me to the front to set the pace for Lance on the flats. Even though we bickered sometimes and my contract was up in the air, there was never a question of loyalty while on the bike. Lance and Johan knew that I would still give everything to help Lance win. And they were right, no matter how bad things were.

A few days into the race, Lance came to me and said, "We know you've been talking to Phonak." Deep down he knew I would do my job for him, but I guess he was still nervous that I would somehow give Tyler important information during the race, or that I would hurt team morale by seeming friendly with him. Or maybe he was just being possessive, because he could be. "I expect that between now and the end of the Tour, you won't talk to Tyler anymore," he said.

I was insulted, but said, "Okay, you're the boss." The Tour wasn't the place to argue with Lance.

The same day, Johan was furious. He had heard about Phonak too. "We've given you all these opportunities, and you act like an asshole, and still we take you to the Tour," he said. "And now you've been out talking to other teams and haven't even given us a chance to make you an offer yet."

"What do you mean, a chance?" I said. "The Tour is here, and my contract is up, and nobody's said a word to me about renewing." I told him that I knew that all the other guys had already signed, because I had asked them. "I figured you didn't want me anymore since, as you point out, I act like an asshole."

"You'll get your offer," Johan said. "You'll get it during the Tour. Just give us a chance."

I was pretty sure I didn't want it.

By outward appearances, things must have looked completely different: On the bikes, we were tearing up the race.

To make things even better, instead of just watching the race on TV at the Martins', my parents and three of my sisters—Charity, Priscilla, and Abigail—flew to France for a week. That year, they had driven to the Tour de Georgia, so they knew a little bit about how bike racing worked, but it was the first time my sisters had ever been on an airplane, and only the second time for my parents (they had flown to San Diego to see me once).

I was worried about them being so far out of their element.

Going to a foreign country can feel strange and unwelcoming sometimes, but for them it must have been like traveling to another planet. But they had good guides to show them around, and I was surprised by how willing they were to support me and immerse themselves in the race.

For the week they were there, every day they'd stand on the side of the road among the hundreds of thousands of fans to cheer as the race went by. It was 100 degrees out, but there—alongside the fat German men with no shirts on, the women in bikinis, the drunk Belgians, and the French fans living out of camper vans—was my family. Dad and my sisters wore long pants, Mom wore her long dress, and all the women wore their Mennonite head coverings. They held up signs that had been printed up by the people of Farmersville that said, simply, "We Support Floyd Landis."

You couldn't miss them if you tried. The whole team thought it was hilarious, and every day we'd look for my family standing along the course. In the first key mountain stage in the Alps, they were positioned on the final climb. Just when I was about to set tempo at the bottom for Lance, he said into his team radio, "Hey, Floyd, there's your family." I looked over my shoulder and smiled at them. Then I took off.

There were only about ten riders left in the lead pack when I didn't have anything left and had to pull off the front. Lance brought out his stuff and attacked to win the stage and take the yellow jersey.

As the Tour went on, something surprising was happening to me. I had never experienced it before: Even though I had worked hard every day early in the race, I was still feeling strong. In fact, I was actually getting stronger as the race went on.

The next day, there was a time trial up Alpe d'Huez. To even have a stage that ended with the famous nine-mile climb was brutal, but here we had to go up as fast as we could, one at a time. It was Lance's chance to put the race away. For the rest of us, it was a day to conserve our energy. "Take it easy, eh," Johan told me beforehand. "You need to be ready for the mountain stage tomorrow."

"No problem," I told him. I was looking forward to an easy ride, because I knew the final day in the mountains would be brutal. It was the longest, most difficult mountain stage of the Tour, with five tough climbs over more than 120 miles.

Lance flew up Alpe d'Huez and won the stage by a minute. José Azevedo, Postal's new climbing star from Portugal, was fourth, and I was twenty-first, three and a half minutes behind Lance. Mine was an unusually high finish for a *domestique*—Triki, George, and Chechu had all finished more than a minute behind me, placing in the forties and fifties—but I had felt relaxed and kept an even tempo all the way.

At dinner that night Johan said in a mocking tone, "Not bad for a guy who took it easy." He thought I hadn't followed his order.

I laughed it off. "You don't think I took it easy?"

"Well, you got twenty-first."

"What is that supposed to mean?" I asked. I didn't know what I had to do to satisfy him. "You didn't tell me what place to get," I said. "Should I have gotten fifty-fourth? Or seventy-sixth? Exactly what place do you consider 'easy'?"

"You know what I mean, Floyd," said Johan. "The race isn't over yet. We need you tomorrow."

"All right," I said. "Tell you what, I'll make sure that you see tomorrow that I took it easy today." Johan gave a wry smile, and we both dropped it after that.

The next day, my teammates and I set a hard tempo early on and burned off all of the exhausted riders who could no longer keep up. The final climb of the day was the Col de la Croix-Fry, and instead of one of the designated climbers setting the pace, I took off.

Only four riders had the strength to follow me: Lance and his three biggest rivals, Italian Ivan Basso and Germans Jan Ullrich and Andreas Klöden. The crowd swarmed around us, forming a tunnel just big enough for me to ride through. Flags waved in my face, and I heard screaming. Water and whatever other liquids spectators were throwing drenched me. I just kept pedaling with absolutely everything I had. It was the last mountain stage of the Tour, time to dig deep to another level of willpower that most people don't even know exists.

The stage ended with a nine-mile ride down the other side of the mountain. At the top, the others were still right behind me, on my wheel, but it was clear that they were hurting. We all were, but Lance knew I was one of the best descenders around and he thought I could make a break. He sprinted up next to me and joked, "How fast can you ride downhill?" He wanted to help me win the stage as a reward for working so hard for him.

"Real fast," I said.

"Okay, ride like you stole something," he said, and dropped back off the pace to distract the others.

I shifted into a big gear and put my hands low on the handlebar to be more aerodynamic as I tried to turn the cranks harder. For a few moments, I was away from the pack, leading a stage of the Tour de France.

Ullrich wanted to show he had some fight left. It hadn't been his Tour. He had been dropped early in the mountains, and Lance had whipped him up Alpe d'Huez. He was sitting in fourth place overall, behind Lance, Basso, and Klöden. He bridged the gap to me, and Lance followed him. Soon, the five of us were riding together again.

With about a mile to go, I tried attacking again to see if I could slip away. I hadn't worked hard all day long just to give up at the end. But I didn't have enough strength to pull away. Ullrich covered again. All of us were at our limit— even Lance—jockeying for position. Klöden attacked and got a small gap on the rest of us. It looked like he was going to take the stage. Then, finally, Lance got mad.

In the last stretch, Lance found something somewhere that let him power past Klöden to edge him out by just half of a wheel-length. Lance crossed the line with his arms spread wide and his mouth open, screaming like a madman.

It was the third stage he had won in three days. He pumped his fists, and the rest of us rolled through the finish line in his wake.

After we got off our bikes, I made my way over to Lance, and we gave each other a big hug. "You were the man today," he said. "You deserved it." He felt bad that I wasn't able to win the stage.

"That's okay," I said. "I did all I could. I had nothing left." I had worked on the front the entire way while Lance and the others sat in my draft, and still I was almost able to beat them at the end. I knew how strong I was, and I was satisfied.

In all the post-stage interviews, Lance talked about what a loyal teammate I was, how strong I had been this Tour, and how he had hoped I'd be able to get away on the descent. I talked about how happy I was for Lance, who was going to win a record sixth Tour de France, and about how well the race had gone for our entire team. And we both meant everything we said.

Two days later, I was pedaling on the stationary trainer to warm up before the final time trial. Sweat was starting to pour off of me, and my tunes were blasting in my ears. I was going into the zone.

Bill Stapleton, Lance's agent and the CEO of the team, walked up to me and signaled to get my attention. "I have an offer for you," he said.

The timing was ridiculous. "Uh, Bill, this isn't a good

time for me to talk," I said, turning down the volume and gesturing toward my bike. "I have a race to do."

"Well, yeah," he said, and just kept talking. "We wanted to tell you that we came up with a number," and he threw out figures for a three-year deal that were lower than the Phonak offer, and well below what some of the other guys on the Postal team were making.

"No," I said, and continued pedaling. "And I'm not going to talk about it anymore."

"Well, what do you want?" he said, sounding offended.

"I don't want to ride for your team anymore," I said. "And I'm trying to focus on the race." I cranked up my tunes again and finished my warm-up.

The thing was, I hadn't heard from Phonak in weeks. The silence made me nervous. I wasn't sure where my offer stood, so I saw the time trial as my only remaining chance to impress other teams. I had to do well, I figured. I needed a job.

I ended up fourth in the time trial, right behind Lance, Ullrich, and Klöden, and I finished twenty-third overall in the Tour—very respectable for a *domestique*.

Afterward, I had some more contract squabbling with Johan and Stapleton and some others, with plenty of name-calling. At one point, I think I was even kicked off the team. But I wanted the hell out. I didn't trust that they wanted to invest in me as their future leader. The team had just announced the signing of a young Ukrainian, Yaroslav Popovych, and made it clear that they were banking on him to be the leader after Lance retired.

Tyler Hamilton sent me a text message a couple of days after the race, when I was beginning to wonder if I was going to have a job at all: "Hey, congrats on your new contract. Sorry it didn't work out with us." I had no idea what he was talking about, so I called him right away. Then I found out the story.

Andy Rihs had mentioned to his advisor, Jim Ochowicz, that I was close to signing with Phonak. In addition to advising Andy, Ochowicz was one of Lance's best friends, dating all the way back to when he was the director of the Motorola team in the mid-1990s. The news of my Phonak deal had gone straight back to Lance.

During the Tour, the same day Johan criticized me for not waiting around for an offer, someone had called the Phonak team director, Urs Freuler, and told him that I was signing a deal to stay at Postal. Phonak figured I was off the market and had stopped calling me.

Once the mess was cleared up, I signed with Phonak immediately.

In cycling, it's silly to have the latest carbon-fiber wonder bike without an efficient pedaling motion to power it. Over the course of three weeks at the Tour, the smallest increase in efficiency can make a huge difference. As long as I was going to a new team with new bikes, I wanted to make the engine that powered the bike—me—more efficient.

That fall, I went to Boulder, Colorado, to have my pedal stroke analyzed by renowned physiologist Dr. Andy Pruitt.

Andy had looked at the simple circular pedal motion of dozens of the world's best riders, including Lance and Tinker Juarez, and helped them improve.

We talked a bit about my hip, and how since my accident my right leg seemed to be shortening. "Let's take an X-ray to check it out," he said. But when he stuck the film on the wall and flipped on the fluorescent light, he was shocked. Even I could tell by looking at it that something wasn't right. The ball of my femur seemed to be flattening out. Instead of being nice and round, it looked more like a scoop of melting ice cream. "This hip isn't going to last long," Pruitt said. Just when I thought my hip was doing better, it was actually disintegrating.

Back home, I went straight to see Brent at OUCH, and he took a look at the X-ray and did a CT scan and MRI. That evening, he came to my house to deliver the results to Amber and me: I had developed severe avascular necrosis in my hip. Amber and Brent looked ill from the news, and it just felt unreal to me.

The next day, Brent and I went to Dr. Chao in San Diego for an orthopedic surgery consultation. Dr. Chao said that typically with AVN, the dead bone wears away slowly over time as it rubs against the joint. But when you make about ten million pedal revolutions a year, it doesn't happen so slowly.

"You'll need a hip replacement," Dr. Chao said. "The question is when. You're so young that the longer you can put it off, the better." More than four hundred thousand

Americans have hip replacement surgery every year, but typically they are retirees who just want to be able to play nine holes of golf, not world-class athletes in their prime. Bo Jackson had a hip replacement in 1992 because of arthritis resulting from avascular necrosis, and it ended his career in pro football and baseball. But there were no examples of pro athletes who had successfully come back from a hip replacement to continue in their sport.

"You know, though, this part is reasonably round," Brent said, pointing to an arc of bone on the X-ray. When he was just eighteen, Brent was in a car accident that shattered the end of his upper-arm bone. He developed AVN in his shoulder two years later, and had been living with it for twenty-five years, so he had his own ideas about what you can still do with a degenerating joint. "You may be able to get another year or two out of this," he said. "It looks like you're wearing a groove in there."

Brent had seen many orthopedic surgeons over the years, and most had suggested an immediate joint replacement. But one had told him, "You might as well leave it and beat the hell out of it—it's dead already." The same doctor suggested that sometimes the repetitive motion wears a new pattern into the dying bone and keeps the joint functioning fairly normally, albeit with pain. Brent had chronic pain, but had gone on to be a college skier and do more than one hundred triathlons, including six Ironmans.

I liked the groove theory. It made sense to me. Maybe it was even an explanation for that clicking pain I had experienced at Paris–Nice earlier in the year: Maybe it was a piece of bone collapsing, and it only hurt because a new groove was forming. Then, once the groove was established, the pain wouldn't be so bad.

I also liked the idea of being able to put off having a hip replacement. The doctors agreed that the main problem with continuing to ride would be dealing with the pain. There was a small risk that, if I waited, a big enough piece of dead bone would break off and lock up my joint, and then I might need an immediate replacement. But I figured, it's already shot, why not use it until it quits?

Brent explained that if I put off the replacement, I'd need a procedure called a core decompression. In it, the surgeon drills a series of holes in the dying bone to try to increase blood flow around the bone and, hopefully, encourage the buildup of some supporting scar tissue. "You actually want scar tissue in there," Brent said. "That will help hold it all together." Still, it was only a stopgap. Decompression wasn't going to keep the hip from failing, but hopefully it would slow the collapse of the bone long enough to let me keep pedaling for a year or two.

My hip wasn't the only thing falling apart. At the Athens Olympics that summer, a Phonak rider tested positive for erythropoietin (EPO), a hormone that boosts endurance. Then, at the Tour of Spain, Phonak's Tyler Hamilton and Santiago Perez both tested positive for "homologous blood transfusion," or blood doping using someone else's blood.

The team suspended all the riders with positive tests. It had no lead rider anymore and was in disarray. Because of all the doping infractions, the UCI refused to give Phonak a license to be in the big leagues, the Pro Tour, for 2005. With no license, the team would need a special invitation to be included in the Tour de France as one of the two wildcard teams selected each year, which didn't seem likely after all the doping scandals.

Andy Rihs called me. "I know it looks bad, but I'm going to stick with it," he said. "Still, I'm giving everyone the option to leave if they want to. I couldn't blame you if you found something better." He was being fair, and yet I could hear in his voice just how much he cared about the team and wanted to see it succeed.

"Who has left?" I asked him, point blank.

"So far," he said, "no one." That was Andy. All year he had treated the riders with so much respect that, even though things were shaky, no one felt like they'd get a better deal if they went elsewhere.

That loyalty spoke volumes, and I liked the guy. With Hamilton gone, there was a chance I could be the team leader, but I still wasn't sure what to do. After the doping mess had erupted, Johan called me and made it clear that I could go back for Lance's last season on Discovery Channel, which was taking over sponsorship from U.S. Postal, if I wanted to. I thought hard about going, despite how bad things had been and how poorly the team had treated me in negotiations. I also knew that it was possible that my hip wouldn't last, and that if whatever team I ended up on found out, I'd be dropped.

In the end, here's how I looked at it: The Phonak team was damaged goods, but with my hip I might be also. I decided to stay and make the best of it. Andy knew that I was his strongest rider and that my salary was very low for a team leader, but I didn't demand more money. Instead, we front-weighted my deal in case the team didn't survive: I'd get six hundred thousand dollars for 2005, and then three hundred thousand for 2006.

The week before Thanksgiving, Brent and I went back to Dr. Chao in San Diego, and he removed the three pins in my hip and drilled the decompression holes. My plan was to have the decompression and race in the 2005 season. If I couldn't train at my normal high intensity, I'd tell Andy that I needed to have a hip replacement, and that it was his decision whether to keep me on the team or to terminate my contract. For now, though, I wanted to fulfill my obligation to the team, and I wanted the chance to see if the decompression worked without bringing Andy any more worries than he already had.

To keep the surgery a secret, Brent made me a fake removable cast for my perfectly fine right ankle. If anyone asked why I was on crutches, the story was that I had twisted my ankle, and that I'd be fine in a couple of days.

CHAPTER 6

To the Limit

"Please stand against the wall," said the Swiss doctor. It was ten days after my core decompression surgery, and I was attending the pre-season team meetings at a hotel near Phonak's corporate headquarters in Stäfa, Switzerland. In only my boxer shorts, which covered my fresh scar, I walked across the room, hiding my limp as best I could. I had ditched my crutches before flying to Switzerland, but my hip was still so sore that I couldn't go up a flight of stairs without using the handrail. I stood against the wall, and the doctor looked me up and down. "Hmm," he said. He was like a human measuring tape. "Your right leg is a few millimeters shorter than your left." It was more like one and a half centimeters, but I didn't argue.

"I broke my hip a few years ago and had surgery on it," I told him. "It's fine now." He nodded, as if that explained it, and made a note on the chart he was holding.

When the riders had arrived, we had received a long schedule that included a bunch of organizational meetings, a tour of the hearing-aid plant, and a team physical. Pre-season team physicals are standard, and typically only a formality—after you've done the Tour, the doctors are pretty sure you're in good shape before they look at you. But for some reason, Phonak decided to be more thorough by including a full orthopedic exam. I had no idea it was coming, and as I stood there, I was scared he'd start asking more about my hip. If he gave it even one close look I knew he'd say, "This thing is garbage."

After his initial examination against the wall, he had me lie on the table to test my flexibility by twisting each leg inward and outward. He did it to my right leg, and I tried not to wince. It didn't move very far, but he didn't say anything about it. I worried that when he did my left leg, though, he'd notice the difference, and I'd be busted. The only thing I could think to do was make it seem like I was stiff all over. When he reached for my left leg, I flexed my hip so that he could move it only as far as he had moved my right. "Seems all right," he said.

As soon as I left, I called Brent. "You won't believe this," I said. "But they had an orthopedic check—and I passed!"

He laughed. "You're lucky they didn't take an X-ray," he said. "They would have asked you how it's possible that you're even walking."

As promised, Andy Rihs made sure that all the riders got the equipment they needed, and we all had open discussions about our racing schedules. A Swiss bike company that Andy owned, BMC, provided the high-tech, carbon-fiber bikes. I even had my very own time-trial bike shipped home for training.

In the meetings, though, it became clear how disorganized the team was after the doping scandals. To demonstrate to the UCI that the team's problems were over, Andy had cleaned house, hiring a new team director, new doctors, and new key management. The team had a fresh start, but no one had worked together before.

The new director was John Lelangue, a former public relations manager for the Amaury Sports Organization, the French company that runs the Tour de France, which recommended him because of his outspoken position against doping. Many team directors, such as Johan of Discovery and CSC's Bjarne Riis, who won the Tour in 1996, are former pro racers. Lelangue did a little bike racing growing up in Belgium, but was never a pro. He was young—only thirty-four—and didn't have any experience with the heat of the battle in the peloton, but his strong suits were developing a good public image for the team and having an open mind when it came to dealing with the riders. Both things were critical.

Andy also instituted an internal team anti-doping program. With the UCI's system, we already gave blood and urine samples during races, a separate blood sample every three months for screening, and urine samples outside of competition anytime collectors visited us. From the time I signed with Phonak in the fall of 2004 until I started racing for the team in early 2005, anti-doping collectors came to my house four times for urine samples, way more than they had ever come before. In addition to all of this, Phonak now required every rider to sign an ethical code agreeing to team blood screenings before and during every race, and giving the team the authority to suspend or fire him for irregularities in the test.

Team screenings were done by the new team doctor, Denise Demir, a German sports medicine physician, using the blood analysis machine the team bought. While preseason physicals done by outside doctors were pretty much a joke, the team doctors are thorough and excellent. They need to be, because the Tour is so demanding that riders need medical attention pretty much every day. Denise did everything for us during races: patched us up after crashes, met us at the finish with fluids, and checked our weight and nutrition. She even supervised the training for some riders. In addition, Denise would bring the blood analysis machine, which wasn't much bigger than a TV remote, to each race. Every few days she'd say, "Stop by my room after breakfast," and we'd file in to get our fingers pricked.

The idea was that if there was any chance a rider was using performance-enhancing drugs, the team could catch it and suspend him before he even had a chance to submit a positive doping test in competition. I never minded the intrusion, because I understood that my team needed to go the extra mile to prove that it played by the rules. While several teams have similar anti-doping efforts now, back in 2005 Phonak was one of only a few teams to do this kind of internal testing.

Despite all of Phonak's positive initiatives, I still found the state of the team very unsettling. I was coming from Postal, which had developed a system for winning that had worked for years, and now, because everyone was new, it felt like Phonak had no system at all. We didn't even know yet if we'd be invited to the Tour de France.

I called my old Postal teammate Robbie Ventura, RV for short. RV always saw the positive in things, and we had become good friends. "I know it's unsettling," he said. "But it's a waste of energy to focus on it. You've made your decision to stick with the team, so now you should concentrate on what you do have control over—your performance."

RV had just retired from racing and was ramping up his coaching company, Vision Quest Coaching, in the Chicago area. "Why don't you visit my lab?" he said. "We can do some testing to see where you are, and talk about where you need to be to become a team leader." I agreed to go. For years I had basically coached myself, calling Arnie for advice now and then or following along with Lance. That seemed to work fine, but I believe that when an intelligent person offers to give you an opinion, it's foolish not to hear him out. I went to Chicago.

The tests at RV's lab measured my output in watts on a

stationary trainer. Watts are the same whether they're powering a light bulb, a blender, or a bicycle. Just about anyone can produce enough power pedaling a bike to light a 100-watt light bulb for a little while. In general, your average male recreational cyclist can produce about 175 watts for an hour, and the average woman 150 watts. An amateur male bike racer can do more like 270 watts, and a female racer close to 200 watts. Top Tour riders can hold about 340 to 360 watts for an hour.

"Of course, you have some phenomenal results," RV said. "There are also some areas where you aren't even close to where I think you should be." On a very hard day, I could motor like a diesel engine at around 280 watts for six hours. Not many racers can do that, and it had served me well as a *domestique* leading the way for Lance. What I lacked, though, was the explosive power that a team leader needs in order to be able to attack on a late-stage climb and pull away from the peloton. My best ten-minute effort was about 435 watts. In an all-out sprint, I could only do about 950 watts. While I didn't need to keep up with top sprinters, who can pump out more than 1,600 watts for a few seconds, I needed to have more punch.

RV suggested that maybe my hip was holding me back. I was impressed that after just a short time analyzing my performance, he had noticed the problem.

"Well, let's talk," I said. I told him everything about my dying hip, and how I felt like I didn't have much time left. "I want to win the Tour."

RV didn't miss a beat. "You can do it," he said. "I really believe that." Having been a pro, RV understood everything it took to race at the highest level—from the training to the race tactics to surviving the travel. He didn't have a champion's talent, so his training and tactics had always had to be exactly right to get the best results he could. He had a lot of good advice to give, so I asked if he would be my coach. "I've never coached a pro at your level," RV said. "It's going to be a learning experience for both of us."

"It always is," I replied. "Or at least it should be."

RV and I talked about the general areas I needed to work on. "If you can hang with the climbers in the mountains and then win the time trial, you'll win races," he said. So I trained on my time-trial bike, visited a wind tunnel to make my body position more aerodynamic, and focused more on climbing and monitoring my power with a PowerTap power meter, since the company that makes it, CycleOps, had recently become a sponsor of mine. I had started using a power meter riding with Lance, but now it became a more important part of my training.

My hip surgery set my training back a couple of months, so it was February by the time I was going full-strength. Around that time, Phonak was finally given a Pro Tour license, which meant that we were back in the big leagues, with an automatic invitation to the Tour de France. Things were starting to look up.

In Girona, I climbed like crazy, and every few days I'd talk to RV about how things were going, and he'd give me his usual positive words to help keep me motivated. There is no way to place a value on a person like that.

Most days, I rode with Zabriskie, who had left Postal and signed with CSC. With Amber and Ryan on their own in California, he stayed in Ryan's old room in the apartment, sleeping in her Strawberry Shortcake sheets for the first couple of weeks. "They're not coming back here," I said. "You should just stay." He brought in his own stuff, and we became roommates. I didn't charge rent, he did all the cleaning, and if there was any cooking, he boiled the chicken and made the pasta. Usually we didn't bother with vegetables; we took vitamins instead. We goofed off a little, but mostly we were either riding or sleeping. And the apartment soon became cluttered with trophies and leader's jerseys.

My more-focused training showed at the Tour de Georgia in April. I won the time trial and finished two minutes ahead of Lance. I guess Lance wasn't happy about that. I wouldn't have been either.

I was in the yellow leader's jersey when we began the race's only tough mountain stage. Lance attacked early and a few of us went with him, including Tom Danielson, a rising star for Discovery who Lance had taken under his wing. Danielson is a climbing specialist, and he attacked on Brasstown Bald, the final leg-crushing climb. I couldn't stay with him, and neither could Lance. Danielson won the stage and took over the yellow jersey. Just before the finish, Lance put in a surge to finish third. I rolled in ten seconds later. When Lance rode by the finish clock, he pointed at it and then turned to point back at me, as if he had just proven something.

I'm not sure why he did it. Probably because he was mad that I had left his team, or maybe he was just trying to intimidate me because now I was his competition. After that, we didn't speak to each other for the rest of the race, or for months afterward.

At the suggestion of RV and the people from CycleOps, I met with Allen Lim, a scientist who had helped develop the latest version of the PowerTap and had done studies on how cyclists produce power in training and races. He had also coached a women's pro team and studied the physiology of high-altitude porters in Nepal.

Pretty much every racer used a power meter in training, but not many used them during races. Allen believed that race data was critical. "If you don't know the exact demands of the competition," he said, "then how do you know how to train for it?" It made sense to me.

In our first few conversations, all we did was ask each other questions about every aspect of training. It was clear after just a few minutes of talking to Allen that he's the type who was always one of the smartest kids in class. He could spout formulas and power numbers and physiology terms for hours. But lying on top of the science geek was a layer of straight talk that I liked. "What do you think it takes to win the Tour?" he asked.

"I know the answer to that one," I said. "Some people

think it's the guy who trains the hardest. And other people think it's the guy who trains the longest. They're all wrong. It's the guy who trains the hardest and the longest." To become strong for something as long and hard as the Tour, you need to give your system more than it can handle, and then let it recover so that the next time, it's stronger than before and resists the torture more effectively. In a way, to become stronger, first you have to kill yourself a little bit.

"That's right," Allen said. "You gotta do the work."

"Okay, so how much work, exactly?" I asked him. I wanted to know the hardest I could train to be as good as I could possibly be without overdoing it.

"Everyone has ideas," he said. "But who the hell really knows?"

"No one's ever written down a fool-proof recipe for ass-kicking," I said.

"Exactly," he said. "And anyone who says they have is talking bullshit." Allen expressed what I had thought for years. Training is an individual thing. Two people doing the exact same workouts won't get the same results in a race. We both knew that the watts numbers could tell me a lot, but that ultimately how I applied the knowledge would have to be based on how I felt.

"So it's a balance between being scientific and winging it," I said. Allen laughed. I felt like I needed his help. "Lance had a team of people around to help him on a daily basis, and I have no one," I said. I asked Allen to come to Europe for my pre-Tour training, and then to monitor how I raced at the Tour.

"I'm in," he said. "Let's do it." Allen was the absolute best choice to advise me on power—not only because of his expertise, but also because he met one vital condition: He had nothing better to do. He had just finished his PhD and was about to move back in with his mother. He was the only person I knew with the freedom to drop everything for three months. "So, what do we do?" he asked.

"I don't know," I said. "But we'll figure it out."

The morning after Allen arrived in Girona, I walked out to the car with a big bag full of clothes, including extra jerseys, shorts, a jacket, leg warmers, and shoes. I could have outfitted three cyclists for an all-day ride. "What's all this?" Allen asked. "Are you planning on spending the night somewhere?"

"In case I need it," I said. If it rains or is hot out, sometimes jumping into the car to change into a fresh pair of bike shorts or dry shoes before going back out to finish the ride makes all the difference. I tossed Allen the keys to our rented Volkswagen minivan. "Meet me in Olot with some food," I said. "I'm doing the Vallter 2000."

Allen trailed behind me. "Wait, where's Olot? What's Vallter 2000? Uh-oh, is the van a stick shift? I haven't driven stick in years . . ." His comfort zone was number crunching and academia. Here, on his first day in a country he'd never been to, he was far away from that.

"Olot's north of here," I said. "You should probably get yourself a map." Then I got on my bike and started riding.

About three hours later, I rolled in to Olot, and Allen was waiting for me looking pleased with himself. He handed me a snack and pulled out his map. "So, first we go through a town called Camprodon, and then you'll make a right at the base of the climb," he said. Vallter 2000 is a ski resort with a nice forty-minute climb up to 7,100 feet. It gets really steep at the top, which is the perfect time to get out of the saddle and practice attacking.

It only took us a couple of days to realize that I was wasting time going from Girona to the mountains and back each day. Allen and I relocated to a tiny house in the heart of the Pyrenees in a middle-of-nowhere town called Mollo. The house had a little bit of furniture and a small TV we never watched. Our first night there, Allen went to boil water to cook dinner and realized that the stove didn't have a spark ignition system. We didn't have any matches. "What do we do?" Allen said. All the shops in the tiny town had been closed for hours.

We searched every drawer in the place. No matches. And then it came to me. "Watch this," I said and wadded up a piece of newspaper. I stuck it in the toaster and pressed the button. The coils turned orange, I blew into the slot, and a wisp of smoke snaked up. The paper burst into flame.

"Oh, we're *men*," Allen said. "We made fire! I feel like the Tour de France has already been won."

"You have to blow on it," I said proudly, "so it gets enough air to ignite." After that, we just kept using the toaster to light the stove. Somehow, matches seemed too easy.

For the next few weeks, Allen was always back there, watching my legs go up and down for hour after hour. In the three months before the Tour, I averaged 200,000 feet of climbing each month. Who knows what Allen was using his PhD brain to think about as he watched me pedal uphill. His whole day consisted of driving along slowly, occasionally looking at a map, and every once in a while leaning his head out the window to yell, "Left turn, Floyd." He was probably the most educated chauffeur in Europe.

In all of our discussions about training, Allen had come up with a theory: There's no such thing as overtraining, only underresting. You can push it as hard as you want, as long as you give your body ample time to recover. I wanted to put his theory to the test by going out and riding as hard as I could until I found my absolute limit—and cracked. If Al was right, I'd rest afterward and be okay.

So Monday I woke up and went apeshit, pedaling like crazy for six hours. Then, I woke up on Tuesday and did it again. On Wednesday I did it again. Each day I rode six hours, averaging somewhere between 250 and 350 watts, and climbing 10,000 feet or more.

On Thursday, day four, I found the limit. It's called "cracking" because it feels like you've been broken apart, and in addition to losing every bit of your physical power it feels like something essential in your will escapes you as well. "Al, that's it," I said. "I'm screwed up. I gotta go to bed." It was only 7 p.m. "Look, if I'm not up in like a day or so, just wake me to make sure I'm not dead," I told him.

At first, Allen thought I was joking. The next day he woke up at 8 a.m., went by my door to listen for any movement, and didn't hear a thing. He made breakfast, went out for a bike ride, made lunch, ran some errands, and hung out. Late in the afternoon, he started to scare himself. "Holy crap," he thought. "What if it killed him?"

Around dusk, he couldn't take it anymore. He went to my door and knocked. Nothing. He knocked again, a little louder. I jolted out of the deepest sleep of my life, pulled out my earplugs, and, before I could think, I shouted, "I'M STILL ALIVE!" I heard laughter through the door.

"It's like you're trying to get over a hangover," Allen said. In a way, I was. I got up to eat some food, and a couple of hours later I went to sleep for the night. Training that hard is not a healthy way to live. It made me grumpy for a couple of weeks, and when you're in the middle of it, it's hard to see how it helps. But it does.

Allen showed me on his computer screen that over the weeks my average wattage was creeping up, sometimes by as much as five or ten watts per week, and I was able to change speeds while climbing much better than before. Even after all those years of training, I had lots of room to improve. I was getting stronger.

The Tour started on the Atlantic coast of France, but the team was first meeting in the town of Tours, in the heart of the Loire Valley. Allen and I were still in the Pyrenees, but we had flights booked from Barcelona to Paris. It takes two hours to drive from the mountains south to Barcelona, where we'd have to sit around for another hour in an airport, fly north for a couple of hours, get our bags, and take an hour-and-a-half drive southwest. The way I saw it, we were facing at least seven hours of travel, much of it going in the wrong direction. It was going to be a complete waste of a day. Besides, I wanted to get in one more hard ride before the start of the race.

By the time Allen woke up I already had on my bike shorts and jersey. "What are you doing?" he asked. "We're supposed to fly out today."

"Not anymore," I said. I explained that I had an idea that would allow me to get in one more day of training. "I'll ride there."

"You're insane," he said, and then he thought about it for a minute. "Okay," he said, "if that's what you feel like."

I threw all my stuff in the van, and Allen followed me over the mountains and down the other side into France and on whatever back roads headed north. It rained the majority of the day, and I kept pedaling, with my rear wheel spraying mud and road grit up my back. Whenever Allen yelled out the window at me, I turned.

Six hours later, I was done. I climbed into the van and changed into dry clothes. My shorts and jersey were trashed. There was no point in carrying them around for the whole Tour, so I threw them away. I settled into the passenger seat next to Allen. We still had a couple of hours more to drive.

"See, that wasn't so bad," I said. "Hey, do you know how I got to the Tour last year?"

"No, how?" Allen asked. He had a glazed look from staring at the windshield wipers for too long.

"Lance's jet." It took a few seconds, but then Allen smiled.

Allen tracked my performance at the Tour that year in a way no one had ever done before. Each day, he downloaded the data from my PowerTap and wrote up an analysis that included the weather, distance, and total feet of climbing, along with my average speed, average power output, spikes in power, and calories burned, which was usually in the 6,000 to 10,000 per day range. He also broke down any tactical factors that affected the race, like how much of an advantage I gained by drafting, and explained all the ways I stayed cool and hydrated in the sweltering heat, including using a gel-filled cooling vest during my time-trial warmup. As part of my deal with CycleOps, it all got published on the Internet. Typically riders like to keep their training or anything that gives insight into their performance a secret, but I didn't care who saw. They're just numbers. They don't tell you what's going to happen in the race.

The Tour began with a bang, because Zabriskie won the prologue and became only the third American ever to wear the yellow jersey, after Greg LeMond and Lance. I called him from my team bus. "Good job, man," I said. "My whole team was cheering for you." All the Phonak guys let out a whoop for him.

As a team, we got along well. But we weren't set up to

win. The first week, some of the guys spent energy trying to get our sprinter, Robbie Hunter, toward the front to win a stage. After that, two of our stronger climbers, Santiago Botero and Oscar Pereiro, tried to get into breakaways to win stages. Even though I was our strongest rider, there were a few days when I drifted back to the team car to get my own water bottles. The *domestiques* sacrificed a day here and there, but ultimately, they weren't sure who to work for.

During Stage 16 in the Pyrenees, we had just ridden up the Col de Marie-Blanque, and I wanted to make a move to try to gain back some time on Lance, who was in yellow by then. There were a few of us spread out at the top of the climb, and American Levi Leipheimer, another former Postal rider who I knew from Girona, said to me, "You should attack here, there's a big downhill." He knew I was a strong descender, and thought I had a good chance to get away.

I sprinted as hard as I could, but the downhill was too gradual. I had misjudged—the steep part hadn't started yet. After about two minutes I realized it wasn't going to work, so I sat up. My old teammate George Hincapie was pulling for Lance, and they caught up to me. "Nice one," Lance said in a nasty tone. "Like that's going to work."

Lance and I hadn't spoken all year. We had both raced the Dauphiné, and he completely ignored me then. For the first two weeks of the Tour, we hadn't even acknowledged each other, which is pretty hard to do in the middle of a race when your handlebars are just a couple of inches apart.

Now he was directing his crap at me, and I didn't feel like taking it. There's no way to sugarcoat my reaction: I told him to fuck off in a creative way that ended with, "—in hell!" Lance's eyes got really big, and he looked at me like I was crazy. The shock only lasted a second, though, because then he started screaming back at me in his own profane way about all the things he hated about me, and about how ungrateful I was after all he had done for me.

George just shook his head and dropped back, out of the line of fire. All the riders behind us tried to move up to hear what was going on. The whole time Lance yelled, I just stared at him, and when he was finished I pointed out that I didn't care what he thought. We went on like a couple of jerks all the way down the hill.

I was mad at myself for falling for it. Lance was trying to intimidate me like he did everyone else, and when I took the bait and responded to him, I was wasting energy that I needed to finish the Tour. At that point, I already knew that I couldn't beat Lance that year. I was already more than nine minutes behind him in the overall. I wasn't as strong as he was.

That became even more evident two days later, on our last climbing day, heading north away from the Pyrenees toward Paris. The final climb of the day was the sharp two-mile grade at 10 percent, the Cote de la Croix-Neuve. Lance attacked and gapped me. I tried to respond, but didn't have enough power. By the end of the stage, Lance had gained another forty-nine seconds. "On that climb, you produced 430 watts for ten minutes," Allen said afterward. "In order to not get dropped by Lance, you would have needed to do 454 watts." At the time, it was frustrating to hear how far I still had to go to win, but having the data was as valuable as Allen thought it would be, because we could use it to figure out what do to the next year.

Lance won his seventh Tour in a row, and I finished ninth. During the final stage into Paris, I rode up next to the Discovery team car to chat with a mechanic. I told him to tell Lance I was happy for him and his impressive win. I understood how hard Lance worked in his training and preparation, but I couldn't even imagine the mental drive it takes to want to win seven Tours. I was trying to win just one, and knew how hard that was.

The year had gone well for Phonak, considering, but Andy didn't want any of the riders to feel restricted by their contracts. Once again, he gave us the option of leaving—and Pereiro did.

Johan heard about this and called to ask if I wanted to join Discovery. I told him that it was worth talking about. "I know we've had our issues in the past," I said. "But I don't think there's anything between me and the team that's not repairable."

Lance had just retired, but was still involved in managing the team, so Johan asked him to call me before we did any negotiating. To Lance's credit, one of the first things he said was, "About all that other stuff, let's forget it." I agreed, and we've been friends ever since.

I didn't go to Discovery, of course. In the end I decided that, while I like Lance and Johan as people, we see things differently as employers and employee. Plus, I appreciated Andy's dedication, enthusiasm, and openness during Phonak's grim time. The attitude of an organization starts at the top, and nobody was more willing than Andy to make things right. He, Lelangue, and I had a meeting to discuss the next season.

"I think we can win the Tour," I said. I acknowledged that I needed to get stronger, but pointed out that the team also had to make some more changes in order for us to even have a chance. "I saw how it worked firsthand with Lance," I said. "Everything the team did was for him. That's the only way it works." If we were serious about winning, we'd have to stop strategizing to win stages and spend every bit of the team's energy on helping the leader.

"You're the strongest," Andy said. "So everything will be for you." Lelangue wanted what was best for the team, so he agreed. The entire team would work for me, and we'd try to win.

CHAPTER 7

The Strongest One Here

Over the winter, I took a hacksaw to some PVC pipe in my garage and tinkered around to try and find myself a little bit more speed. My time trials had come a long way, but I could feel that something about my position wasn't quite right. If I could shift my weight forward and pull in my shoulders a bit more, I'd be smaller in the wind. I glued halved pieces of the pipe side by side and used zip ties to fasten them to the end of my time-trial bike's handlebar, making a homespun model of how the position would work. My elbows and wrists practically touched when I set them in the pipe. "Those look like handcuffs," Allen said when I showed him.

My project wasn't 100 percent about speed, of course. A

rocket scientist can put a rider in the most aerodynamically efficient position, but it may be so uncomfortable that the rider can't produce maximum power. With my hip, I didn't have much choice. I needed the angle between my pelvis and leg to be wide enough so that the joint could tolerate the force of each pedal stroke.

A bunch of my teammates met me in San Diego to go to the San Diego Air & Space Technology Center wind tunnel. We had boxes of bike parts from BMC, and Allen and the aerodynamics experts spent a couple of days using clay models, cardboard, and duct tape to figure out which time-trial position would work best for each of us. They considered hundreds of details about my equipment, from the shape of my helmet and water bottle to which wheels I should use. Then I got on my bike in the tunnel and pedaled while they shot wind at me and measured my aerodynamic drag.

In the end, we made changes to just about everything about my body position from the year before. My fastest setup? It was pretty close to what I had come up with in my garage. "I told you so," I said to Allen, and he just shook his head.

Then one of the other scientists had an idea. If I could try one more position with my hip angle tighter, I'd probably be more aerodynamic. "No," I said. "That's it. I'm done." I walked away before he had a chance to argue. He probably thought I was just another pro athlete with an oversized attitude. In reality, I knew that the position he was suggesting would put too much force on my hip, and I was nervous that if we started testing it, everyone would realize how weak it was.

From the tunnel, we all went straight to our first race of the season, the inaugural Tour of California, which starts in San Francisco and ends in the Los Angeles area.

Everything about the team was better than it had been the year before. We were all used to one another now, and some of us were good friends. Our top sprinter, South African Robbie Hunter, spent a week at my house training before the race. I took everyone to In-N-Out Burger and passed around Monster energy drinks, which you can't get in Europe, to get everyone addicted. I always travel with portable speakers, and I'd try blasting my music on the team bus. The European guys liked Bruce Springsteen, and could even tolerate Metallica on occasion. Johnny Cash, not so much.

There were other positive signs. Allen and Denise talked a lot about training philosophy, and Denise was using some of Allen's ideas in other riders' training plans. And John and I had begun working together as sort of co-directors of the team. We collaborated on race strategy and agreed that he would handle all of the team logistics, while during the race I would decide most of the tactics.

Finally, with hip surgery behind me, I had a solid winter of training. I also had a new secret weapon: Max, Amber's eighteen-year-old brother. Max had moved in with us and needed a job, so I made him my training assistant. It had been so nice to have Allen in the car behind me in the

Pyrenees to give me whatever I needed, so now when I trained at home, Max drove behind me every day, blasting tunes and talking on the phone and handing me food, water, or anything else I needed. It made a huge difference. Instead of riding up Palomar once and then going home because I grew cold on the descent, I'd ride up and down four times in a row. Each time, Max would hand me clothes at the top to put on for the cool ride down, and at the bottom, I'd take them off, turn around, and head straight back up again.

Everything was falling into place. The only thing left for me to do was win. Perhaps the most important thing I learned from Lance is that when you're assertive in your attitude and tactics in a way that says, "This race is mine," it's hard for others to stop you. If you want it, you have to claim it. That was my objective for 2006.

My new time-trial position proved itself in the Tour of California. I won the time trial and took over the leader's jersey. I had my baseball cap on backward, the way I like to wear it, but the team's PR person told me to turn it around before I stood on the podium for the jersey presentation, so I did.

When I stepped onto the team bus afterward, heads turned up and smiled. High-fives came from all corners. Nothing motivates teammates like a yellow jersey. I sat down with Robbie and Miguel Ángel Perdiguero, a strong tempo rider from Spain. Perdi, Robbie, and I loved talking tactics. "It's time to go to work," I said. There were a bunch of guys less than a minute behind me: George, Levi, Zabriskie, and his CSC teammate, American Bobby Julich. We were going to defend the jersey for the rest of the race. It would be great practice for later in the season.

The next morning I sent all of my guys right to the front. Every time a rider from CSC, Discovery, or Levi's Gerolsteiner team would attack, we'd cover the move. If there was a break-away, Robbie, Perdi, and I would organize the chase. Every-thing the team did was about preserving the jersey, and it worked. It was the biggest win of my career. I was happy to show that I was strong, but even better was that we showed how strong our team was and that we knew what we were doing tactically.

The next race was Paris–Nice. In the first hard climbing stage, the pace dwindled after we had been racing for a cou-ple of hours. There was a half-hour climb coming up, and then a ten-minute descent to the finish. It was rainy and cold, and everyone felt bogged down in their heavy, wet clothes.

In other words, the conditions were perfect for me. When it's miserable out, it messes with people's minds. They lose focus and lose their will, like they're waiting for the race to end. When things are like that I smile, just for the mental advantage. I began to peel off all my extra clothes. "Are you high on crack?" Zabriskie asked as I tossed my vest to the side of the road. "You'll freeze," someone else said.

"What do you mean? It's beautiful out," I said. Four rid-ers attacked at the base of the climb, and I went with them. Without all those heavy, wet clothes to drag me down, I was much lighter than everyone else.

Halfway through, I accelerated and dropped everyone but this one Spanish guy, Patxi Vila of Lampre-Fondital, who was thirteen seconds behind me in the overall. I could have dropped him, too, but he made me an offer: If I helped him win the stage, he'd help me win the race. "Let me sit now," he said. "I'll work on the downhill."

It was the only way we were going to stay away from the group, so I let him draft on my wheel for the rest of the climb. Then, along the flat crest, we took turns pedaling hard and drafting to stay away from the chasing peloton. As we started the descent, I heard John on the team radio. "Floyd, you have plenty of time," he said. If I maintained my position, I'd be far enough ahead to take the yellow jersey. "Plenty of time," he said again. "No risks, eh?" As our speed picked up, I became cold, but I just ignored it and stayed relaxed. As promised, I let Vila win the stage. And I claimed the overall lead.

Before I stepped onto the podium to receive the yellow jersey, I turned my cap to face forward.

In the team bus afterward, the wet and cold didn't seem to matter anymore. "I could have put ten minutes on them today," I said, and my teammates smiled.

One rider new to Phonak, Axel Merckx from Belgium, was sick with an infection and felt terrible. "If it wasn't for the yellow jersey, I would drop out now," he said. It was clear he was hurting. Axel had been a pro for thirteen years, and had been around the peloton his entire life. His father, Eddy Merckx, won the Tours of France and Italy five times—each.

During the 1960s and 1970s, he won more than five hundred races and was known as "the cannibal" for the way he would attack early in a stage, ride alone all day long, and put seven minutes on the entire field even though he was already leading the race.

Axel wasn't a champion like his dad, but he was the ideal teammate. He had helped me stay near the front all day and delivered me safely to the base of the final climb, even though he was sick. And now he was going to stick it out and help us defend, even though he didn't have anything to give. "It always looks better when the whole team is in the front," Axel said. "Even if I'm bluffing."

Really, I shouldn't have won the race. Two days later, attacks split off at the very beginning of the stage. Axel, Frenchman Nicolas Jalabert, and Koos Moerenhout, a Dutch rider new to the team, tried to keep things under control, but a big breakaway of twenty guys escaped up the road. Soon, they had built a four-minute lead. I rode up to Robbie. "How are you guys today?" I asked, thinking about how we'd organize a chase.

"Everybody's fucked," he said. Axel was feeling worse, the rest of my team was wiped out from chasing attacks the day before, and the weather was still miserable.

"Okay, just let them go," I said. "No big deal." There was no reason to get angry with my team. If they couldn't go, then they couldn't go.

Other riders asked me why my team wasn't chasing. They were worried about losing their own high placings, but nobody wanted to do the work themselves to catch back up. They wanted a free ride on the Phonak train. "Oh, I don't care," I said. "I had the lead for a couple of days, and that's good enough for me. I already won a race this season."

Of course, I didn't really want to give up so easily. There was a patch of ice on the road past the feed zone where riders could only get through single-file, so the race stretched out and the road twisted and went up and down. It would be hard riding if someone attacked.

I called Axel over. "Everyone thinks we're done," I said. "When they're strung out at the ice, we're all going like it's a sprint—just for ten minutes, just bluffing." It was a jack-ass move, because there wasn't much likelihood that it would do anything besides make people mad. But at least we'd be trying something.

Axel went, then Robbie, and then me. Each Phonak rider took a pull at the front. The rest of the peloton was eating and drinking, not expecting the attack, so water bottles and food went flying, and splintered groups scrambled to chase us. After about twenty minutes, my team sat up and pedaled easy, as if nothing had happened.

Either the other teams were mad enough, or they had momentum and didn't realize it, because a big group started to chase. My team sat in the draft and took an easy ride. In the end, the peloton caught the breakaway and I stayed in the lead. We couldn't believe it had worked. "We tricked them into chasing," I said later as we were getting warm in the team bus.

The next morning, I was in a good mood, and after breakfast I was singing "Man in Black" in my best deep Johnny Cash voice. *"Well, there's things that never will be right I know, And things need changin' everywhere you go."*

"Okay, keep racing your bike," Axel said, breaking into a big smile and raising his hands as if asking for mercy. "Don't become a singer, you know?"

That day none of the contenders even attacked. They gave Phonak complete control, and I won my second race of the year. It baffled me. "Nobody even tried," I said at dinner that night. "It's like they don't even want to win, like they're waiting to see what happens and taking what they can get."

I flew back to California to spend some time training at home before the Tour de Georgia. David was closing his restaurant to open an upscale one, Hawthorn's, in a much bigger space next to a renovated theater. I gave him my yellow jersey from the Tour of California to display on the wall along with several others I had given him over the years. "Look at you, going big time," he said. I asked him how the re-opening was going. "Oh, it's going," he said. There were some delays, but he'd get through it.

His plan was an ambitious one. "You've got to follow your dream," I told him, giving him the same advice he had always given me.

My riding continued to go well. One day, I rode six hours with Max trailing behind me, averaging 320 watts for the first three hours and 315 for the second. They were my highest numbers ever. Another day, I maintained 470 watts for ten minutes or, by Allen's figuring, more than enough power to stay with Lance during a late-stage attack.

On the bike, my hip was cooperating better than it ever had. Off the bike, though, it was driving me insane. I couldn't sleep, it hurt to walk, and I couldn't even throw my right leg over my bike. Overseas flights when I had to sit for long periods were the absolute worst. I just wanted the pain to stop. I learned that enduring chronic pain is a challenge greater than the hardest five-climb, leg-destroying Alpine stage of the Tour de France. The way it wears you down is similar—the discomfort goes so deep and lasts so long that if you allow yourself to start thinking about it, you want to quit. The difference is that after five or six hours, a bike race ends. Pain from my hip never did.

I went to Dr. Chao to see if he could do anything for me. I had developed severe osteoarthritis, the exact same problem that plagues grandparents and people in nursing homes across the country. I'll tell you, it's serious pain. "I've been thinking more about that hip replacement," I said to Dr. Chao.

At first, Dr. Chao discouraged me. He hadn't heard me complain to the extent that other patients did, and he knew that I had won two races already. He figured that if I was really in that much pain, I wouldn't be able to race so hard.

"No, I'm done," I said. "I'm sick of this." For me, that was real bitching. He knew I was serious.

We talked about timing the hip replacement surgery for

after the Tour de France; until then, Dr. Chao, Brent, and I would research to figure out the best kind of procedure for someone so young and active. In the meantime, Dr. Chao would give me a cortisone shot. "It's a last resort," he said, "but you may get some temporary relief."

Cortisone is a steroid that reduces inflammation in joints and tendons. Dr. Chao and I had decided not to use it in previous years because there's a theory in the medical community that repeated use of cortisone can cause long-term joint damage. But by then, my mind was made up: This was my last chance with my bad hip. There was no reason to try to save it any longer.

Even though cortisone is a steroid, it's not in the same family as performance-enhancing steroids. All it does is reduce chronic arthritis pain, not make you faster. Still, it's on the list of WADA-banned substances. I'd have to file a medical exemption with the UCI stating that I needed the shot for an existing medical condition—and I'd have to tell my team I was using it.

It was time to explain the whole story of my hip to Andy. Because we had been winning races, Andy didn't think it was a big deal that I hadn't told him before. I explained that I was going to need a replacement after the Tour. Until then, I was fine to race. "Yes, it seems to be working now," Andy said, giddy with the team's results so far. "After the Tour, whatever you need."

Dr. Chao gave me the first cortisone shot before the Tour de Georgia. It was a smart decision. For the first time in a long time, my hip didn't hurt at all. There had been times in the 2005 Tour when after a stage it hurt so much that I felt like I was going to vomit. After the shot, my hip simply wasn't a factor.

By then, the team was used to winning, so everyone started the Tour de Georgia with an air of confidence. And as for me, I expected to win.

I won the time trial and took over the yellow jersey. This time on the podium, I refused to turn my hat around. I stood there smiling away in my backward hat and big sunglasses. It was my little way of saying, "Look out, this team is doing it our own way, and no one's going to stop us."

Afterward, I had to report to doping control to give a urine sample. Denise was waiting with me, and there were fans crowded around the fence asking for autographs. One asked me, "Do you do any running as part of your training?"

"Run? You must be kidding," I said. "I can hardly walk." The fan chuckled, took his autograph, and walked away.

I turned to Denise. "He thinks that's funny, but it's true," I said, which she thought was hilarious. As the team's doctor, she was baffled at how I had ridden all last year without pain medication. I just shrugged. It felt good for my team to know about my hip. In a way, it gave the riders and the staff added confidence in me. If I could ride through that, they figured, I could do anything. It also created a sense of urgency. It had to be 2006, or it might be never.

Two days later, on the stage to Brasstown Bald, it rained in the morning, but I smiled the whole time. My team rode on the front to protect me, and on the climb Danielson of Discovery set a blistering pace that whittled the field. But that time, he couldn't drop me. I took the lead toward the top and kept looking back, waiting for his final move. All I had to do to keep my yellow jersey was not lose time to him. He shot around me to win the stage and I stuck on his wheel with a big acceleration. No problem.

After the stage, Brent, who had flown in to watch, said, "You're like an old junkyard dog. All day long you limp around and can hardly move, but then when there's an intruder who comes to challenge you, you're a rabid animal." I was the strongest one there. And I won my third race of the season.

After a rest week, Allen and I headed back to the Pyrenees for a training session. We rented the same tiny house in Mollo, but this time we knew what we were doing. Allen even brought matches for the stove. All of the data Allen gathered confirmed what we had seen in races so far: I had developed a leader's ability to respond to attacks and strike late in a stage.

A little more than a month before the start of the Tour de France, Spanish newspapers reported that authorities had raided the labs of a Spanish sports medicine doctor, Eufemiano Fuentes. It was like a Spanish version of the 2003 BALCO doping scandal in the U.S., when a Bay Area laboratory bust exposed a systematic doping ring that included athletes from several different sports. The newspapers reported that in Fuentes's lab, the authorities found anabolic steroids, the growth hormone EPO, and bags of blood with code names written on them, presumably for blood doping. There apparently were files with coded calendar pages, presumably doping schedules, with symbols and code names for the athletes' identities. Fuentes supposedly treated cyclists as well as athletes from other sports, such as soccer and tennis.

My first thought was, *Oh, no. Not again. This is the last thing the sport needs.* The allegations were astounding. Spanish police suspected that, in all, fifty-eight cyclists from several different countries were part of the doping ring, which was given the name Operación Puerto.

Two of those named on the list of riders suspected to be involved with Fuentes were my teammates, and had been part of Phonak's 2005 Tour de France team: Santiago Botero and José Enrique Gutierrez. Botero was a strong climber, and Guti was one of the best all-around riders and climbers we had—he had just finished second place in the Tour of Italy, behind Ivan Basso, the week before the scandal erupted.

John Lelangue had to decide what to do, and he called me for my opinion. The idea of punishing our riders in any way before having definite proof that they were involved sickened me. "Where's the evidence?" I said. "All we have to go on are media reports."

"I know it's not fair," John said. "But let's think about the Tour. We can't risk hurting the team." I agreed. We both knew that if Botero and Guti were at the Tour, they would be the focus of a lot of media attention. Not only would it be a distraction for the riders, but John had the team's public reputation to protect after Phonak's past problems.

"I understand that, and I'll support any decision you make," I told John. "I'm just sorry you have to make it." As for our Tour team, we still had some decent climbers, such as Axel and Victor Hugo Peña, who had just placed a strong ninth in the Tour of Italy.

Phonak issued a statement saying that the team was sidelining Botero and Guti "until the examinations bring more clarity to the issue." John added that they weren't being fired or even suspended, but that they wouldn't be selected for future races "in the interest of the team and to ensure calm for all team members for the coming races," he said. Of course, if further investigation showed that they were dopers, they'd be fired.

No other team took such a proactive approach.

Once the decision was behind us, I didn't think much about it. It didn't involve me or my team—not anymore anyway. Koos, Robbie, Perdi, and I met John and Denise in the Swiss Alps for a mini training camp before the Tour. The weather was terrible. The temperatures were frigid, and it snowed like crazy—the kind of weather that even changing into dry shorts and shoes can't improve. In a race, I love conditions like that because I know it bothers everyone else so much, but in training it just wears me down. I still did the hard riding I needed to do, but afterward I felt like I had been sapped twice, once from the riding and once from the cold.

By the time of the Dauphiné, a few weeks before the Tour, I still didn't feel recovered. "John, I'm not going to win this race," I told him beforehand. "We shouldn't plan the team around me. Just tell them I'm not feeling good and not to worry about it."

"Well," he said, "give it a chance." John knew that sometimes the legs come around. He had also grown accustomed to winning, and didn't want to give up so quickly. "Just see how the time trial goes."

The next day, I ended up second in the time trial. Zabriskie won. "See," John said, "you're good." He told the team that I felt good, to try to motivate them for the mountains.

"To be honest with you, I don't know how I got second," I told John. True, it had gone better than I expected, but I still felt awful. "I'll see how it goes tomorrow. If I'm good, then I'm good, but I wouldn't count on it." The next day was the mountain stage up one of the classic French climbs, Mont Ventoux.

My team rode straight to the front about 10 miles before the Ventoux, to put me in position to attack. After just a few minutes of climbing, riders from other teams started attacking, one after the other. First, Oscar Sevilla of T-Mobile, then Discovery's Azevedo went shooting up the road ahead of me. There was nothing I could do. I couldn't even will myself to respond, so I sat up and went easy the rest of the way up the mountain.

I could feel the doubters around me, in the peloton, in

the press—everywhere. "Too bad, he peaked too soon," they were saying. "He won all those races early in the season, and now he's done—cooked. We knew it wouldn't last."

Deep down I knew that all I had done was taken it to the limit in training. When I called RV, he agreed with me. "All you need is some recovery time," he said. "You have to trust yourself. You'll come around." Even though I knew from experience that I had plenty of time to recover, it was still unsettling to feel that way so close to the Tour. No one is immune to doubt. At that point, it was stress I didn't need.

I called Amber and told her things just didn't feel right. "Do you want me to come see you?" she said. We talked for a while, and I decided that if she was going to bother to fly all the way to Europe, I should just fly home instead. But here's the thing: No one ever goes home before the Tour. Flying overseas takes too much out of you. There's too great a risk of jet lag or catching a nagging cold that could wreck your whole Tour. It's unheard of for a contender to fly home in June. But I knew it would be better for my head if I were in San Diego, where there would be plenty of sunshine— and my family. "Okay, well, why don't you quit and come home," she said.

"No, I won't quit," I said. "Not now." People on the outside were doubting me already, that was a given. But I figured that if I dropped out of the Dauphiné, even my teammates might start to worry. I went to John and told him I wouldn't be going back to training camp with the guys after the race. "It's no big deal," I said. "I just need to get away to someplace sunny."

"Okay, whatever works best," he said. He probably assumed I was headed to southern Spain, and didn't make anything of it. I spent the rest of the Dauphiné hanging out deep in the peloton, telling jokes, and saying it was just a training ride.

Meanwhile, Brent sent me a first-class ticket, and after the race ended I flew home. We didn't tell anyone where I was going.

Max had started to work at OUCH Medical Center, but Brent gave him two weeks off, and he and I got our band back together. I rode, and Max followed behind blasting tunes. The first few days I was grumpy. Then one day after training I overheard Max say to Amber, "I don't know what he's worried about. His fitness level is fine." Max had spent so much time driving behind me that he knew my usual pace. I never thought he was paying so much attention. I knew he was right, but it was still nice to hear his confidence.

Slowly, my arms and face got tan from the sun, and I started feeling great. Amber could tell that I was finally myself again. "You're ready," she said. "Make it count." I went to see Dr. Chao for another cortisone shot. Five days before the start of the Tour, I flew back to Europe.

CHAPTER 8

A Wide-Open Tour

From the standpoint of trying to win the Tour de France, John made a wise decision to leave Botero and Guti off of our Tour team. They would have been barred from racing anyway.

Just two days before the start of the race, organizers pressured all of the team directors to meet and decide what to do about the riders under investigation in Operación Puerto. The team directors unanimously agreed that any rider on the list of suspects provided by the Spanish authorities should be banned from the race. They basically had no choice under the UCI code of ethics, which states that no team can allow a rider to compete if he's under investigation for doping. No one was allowed to replace those riders to field a full nine-man Tour squad. They would just have to race with fewer riders.

Among those kicked out of the race were every single rider who finished in the top five behind Lance in the 2005 Tour: Ivan Basso, Jan Ullrich, Francisco Mancebo, and Alexandre Vinokourov. Even more outrageous, Vinokourov wasn't even under suspicion for doping—he was booted on a stupid technicality. There's a UCI rule that teams need to have a minimum of six riders. So many of Vino's teammates had been named in the doping scandal that there weren't enough riders left, so he and the three remaining riders on his team were sent home, even though they weren't even suspected of anything. In all, thirteen riders were banned. Only 176 started the race instead of the usual 189.

I hated everything about what was happening. First of all, it was a complete embarrassment for the sport that all of this happened so close to the start of the race. Tour officials had known about the scandal for more than a month, but apparently the best plan they could come up with was to force the teams to make a decision just forty-eight hours before the start.

As for the ruling that the teams agreed on, I believe that cheaters should be sent home. But in America, people are innocent until proven guilty, so to me, barring those riders from the race was unjust. Nothing had been proven against them, and investigations weren't complete. They were kicked out based on suspicion, not proof. No one knew if any of the ejected riders had doped—but whether they had or hadn't, I knew I could beat them, so I wasn't happy they weren't in the race.

Of course, all the press wanted to talk about was doping. Reporters would ask me what I thought, and I didn't have an answer. I hadn't seen any evidence, and I certainly didn't know enough to pass judgment on anyone. The only information I had was what was in the press. As much as I would have liked to offer up a solution for how to make the anti-doping system more effective at catching cheaters—and how to make it more fair to everyone—I didn't have the answer.

I knew that it wouldn't do me, my Phonak team, or the sport of cycling any good to speak out against the system two days before the start of the biggest race of the year. I wouldn't talk about it, and the press wrote that I refused to come out against doping.

I just blocked out everything around me and focused on the race. It was time to control the things I could, and do the best I could to adapt to the things I couldn't.

The prologue was only seven kilometers—about eight minutes of all-out sprinting to show who was at their peak and who wasn't. I had previewed the course a few times that morning to learn all the tricky corners, and the team mechanics had checked over my time-trial bike to make sure everything was ready to go.

Riders start staggered one minute apart, so just as the rider ahead of me was taking off down the start ramp, I rolled into the staging area and came to a stop by one of my mechanics, who leaned over the bike one last time and spun each wheel with a towel to be sure there was no debris on my tires.

"Your tire is cut," he said. "I want to change the wheel." I must have rolled over a small piece of glass or metal cruising from the bus to the start.

"All right," I said. A blowout could mean a high-speed crash that could end my whole Tour, or at the very least mean valuable seconds lost in changing to my spare bike from the team car, which would be following behind me.

The mechanic undid the bolts, replaced the wheel and tightened the new bolts as I stood there. I knew we were cutting it very close to my start time, but John didn't say anything into the radio, so I figured we still had a few seconds. I pedaled up the ramp to the start and stopped at the table to sign in. The official was all stressed out and said, "Just go!"

I thought, *Oh, I guess I missed the start,* but I didn't worry. If I did miss it, then the only thing I could do was try to ride hard to make up the time, so that's what I focused on. Worrying would just waste energy on something in the past.

In the end, I finished ninth and was nine seconds behind the stage winner. It was a lousy finish for someone who was supposed to be one of the overall favorites, but afterward John said to me, "You were nine seconds late," and shrugged his shoulders. He knew that screaming into the team radio would have only distracted me, so he'd let it go.

I'm sure it didn't look so good from the outside. I probably looked sloppy or conceited. "The start of the Tour? Oh,

Landis will be here in a little bit, once he's done with other pressing matters." But what else could I do? The truth is that I dodged a bullet, and my team protected me as efficiently as possible. Losing nine seconds wasn't good, but it was far better than the potential alternatives. Besides, without my wheel change, I might have won the prologue. I took that as a good sign.

Without Lance in the race, the whole Tour was wide open. There was no one clear leader or team to bully the peloton. Phonak wasn't a superteam like the Postal Service and Discovery teams were during the Lance years. But the thing was, no one else had a superteam either. While Discovery was still strong even though Lance had retired, they had three or four possible contenders but no clearly defined leader, a strategy that simply wouldn't win them the Tour. I knew that from last year.

One advantage I had over the other teams was that the riders on Phonak believed 100 percent that I could win, and they had no personal ambitions whatsoever. Maybe some of the other guys believed their leader could win, but they didn't race that way. T-Mobile was better than we were on paper: Even with Ullrich and top lieutenant Oscar Sevilla gone due to Operación Puerto, they were still led by Andreas Klöden, who had beaten Ullrich in 2004 anyway, and other strongmen, such as Matthias Kessler and Michael Rogers, to back him up. During Stage 3, a very hot day as the Tour wound into Holland, Kessler and Rogers beat themselves up by working hard to finish first and second in the stage.

My mom would always make something special for nearly any occasion.

This duck was mean and quacked a lot for no reason. I think we named it Dick.

Photo by Paul Landis

Thank you, Easter Bunny!

Photo by Paul Landis

This certainly looks dangerous by today's standards.

Photo by Paul Landis

I got my first real sponsor, GT Bikes, after I won the Junior National MTB Title.

Photo by Paul Landis

This is my first team, sponsored by Green Mountain Cyclery.

Blue Train coming through—our U.S. Postal team dominated
in the team time trial at the Tour de France.

Two workers (me and George) riding in from a stage
of the Tour—our job was done for the day.

I am proud of the job I did working to help Lance win.
Stage 17 of the 2004 Tour was one of my best efforts.

Photo by Dave Wrolstad

This is some of my teammates and me from 2005.
It can be hard to look tough in green and yellow, but we tried.

Photo by Beth Seliga/www.3catsphoto.com

I really enjoyed racing and winning the Amgen Tour of California.
I think it is already one of the best races in the world.

This is me and my girl.
I am a lucky dude, for sure.

In our suite at the Le Meridian, Ryan
displays her new favorite shirt.

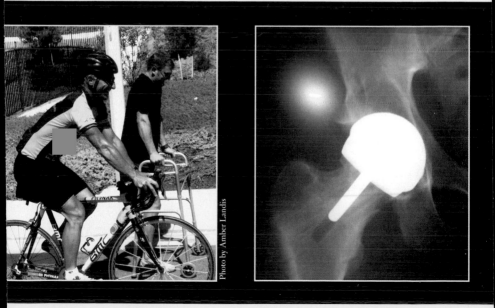

...ays after surgery, on a stroll with Dr. Kay.
...y new hip was great from the beginning.

This is my new Birmingham hip. It looks
simple and clean on the X-ray and really works.

I had finally made it. Victory at last.

My teammates, on the other hand, used all of their energy to make my ride easier. "Today, you only lost three hundred grams of water weight," Allen told me when I stepped on the scale after the stage. "The rest of the guys lost between two and three kilos." He made the analogy that my team was like a crew of worker bees flapping their wings to keep the queen bee cool. All day, my guys had drifted back to the team car to fetch more water and sports drink for me, and then ridden up through the pack to make the delivery. That day I drank close to twenty bottles and stayed completely hydrated.

Every night, Allen analyzed the power data, not just for me this year but also for Robbie, Peña, Koos, and Nicolas— they all raced with PowerTaps now. One thing Allen had determined in analyzing cyclists' power output is that it's less stressful on the body to put in one consistent effort than to keep surging and slowing down. Allen noticed from the data that out of all of our riders, Robbie was putting out the most consistent power with the fewest spikes. When I tried following Robbie's steady wheel, my day felt a little bit easier.

In addition to Allen's daily analysis, I had help from RV, who put his coaching business on hold to come to France for the entire race. Every morning, he'd scout the course and call me to warn me about any hills or turns that were tougher than they seemed to be in the course book. The information was invaluable. "Floyd, this race is going to break up on this hill," he'd say. "Be in the front when you get here so you don't get caught in the back and lose time." After each stage, whenever I needed a positive word, RV would visit or call.

Two days before the first mountain stage, it was time for another cortisone shot. The injections had been working perfectly. I was pedaling essentially pain free for the first time since I could remember. Dr. Chao and Brent met me in my hotel room and gave me a shot to last me the rest of the race.

There are two days off during the Tour, spaced out to give riders and team management a much-needed break. Typically, not much happens during these days for the riders. We go for a two- or three-hour ride—if you don't ride, your system goes into rest mode and you feel terrible during the next stage—get massages, rest, and do interviews. But I was going to use our first day off to set off a firecracker in the middle of the Tour.

I announced that I needed a hip replacement. There were two reasons to make it public at that time: I was launching the Floyd Landis Foundation to help fund research and treatment of AVN and osteoarthritis, and I wanted to get people excited about it. But I also wanted to make as big a scene as possible so that joint-replacement experts around the world who had ideas about what hip I should choose could offer opinions or insight that Brent, Dr. Chao, and I hadn't considered. What better way to do it than during the Tour?

It worked. But the news also shocked many people who couldn't believe I could pedal at all, much less be a favorite in the Tour de France. My hip practically took over the race. Reporters constantly asked me, "Floyd, how's the hip today?"

Or, no matter what had happened in the stage, they wanted to know, "Did the hip bother you today?" Or, "Were you able to sleep last night given your hip problem?" It was practically to the point that, if I yawned, reporters wanted to know if my hip was responsible.

They asked the other teams about it too, which I'm sure drove them crazy. Johan even came out and questioned my judgment, saying, "It's not wise to reveal a weakness in the middle of the race." I found that quite amusing. I had made it clear that my hip wasn't a limitation in racing; it was a chronic condition that was painful and required a hip replacement after the Tour. I didn't feel like I was revealing a weakness. If anything, it was my way of saying, "Yeah, I have a problem. But I'm going to beat you anyway."

Still, it was nice to have it out in the open. Once we were racing again, Zabriskie rode up to me during a flat section, wiggling his butt out of the saddle and singing his own special version of "Hips Don't Lie" by Shakira. "Hey, Floyd, you know my hips don't lie . . ." I had told him about my hip more than a year before, so he knew all about the pain and stress I had been through. Even though we were racing together every day, we hadn't had any time to talk, so this was his way of congratulating me on the announcement.

The first big test of the Tour was the Pyrenees. Stage 11 was a monster, 128 miles of riding with five of the toughest climbs of the race all packed into one day. My team was strong over the first peak, but from there guys just kept falling off the back. I knew there would be no one left to pace me up the last climb of the day. We didn't even say anything over the team radio. There was nothing to say. They were having a bad day.

With three miles to go up the Col du Portillon, the third climb of the day, the T-Mobile team went to the front to set pace for Klöden. I felt good, so I went with them alone. Riders were spit out the back one by one, including the yellow jersey at the time, French favorite Cyril Dessel.

On the descent, a few of the stragglers caught back on, so there were about twenty-five of us at the base of the final climb to the summit at Pla-de-Beret. Other favorites had teammates around them, and I still can't believe someone didn't organize an attack to try to finish me off then. I had won three big races during the season and was one of the clear favorites to win the Tour. But instead of trying to gang up on me to end my chances right there, they just let me stay in the group. Soon, only a pack of five remained: me, Levi Leipheimer, Denis Menchov, Cadel Evans, and Carlos Sastre.

Occasionally, Levi would stand in the saddle and launch an attack, but each time I was able to use a short burst of power to mark the move and stay with the remaining riders. Rather than push hard to win the stage, I hung back to take third place, while Menchov won the stage and Levi took second. I finished just on their wheels, which was good enough to put me in the yellow jersey for the first time in my life.

On the podium, a model in a yellow dress presented me with the traditional bouquet of sunflowers and a stuffed yellow lion. The Tour is big on ceremony, so I added a special touch to my usual podium getup of a backward baseball cap and sunglasses—a pair of white loafers, just to complete the look.

Afterward, I told all the reporters that I felt good, and that "we told most of the guys that it wasn't necessary to have the whole team there with me." It was part of the plan, I explained, to let my teammates save themselves for later in the race.

In reality, this was the only bad day my team would have all race. I stepped onto the team bus and placed the yellow lion in the windshield to be our mascot. "We didn't mean to leave you alone," Peña said. "I should have been there." A couple of the other guys apologized. The team was down.

"Look, we can't change today, so don't worry about it," I said. "I need people in the Alps, and I'm sure you guys will be better then. Plus, we're in the lead. Can you believe those idiots let us have the lead?" My teammates had given me their full confidence in me as their leader, and now they had mine. It was time to look forward.

Now that we had the yellow jersey, our main focus became giving it away. It was an unorthodox strategy—in the Tour a leader's team may let the jersey go if another team attacks, but we worked together, actively trying to get rid of it. Attempting to keep it took too much energy from the entire team, and I knew we needed to save everything for the Alps in the Tour's final week.

Stage 13 was 143 miles, the longest stage of the Tour

with a few rolling hills through the south of France. CSC's Jens Voigt and Oscar Pereiro, my former teammate now on the Spanish team Caisse-D'Epargne-Illes Balears, rode away from the group early to get a huge lead on the peloton, and we let them go. Voigt specialized in launching breaks and winning individual stages, but he wasn't a threat to win the whole Tour. Pereiro's Tour was over. In the stage to Pla-de-Beret, he had blown up and lost more than twenty-six minutes. But still, he and Voigt were flying. If we could ride slowly enough, we could give the yellow jersey to Pereiro.

My teammates rode at the front of the peloton. "Hey, guys, sit up," I said into the team radio, and they pedaled easy. At one point, I even told them to hit the brakes a little to allow Voigt and Pereiro to get even more time.

With about five miles to go, Menchov's Rabobank team pedaled to the front to try to speed things up. They wanted me to stay in the yellow jersey so that my team would have to waste energy defending it. The Rabobank team was hoping that Menchov, who had been so strong in the Pyrenees, would be able to beat me in the Alps if my team was worn down enough. So I rode up to the Rabobank guys. "Maybe Menchov is strong enough to win the Tour," I said. "But if you work now and I keep the lead, then I'll race just so he loses. I promise you that."

"Fuck you, you can't do that," said Michael Boogerd, one of their top *domestique*s.

I told him that I not only could, but that I was just crazy enough to do it. I wouldn't win, but neither would Menchov.

"I'll attack every single day to make sure of it," I said. "I don't care. I'll make your lives hell." They gave in and stopped working. It's funny to me when trash talking works. If I were them, I never would have listened to me. But I had developed a reputation for being able to cause suffering in the peloton, so I had control.

Voigt and Pereiro finished twenty-nine minutes and fifty-seven seconds ahead of us. Pereiro catapulted from forty-sixth place in the standings at the beginning of the day to wearing the yellow jersey at the end. I couldn't believe that the other teams had just sat there and let us get away with it. Now Pereiro's team would have to do the work to help him stay in yellow.

I was pretty pleased with how clever we were, and the team loved it too. Apparently, the French newspapers were unimpressed. Their idea is that once you have the yellow jersey, you should ride with panache to defend it, because it's such an honor. "I don't care at all about what people think about how we did it," I said in a press conference. "If you understood how cycling works, you wouldn't question that." I tried to explain that I would use any tactic necessary to wear yellow in Paris, because that's the only thing that mattered to me. I don't think that sat well with tradition either. *Oh well,* I thought, *that's their problem.*

On the second rest day, I went for a two-hour ride and decided to clean out the engines a little bit by riding up a short hill as hard as I could. It takes some motivation to ride hard when you just want to sleep all day, but I knew from experience that if you push yourself just a little, you feel better the next day in the mountains. So I punched it. My power meter said I rode at 460 watts for ten minutes. It was my hardest effort of the entire Tour. I felt ready for the next three days in the Alps, the mountain stages that would decide the race.

Attacks were coming fast from all directions. Pereiro's team was trying to take control, but Phonak was working on the front, too. "Axel, we need you up here," Robbie said into the team radio. Robbie had become my workhorse setup man, but he had developed a serious saddle sore. It was no laughing matter—without antiseptic cream in his shorts, it was too painful for him even to sit down. Still, he led me over the first few climbs of each mountain stages with his even cadence.

Axel had been hanging out in the back, saving himself to help me on the last climb of the day, Alpe d'Huez, but when Robbie called, he went straight to the front to help. Almost immediately, a breakaway of about twenty-five riders splintered and pulled away, and Axel snuck into that group.

Even though Axel was ahead of me, he was riding only for me, not for himself. It was intentional. By being ahead of the peloton, he was a sort of an insurance policy that I'd have a teammate late in the race to protect me.

When Axel finally hit the bottom of Alpe d'Huez in the breakaway, I was still three minutes behind him in the peloton. John said into the team radio, "Floyd is coming up with some others." Axel heard. Instead of continuing on and trying to snag his first ever Tour stage win for himself, he slowed down to ride at an easy tempo to wait for me. He took a long drink from his water bottle, enough so that he wouldn't need more for the rest of the climb.

Meanwhile, at the base of the Alpe, Perdi ratcheted up the speed so quickly and quietly that he surprised the peloton and dropped everyone—even me, for a few seconds. He had seen that Pereiro, in the yellow jersey, was hurting, so he went after him. I regrouped with some of the other strong climbers, such as Klöden and Levi, but thanks to Perdi, Pereiro was losing time to us already.

I caught a glimpse of Axel ahead and realized what he was doing. When I came upon him, he handed me his half-full water bottle without a word and took off as hard as he could to lead me up the mountain. All of a sudden, I went from having no water to having half a bottle, and from battling the other team leaders all by myself to following a friendly wheel. It not only helped from the standpoint of hydration and drafting, but the feeling of support was a huge mental advantage—and a disadvantage to the others who were watching me rest.

Axel lasted about two miles before pulling off, and from there I rode hard enough to keep the overall race contenders behind me, but not so hard that I sapped myself. By the finish of Stage 15, I had put more than a minute and a half on Pererio and averaged about 410 watts on Alpe d'Huez. I was in yellow again, and Amber had just flown in from San Diego to follow the last week of the race, so this time I gave my sunflowers and stuffed lion to her.

Tactically, my team was perfect. There were still two brutal mountain stages to go, but I knew I was the strongest rider in the race. There was no strategic reason now to give up the yellow jersey. We'd try to defend it all the way to Paris.

After even just a few days of the Tour, you rarely wake up feeling well. In fact, you feel miserable. The last place you want to be is sitting on that saddle, pedaling. Your legs feel powerless, and it's hard to figure out how you'll possibly be able to put your body through another day. But you line up anyway and hope that after an hour or two, you'll begin to feel a little less miserable—or that you'll at least be able to go fast.

I felt this way as we started rolling on Stage 16. The problem was that after suffering up the first climb of the day, the massive, 27-mile Col du Galibier, I wasn't coming around. The pavement was baking in the 90-degree heat; I was sweating all over the place, but never felt like I was cooling off. I tried to force myself to drink to stay hydrated and eat to keep my energy up, even though the thought of food made me feel nauseous at that point.

There was just no stretch of flat. We went from climbing to descending, back to climbing again. If only there were fifteen minutes of flat road where I could tuck in behind Axel and eat some food and rest, I thought maybe I'd shake the feeling of misery. But there was nothing.

You can tell when someone isn't right in the peloton, and I was giving all the telltale signs: I was a little pale, my elbows stuck out a bit, my shoulders rolled forward, and my chin drooped a little. I tried to hide it from the beginning, but it wasn't working. At one point Axel pulled beside me and whispered, "Are you okay?"

I completely ignored him and withdrew from everything in the world but those turning cranks. One pedal revolution, then another, and then another—that was my focus, while deep in the back of my mind I still had hope that maybe my body would come around for the final climb, La Toussuire.

It didn't. When the first attack went, I couldn't go. To Pereiro and the other riders around me, I was like a limping animal straggling in the back of the pack. They knew I was weak, and they went in for the kill.

"Keep your tempo. Stay calm, stay calm," John said into the radio, trying his best to sound calm himself. I pulled out my earpiece. There was nothing I could do to get my body to move any faster. The attackers became smaller in the distance ahead of me.

Axel had fallen off the pace only a few minutes before. When he heard John on the radio, he knew right away that something was wrong with me. He started to hear fans on the side of the road scream to him, "Landis is dropped!" Then he looked up and saw the Phonak team car just two switchbacks ahead, which meant that I was right there, in front of the car, instead of minutes up the road with the leaders.

My gaze was downward, directly in front of my wheel,

then all of a sudden there was a Phonak water bottle in my face. Axel was handing it to me. He had already ridden to his limit, but when he saw I needed help, he stood out of the saddle and pumped his legs as hard as he could to catch me. I threw my empty bottle to the side of the road and replaced it with Axel's. He rode in front of me to try to pace me, but his adrenaline was pumping and I had nothing. I couldn't hang on, and it was embarrassing. "Just go," I said.

"Go where?" he responded, confused at the suggestion that he should leave his team leader behind. He slowed down a little. "It's not over. Stay on my wheel and we'll get there," he said. He paced me all the way to the top. "You take a drink," he'd say every couple of minutes. "We'll get there." It took roughly forever.

Axel and I finished more than ten minutes behind the stage winner, and I plummeted from first to eleventh in the standings. Pereiro was back in the yellow jersey, and ahead of me by eight minutes and eight seconds. It may as well have been an hour. I had blown my chance to win the Tour.

My wheels came to a wobbly stop. I slumped over in the yellow jersey that I thought I'd never wear again and put my forehead on the handlebar to hide my face. Instantly, I was in the center of a huddle of photographers. My head pounded and I felt heat radiating from everywhere—the pavement, the photographers, my own body. Then I felt a cold wet towel on my shoulders. It was Denise. "Come on," she said, and pulled me out of the crowd and rushed me to John's waiting team car. He drove me straight to our hotel.

CHAPTER 9

Stupid for Trying It

Despite the heat, I was freezing cold from dehydration and too tired to even stand up in the shower, so I took a hot bath, lying there for half an hour, just spacing out. When I finally got back to my room, Amber was there.

"I'm sorry," I said.

It just came out. At the time I wasn't sure why, but I suppose part of it was that she felt so bad for me, and I hated being the cause. But I also think part of it was that I wasn't the only one who had made sacrifices all those years to pursue my dream: She had also been broke early on, and endured all the months apart, and she had put up with my hip for as long as I had.

"Stop it," she said. "What could you possibly have to be sorry for?"

"I don't know what happened," I said. Neither of us really knew what to say to make the situation better. I'm not sure there was anything that could have helped. I lay down on the bed to rest, and we just hung out.

The team was staying in a small ski condo complex right on top of the mountain. Our little house had suites and adjoining rooms. Five of us riders were staying in one part: me, Robbie, Axel, Perdi, and Koos. Denise, John, and other team management were in the other.

One by one, between eating and showering and seeing Denise for medical attention, my teammates quietly knocked on my door to talk to me. "Hey, shit happens. No matter what, I've got your back," Robbie said. Then came Koos. "One bad day doesn't make a difference." Then Axel. "You made me a better rider than I actually am by believing in you, and I still believe in you."

I didn't know what to tell these guys, who for more than two weeks had thought only of me instead of themselves. All I could do was thank them for everything they had done. It was unacceptable to me to be in that situation, but there was nothing I could say to change it. They all showed their continuing loyalty to me, and there's no way to express how much I appreciated that.

"This is the most humiliating thing I've ever experienced," I said to Amber when we were alone again. I was already starting to rebound physically. I'm not sure what happens to the body when it shuts down and you can no longer get it to perform the way you want it to. But it seems like once you refuel and give it a chance to rest, it tries to overcompensate, just in case you're crazy enough to push it that hard again. It's quite common for a cyclist to have a terrible day, and then come back to have the next day be his best. I had been eating and drinking since the moment I got back to the condo, so my body felt much better, which meant that now I felt even worse about letting everyone down.

John stopped by and said that the press had been calling. Did I want to speak? Not really, but I knew that they'd corner me sooner or later, so I might as well deal with it sooner. Hiding is weak anyway, and I wasn't going to move past the experience until I faced the questions. The team called a makeshift press conference right outside our condo. Amber left to go to her hotel, and I walked out the door to face cameras and reporters stacked ten deep, waiting to fire questions at me.

I had no excuse for what had happened, so I refused to make one. "Sometimes you don't feel well, and today was not a good day to have a bad day," I said. "What can I say? My team was good, but I suffered from the beginning, and that was all I could do."

"Was it your hip?" someone asked.

I actually laughed at that one. "No."

"Where do you go from here?" It was a silly question. Everyone was looking for some grand revelation or fundamental change in me as a person just because of what happened during the last half hour of a day's bike race.

"Uh, from here? Stage 18, 19, or whatever's next," I said. I had lost count. "Look, bike racing is a big part of my life, but today doesn't change anything about who I am or what I'll do next." I was going to come out fighting the next day, because my teammates had helped me come all that way, and I owed it to them not to give up. But being more than eight minutes behind pretty much meant the end of my hopes for the yellow jersey. I freely admitted that. "I'm happy for Pereiro," I said. "That's the way the Tour went."

I walked back inside, frustrated with myself. Robbie and Perdi were sitting in the common area, and Allen had showed up. "Who wants to join me for a beer?" I said.

It may sound surprising that in the middle of killing ourselves in the Tour that I would even consider drinking alcohol, but it's more common for riders to drink than most people would think. Europeans have a different view of alcohol. Wine or beer flows freely at every meal. It's part of their culture. While it's rare for a pro rider to have a glass of wine with dinner during a race, it wouldn't be a scandal if he did. Plus, at that point, I didn't care much about anything. I wanted to forget about what had happened and feel like a normal person, if only for a little while.

A group of us slipped out and walked maybe fifty yards down the hill to a busy sidewalk café. We sat at a table smack in the middle of the patio, with cycling fans all around us, and ordered a round of beers. "Look, there's a whole world going on out here," Allen said. Everyone was trying to be supportive and tell me not to worry about it. At one point, they all raised their glasses to toast me.

"Yeah, here's to me for that amazing display of crap today," I said, raising my eyebrows. We ordered another round. Every few seconds my cell phone would ping with another text message from a friend. "Oh, this is the best thing I've heard all day," I said. "It's from Vaughters." Jonathan Vaughters was an old Postal rider who now managed a domestic racing team in the U.S. I read it out loud. "I know everyone's telling you it's okay and to keep it in perspective, but this sucks ass!" It was the absolute truth.

By that time people around us had noticed who we were and had started crowding in to take pictures. We'd only been there fifteen minutes, but we split before things got out of hand.

On the way back to the condo, I got another text, from Arnie: "Character is not determined by your actions when things are wonderful." I felt a little rush when I read it, but I kept that one to myself.

At dinner, it was as if someone had let the air out of the tires. Everyone on the team, from the riders to the mechanics to the massage therapists, had been carrying themselves with pride, acting like winners. Today, I had sapped their motivation.

Later that night, Perdi, Robbie, and I were hanging out in the condo, listening to some Johnny Cash, when Denise came out with a bottle of Jack Daniel's that she kept on hand for the staff, in case anyone had a particularly rough day. "Why do you torture us with that?" she said, referring to the music.

"Come on, you gotta love Johnny Cash," I said. "Hey, pour me some of that." She got glasses for everyone and poured a round. No one said much, and I just listened to the music, thinking that Johnny Cash has the perfect soundtrack for the desperate man, but not taking it deeper than that. "I can't believe this," I said, finally.

"Look, Floyd, you've said this whole time that you can put ten minutes on all of these guys," Denise said. "Now you just have to do it in one day."

I liked her enthusiasm, but I am a reasonable person. "I'm afraid that's impossible," I said.

"It is possible," Perdi said. "If anyone can do it, it's you."

"Well," I said, "no matter what, tomorrow we've got to make them remember we were in the race." Maybe we weren't going to win, but I figured we could shake things up so that whoever did win had to work hard for it.

"We should win the stage at least," Robbie said.

"Don't wait until the last climb to attack," Perdi said. "That's what everybody does. We should attack halfway in. They'll be so surprised."

I started to smile.

"What if he goes on the first climb?" Robbie said. "We make it as off-the-charts as possible. They'll think he's stupid for trying it and they'll let him go."

Something changed in me right then. It was a crazy idea,

but I figured that if I had a good day, it just might work. "If I'm going to make back enough time to win the Tour," I said, "then that's the only possible tactic for us to try." Anything else, and we'd be eliminating the option of winning.

Having been in the position of working for a team leader, I knew how tired all the *domestiques* would be at this point in a three-week race. If we attacked like hell, they'd fall off the back of the peloton and not be able to help their leader with anything. Then, once I escaped, the only way anyone would catch me was if a bunch of leaders from different teams made a deal to work together to chase me down. But the team leaders would all be tired, too, because of how hard they had attacked today once I was dropped. It wasn't so far-fetched to believe I could escape to win the stage, but how much time I could gain back in the race for the yellow jersey ultimately depended on how well the pack organized to chase me.

"Here's what we do," I said, pulling out the course book. "We're going to need absolutely everyone." I opened it to the map of Stage 17, and the guys gathered around. I pointed to a spot just before the base of the first climb. "Here's where Perdi sets the tempo." Perdi was the best at sneaking the pace up without anyone in the peloton realizing what was going on until we were going full speed, just like he had done at the base of Alpe d'Huez to drop Pereiro. "They'll think we're just doing it to be a bunch of jack-asses," I said.

By the bottom of the climb, the pack would be strung

out, and Robbie, whose specialty was a world-class fifteen-minute burst of speed, would blow the peloton apart. Before any of the race leaders would be able to mobilize in any way, I'd be on the front, surrounded by all of my guys, pulling away. "You just have to give me everything to get me away on that first climb," I told them. "Then I'll take it from there."

The mood in the room was completely different. It was back to normal, and we were all so excited for the next day that we ended up staying up far later than we probably should have.

The warm sun came through the window early the next morning. It was going to be another hot one. I woke up perfectly calm, feeling like I had absolutely nothing to lose. As I was gathering my things to pack, with Metallica blasting from my portable speakers, I started getting angry to pump myself up. Then I came across a book of Jack Handey quotes a friend had sent me during the race and thought I'd better not pack it quite yet. It might be useful.

Allen had been crunching numbers all night. He came to my room with his scale and his computer, all excited to share his analysis and talk about details. He hadn't been in the room with us the night before, but on his own he had come up with the idea that I could still win the Tour. "I have two pieces of paper," he said. "One is a list of all the possible reasons that yesterday might have happened, and the other is a list of why you still have a chance. Which one do you want to see?"

"Forget yesterday," I said. "Let's talk about how to win." He told me how much power I had produced on all the climbs in the Tour up to that point. The watts numbers weren't that impressive. They were lower than those from last year's Tour, and not even close to what I had done in training throughout the year. "I'm not even close to my limit," I said. Then I pulled out the Jack Handey book, and we cracked up reading it for a good long while. I felt like myself again.

My team's attack at the first climb couldn't have gone any better. Riders popped off the back one by one, so there was no opportunity for them to gather and discuss what to do about me. I watched my power meter and saw that I was cranking above 500 watts for a few seconds, so I settled into a ten-minute effort at 430 watts, not quite as hard as my rest-day climb at 460 watts.

Mentally, we had already delivered a severe blow. I tried to increase my lead as quickly as possible because I wanted to be completely out of sight by the time any of the chasers got to the first descent. My average for the entire climb was about 400 watts, close to the 410 watts I had done on Alpe d'Huez two days before. You can only do a climb at that intensity one time in a stage. I was using up my speed card in the beginning of the game. Nobody else would be so bold. They all just wanted to wait and see what happened.

The entire day was a perfect blend of tactics and technology. More than any other team, we used the information from our PowerTap power meters to help us make strategic decisions. Typically, we'd look at the data only after a stage—in the race itself, you're up against the other riders, not your watts numbers. But that day I watched my watts carefully to pace myself. If I had let my adrenaline be my guide, I would have gone too fast in the beginning and cracked for sure. If I had let my attention wander toward the end, I would have slowed to the point that I might have been caught. Instead, I watched my power meter—at first to keep me from going too hard, and later as a motivating force to keep me pedaling hard enough. There's no way I would have been able to pace the stage without it.

Once John caught up to me in the team car, I kept taking bottles and squirting the freezing water down through the vents of my helmet. It dripped down my head and all over my body. I was completely drenched, but it made me feel so much better in the oppressive heat. The benefit was almost like having air-conditioning. Allen later estimated that I was creating a microclimate for myself that was thirty degrees cooler than what the other riders were pedaling in. It was a huge advantage.

What did I think about for all that time alone out there? Honestly, not much. It's not like I reviewed my life history or thought about how my performance would affect the rest of my life, or even the rest of the Tour. Instead, my whole focus was the road and my power meter.

I didn't have any idea at the time, but all across France and the U.S. and the rest of Europe, people stopped whatever they were doing and turned to the screen to watch me. As the stage went on, the question, "Can he do it?" slowly became the exclamation, "He's doing it!" In San Diego, Arnie was up early, watching and thinking to himself, "It's going to work. I knew it." In Farmersville, my mom was alone at the neighbors' house watching their television, dancing out of her chair and gesturing toward heaven. By the time I reached the top of the Joux Plane, it was apparent I wasn't going to crack, and even the doubters believed. The announcers on TV were already calling it the most spectacular comeback in Tour de France history.

Many have said that my performance in Stage 17 was superhuman, but it wasn't. For five hours and twenty-three minutes, I averaged 280 watts. It was a strong ride, but I had two stages in the 2005 Tour when my average was higher. And during my most intense training periods, I'd do a ride like that about once a week. At our freezing-cold Swiss team camp a month before the Tour, I averaged 270 watts for six hours and thirty minutes on one ride that included 17,000 feet of climbing—all at more than 6,000 feet of altitude. Stage 17 didn't have nearly that much climbing. The bottom line is that most cyclists just don't train that hard, because it's difficult to will yourself to do it.

By the end of the stage, Pereiro was still in the yellow jersey, but I was only thirty seconds behind. There were three stages left, including a 35-mile time trial. Pereiro wasn't a time-trial specialist, and I had already beaten him by one minute forty seconds in the time trial in the Tour's first week. Unless something went catastrophically wrong for me, I'd be able to make up plenty of time win back the yellow jersey.

There was no chance to celebrate with the team until dinner that evening. Once we were all together, the mood was exactly the opposite from what it had been the night before. We were all simply dumbfounded, and how depressed we had been the day before seemed funny. We didn't analyze. We just laughed.

"The strategy was perfect," Peña joked. "I worked for only half an hour, and then I got to take the rest of the day off." Robbie said that they kept getting updates way back in the pack, and every time they heard that my lead had grown, my teammates would all pedal a little stronger, proud of what they had made possible. The only bad news was that after Perdi set his tempo, he'd had to drop out of the race. Not only had he crashed the day before, but he was coughing up a lung from a cold that had developed into severe bronchitis. That night, though, he was as proud as the rest of the guys.

Later, as I unpacked my things in my hotel room, RV and Amber came to visit. "That was unbelievable," RV said. "No one can touch you, my friend."

"Don't forget the time trial," I reminded him. "I still have thirty seconds to make up. The race is far from over." As I pulled things out of my bag, I found the yellow jersey I had worn in Stage 16. "This one means more to me than all the others," I told him. "Because I wouldn't have had today without yesterday."

♦ ♦ ♦

The next day, the race left the mountains and headed west to the plains to finish in Mâcon. The stage was mostly flat, but sweltering with temperatures well above 100 degrees again, and the pace was fast. I had blown apart the entire race the day before, and my solo exploit was the talk of the peloton. "I chased for ten minutes, and still I lost two minutes," T-Mobile's Kessler said, shaking his head. "I am wondering, is Landis in a car?" Another rider, Salvatore Commesso of Lampre-Fondital had a look of astonishment on his face and told me how unique my ride was in his thick Italian accent, "I see this first time now." Axel mentioned that his dad had called and told him he had placed a one-hundred-euro bet on me to win the whole Tour—and he had done this just a few hours *after* my bad day on Stage 16, when the odds were seventy-five to one.

The whole scene was outstanding, but I felt trashed. My teammates were all on the front of the pack again to make sure I stayed out of trouble, so keeping up wasn't the problem. The concern was that maybe I wouldn't recover quickly enough to do as well as I needed to do in the time trial the next day. The team went back into "cooling the queen bee" mode, constantly handing me water and sports drinks from the team car and keeping me safe in the draft.

The morning of the time trial, I woke up early to pre-ride the course with RV and Allen. The three of us had started a tradition this Tour of going out to scout all the tricky turns and rises before all of the races against the clock. As we rode, John drove behind in the team car to take notes on the course, so he could remind me on the team radio of all the spots where I should be careful.

I had serious business to do, but still we were like kids on our bikes, pedaling by the sunflower fields, through the suburban neighborhoods, and past the small towns along the route. My start time wasn't until three in the afternoon and it was only eight in the morning, but already fans were beginning to line the street. Every so often we'd hear "*Allez, Floyd,*" or something in French that I didn't understand, followed by "Lawn-dees."

"Hey, RV," I said.

"Yeah."

"Unless I crash and my leg falls off, I'm going to win the Tour de France," I told him.

"I know," he said, smiling. As if on cue, it started to rain, and then a couple of seconds later his rear wheel slid out from under him on the wet pavement. He managed to keep the bike upright, though John had to slam on the car brakes to keep from running over him. "Whoa, I hope that's not a sign," he said. "Please be cautious today." I promised him that I would. We kept riding along like we were taking the long way home from school, and the rain stopped. It wouldn't be a factor in the race.

After food and a nap at the hotel, I headed back to the start area and stepped onto the team bus. It was another blistering day, and I had felt so good with all that water on me in Stage 17 that I used a cooling vest as I waited for my start, to keep my core body temperature down. I put on my skin-suit and did a light warm-up so as not to overheat, and blasted "Fist of Rage" by Kid Rock over and over to get pumped up. I made sure that I showed up at the start ramp with plenty of extra time to let my mechanic inspect my bike and wipe down the tires with a towel.

Riders start in reverse order in a time trial, so because Pereiro was ahead of me, I'd start before him. There were three intermediate time checks along the route. I'd go through them first, and Pereiro would get to hear my progress to gauge how he was doing. The whole thing would take just over an hour, all out.

I could have tried blasting the first section to gain time on Pereiro and deliver a mental blow at the first time check. But I didn't want to mess with my normal routine. If I just went out and raced it like usual, focusing on myself instead of what Pereiro was thinking or doing, I figured I should be able to gain enough time.

I rode up the start ramp, signed in, and waited for my countdown. I was motivated and ready. When I got the signal, I shot down the start ramp and into the empty street. For one more day, I'd be all alone in my race for the yellow jersey.

At the first time check, I posted the fastest time of any rider by one second. A few minutes later, after Pereiro went though the check, John said on the radio, "Ten seconds on Pereiro. Ten seconds. Don't forget to drink." I took a drink. Pereiro was still too close.

John kept calling out all the features of the course. "A short rise . . . left turn ahead . . . stay wide . . . perfect . . . you're taking the right line." I didn't even have to lift my head out of its aerodynamic position into the wind to look at the road ahead. When I passed through the next time check, I had slipped to second in the stage, but I didn't care. Then I heard, "You got it! Fifty-seven seconds on Pereiro!" I stood out of the saddle and cranked for ten strokes up a rise before settling back in. At the final time check, I had ninety seconds on Pereiro, enough time to give me the yellow jersey by a minute. "No risks here," John said. "That's it." A few more turns in the road, a few more cranks out of the saddle, and that *was* it. I crossed the finish. Pereiro still had to finish, but I knew I had it.

I was back in yellow, with my backward hat, shades, and loafers, this time for good. From high on the podium I chucked my bouquet of sunflowers in an arc through the air. Amber was standing about fifty feet away at the side of the massive crowd. Like it was no big deal, she reached up and made a perfect catch. No matter what was thrown her way, she could handle it.

Fifty-seven seconds. That ended up being the difference between me and Pereiro. Hold your breath, and fifty-seven seconds pass like that. That three-week, 2,000 mile race took me eighty-nine hours, thirty-nine minutes, and twenty-eight seconds. And the guy in second place was less than a minute behind me—all that stress, sweat, blood, energy, and devotion to gain an edge of fifty-seven seconds. Still, the gentleman's rules of the Tour dictate that, as long as the time gap between the lead and second place is substantial enough that there's no reasonable chance for the second place rider to gain enough time to take back the yellow jersey, there will be no attacking the last stage in to Paris. So even though there was one last stage, the race was over because the course was table flat, which left no chance for a breakaway.

The evening after that time trial was the best one of the entire race. While checking over the bikes, our mechanics sang and wrapped each rider's bike with yellow handlebar tape to match my winner's jersey. At dinner it was just us—the riders and team staff—together as we had been the past three weeks, our last gathering before the crush of sponsor parties and publicity obligations after the race. We celebrated with champagne and beer, and everyone was relaxed and savoring the time we had left together. I think Andy Rihs was the happiest man in the room to finally win after all he had been through to keep the team together. There was a spirit to the way we did it, and we all felt it that night. We weren't a machine. We were more like a family that looked after one another.

The only thing that hadn't gone right for our team that day was that Robbie didn't finish the time trial within the mandatory time cut—the poor man's backside hurt so much from his saddle sore that he rode the entire way standing up. He wouldn't be allowed to ride into Paris with us.

The next day, the world joined us in the celebration. Tens of thousands of people lined the Champs-Élysées. We finished the stage and our team pedaled a victory lap around the Champs. Andy joined us, laughing and smiling and slapping me on the back, like I was his own son. It was my fourth time being out there on a winning team, but this time I was the one in yellow. This time was mine. At the final awards presentation, Ryan came up onto the podium with me, in front of the sea of fans. She had flown to Paris with David and Ms. Rose to see the finish.

Later that night, it was time for the Phonak sponsor party. When I was on Postal, the parties were always formal affairs, with assigned seating to make sure that the riders gave sponsors enough face time. But at the Phonak party, people laughed and danced and mingled freely—though I was too tired to even stand and socialize, so I mostly sat in a chair. Someone had the deejay play Kid Rock for me, and then on a big screen they showed a highlight reel of our team from the Tour. All the highs and lows were there, ending with our triumphant parade around the Champs-Élyseés. I leaned over to Amber. "When you put it that way, it does seem pretty unbelievable," I said.

I'd love to say that on the night of my big victory I experienced a high like never before and that I partied all night and the world seemed wonderful. But in truth, the initial rush wore off, and I was feeling crushing fatigue that the Tour inflicts. I needed to go lie down. "That's okay," Amber said. "Because when we get home, we're going to throw a party like you have never seen. We'll get the real Kid Rock to come play." We slipped out while the music and dancing were still going strong and went to our fancy complimentary hotel suite to go to bed. There would be plenty of time to celebrate later.

CHAPTER 10
Having It All

Amber and I woke up in the presidential suite at the top of the Meridien hotel in Paris, in crisp sheets and a king-size bed. I started to laugh. "I won the Tour!" I said.

"You did," she said. "You did it!" We kept saying it over and over. It wasn't real yet, and I felt like a little kid who had snuck into a grownup's palace, especially after three weeks of cramped European hotel rooms in tiny towns. Amber said, "Let's live like rock stars."

Ryan was flying home that morning with Ms. Rose and David, so we all gathered together and ordered room service for breakfast. Ms. Rose joked about how David and I had pressed our heads together to listen in on the same phone when President Bush had called the day before to congratulate me.

"I looked over, and there were two heads with the same laugh," she said.

Afterward, I took a long bath. Amber flipped through the hotel amenities book. "No way," she said. "They have a hotel hairstylist!" She called, and a guy came up to the suite and gave me a haircut.

For the rest of the morning, we entertained visitors. Zabriskie and his wife, Randi, came up. Amber told them about the haircut. "We're ghetto," she joked. "We're going to enjoy it while we got it."

Allen came by. "Can you believe it? You won it on the bad hip."

"Next I'll win one on the fake hip," I said. "And then I'm done." I was completely, deeply exhausted, but the feeling couldn't have been better. Finally, after so much focus and so much energy devoted to training for fifteen years, I could kick back and just enjoy my success.

I had everything I had hoped for and dreamed of. And there was something about the fact that I thought I had lost it all just a few days before that made the victory so much sweeter.

We finally left the hotel to have lunch in a small café tucked away on a side street with Robbie and his wife, Claudia, and a few others from the team. Robbie and I were talking smack about all the stuff we wanted to buy. By most peoples' standards, I had been well paid over the years, but winning the Tour would mean serious money—millions—in endorsements and sponsorships from all over. Even Budweiser had called me about an endorsement deal. It would be life changing. And Robbie would get his share of the Tour-winning prize money, plus an extra Floyd bonus. Robbie mentioned extravagant vacations he and Claudia wanted to take.

"Man, I want a Mustang," I said, "A black one! Oh, I'm going to get so many speeding tickets." After being in the fancy hotel, it was a nice change to feel normal again and to be back goofing off with the team.

After we ate, Robbie said he needed to buy a pair of shoes, so we walked around the corner into a Nike store on the Champs-Élysées. . . . It turns out that the day after winning the world's biggest bike race, people will notice you when you're walking just a few meters from the finish line. A crowd formed and started to mob me. It was open season. During the race, the barricades and my team staff had protected me from the crowds, and I guess I figured that once the race was over, the crowds would go away, too. People wanted autographs and pictures, or just to touch me. They were pushing one another to get closer, so Amber and I got the hell out of there and jumped into a cab to go back to the hotel.

After we'd been driving a couple of minutes, I noticed that the driver kept looking in the rearview mirror. He looked at me, then Amber. Me, then Amber. She saw him casually reach over to the front passenger seat and flip a page of his newspaper, then another. There on the page was a big picture of Amber and Ryan. "This is you," he said, and handed the paper to her. When we got to the hotel, he asked to take a picture with us, so we did. I shook his hand, and then we went back into hiding.

The next day, we snuck out of the hotel and took the train to Holland. There's a Tour de France tradition for the riders to do a few short races after the Tour, as a way to show off cycling's best riders to the rabid fans in the rest of Europe. Riders do it for the money—as the yellow-jersey winner, I was getting paid sixty thousand dollars per race just to show up—but it's also a good way to keep riding.

It sounds counterintuitive, but after three weeks of racing so hard, it actually feels terrible to stop and do nothing. It's much better for your body to go out and do a few short rides. Besides, the races are only exhibitions. I "won" the first one in Holland, and there's no way I could have won a real race after the Tour. I had two more scheduled over the next two days—one more in Holland and then one in Denmark. I'd wave to the crowds, show off the jersey, and then finally it would be time to go home.

The next morning after breakfast we were sitting in the hotel, relaxing with Robbie and Claudia. Robbie was teasing me. "We're on the Champs-Élysées the very next day after the race," he said, "and it doesn't occur to you that people would recognize you."

"Well, I had my sunglasses on," I said.

"Half the world knows those sunglasses from the podium," he said. "Besides, your face isn't exactly forgettable."

They left, and my phone rang. It was John Lelangue. "I

need to see you," he said. I didn't think anything of it. We had plenty to talk about concerning the team for the rest of the season, so I told him to come up to the room.

We went into the office of the suite and sat down at the table. He paused for a minute. "Uh," he said. "Um. We received a fax at the team headquarters today," he said. "It said you had an A sample that tested positive during the Tour." That was all he knew. He didn't even have the piece of paper with him.

"Huh?" was all I could think to say.

"Yeah," he said.

I was stunned. It made no sense, so I started asking questions: "For what? When?"

"I don't know which stage," he said. "I don't know what." He shook his head. "I don't know," he said, quietly.

"John, this is a huge mistake," I said. "I need to know exactly what's going on." Immediately, I wanted to know all the specifics so I could figure out how the error was made. My first thought was that maybe it had something to do with the shots for my hip, that somehow the cortisone was tripping a drug test to show a false positive.

Whatever it was, I wanted it to be resolved quickly. I had seen enough of these stories to know that even though it was just a mistake, once the media picked up on the story it would be a disaster.

"All right, I'll go try to find out more," John said. "But we need to figure out how to get out of here." I had a race that afternoon. The press was there, and they were expecting me.

I went back into the suite in a cold sweat. I was in total shock. I couldn't even think, but I knew I had to tell Amber. I went over to her and sort of lay on top of her on the couch. "I have something I have to tell you," I said.

She could sense right away that it wasn't good. "Get off of me!" she said. "What? What!"

I told her. She was as floored as I was. We just sat there, for almost an hour. Every once in a while one of us would say, "It must be the cortisone. I bet it's the cortisone." But we didn't know anything about how drug testing worked, and we didn't have any information about the results of my specific test. We had no idea what to do.

I called Robbie and told him I needed to see him. He could also tell something was wrong and came straight back up to my room. "It's bad," I said. "There's a positive."

"It's not possible!" he said, and then sat there processing the news for a few seconds. "Okay, who is it?" He thought I meant that someone else on the team had tested positive.

"No, you don't understand," I said. "It's me."

"No," he said. "There's no way." From his reaction, you'd think I had told him that the positive was his. "We're going to fix this," he said. "We'll fix it."

But first thing was first. I had to drop out of the race that was taking place in a few hours. I hated the idea of making up an excuse, but we didn't have a choice. According to the UCI code of ethics, once a rider is under investigation for doping, his team isn't supposed to let him race. So Robbie called the organizers and said that I had hurt my hip and that

I was on my way to see the team doctor, who had ordered me to stay off my bike.

John came back to the room and told me that my A sample showed an illegally high testosterone-to-epitestosterone (T/E) ratio after Stage 17, my big comeback stage. They called it an "adverse analytical finding." Each urine sample a rider gives is divided into an A and a B sample. If the A test shows an illegal limit, then the rider can request that the B sample be tested to double-check the results. A rider isn't considered to have tested positive until both samples have been tested.

I was completely unprepared for the situation, with no idea how to defend myself. The T/E ratio test is one of the oldest in drug testing. Because the amount of testosterone in a person's body varies quite a bit from person to person and is difficult to measure, the test compares the ratio of testosterone to another similar hormone, epitestosterone. The theory is that if someone dopes using testosterone, the ratio spikes. WADA's legal limit is four to one.

Of course, I didn't know any of that at the time. I didn't know how the test worked, or what the legal limit was, or even what epitestosterone was. Why would I? The specifics of the doping rules never concerned me. I had always just peed in the cup, as I was instructed. My philosophy was, "Here you go, take all the urine you need to do your job. I'm not using it anymore." So the only thing I knew when I got the news was that I needed help, fast.

♦ ♦ ♦

Almost immediately, John's phone started ringing with calls from reporters. "We've been told there was a positive at the Tour," one said. "I've called every national cycling federation, and the only one not picking up the phone is the U.S. Federation." Another said he had information that the positive came from a rider who had finished in the top ten. Someone who knew the test results was alerting the media.

After a few hours of phone calls and planning, we contacted a law firm in Madrid that had recently represented a Spanish rider, Inigo Landaluze, who had tested positive for testosterone in 2005. Landaluze had been acquitted of the charges in May, so I figured, perfect. These lawyers had the right experience. The lead guy was going to fly to Paris to meet with me the next day.

Amber and I snuck out of the hotel, just like we'd done the day before. John drove us back to Paris, but instead of his personal car he had a white Phonak team car with a giant green-and-yellow ear on the hood. We were a moving target. Amber and I huddled low in the back the whole way.

We ended up at the same place we had been just the day before, but across the street from the Meridien, in the Concorde hotel. John's wife knew the people at the hotel and set us up on the top floor, where you need a key to gain access, so it would be secure. We went in through the back door. The room had the same view of the Eiffel Tower and the Champs-Élysées, but the world felt completely different.

That night, there was a thunderstorm outside. Amber

stood by the window, mesmerized. "The rain is beautiful," she said. Then, after a minute . . . "How am I going to tell Ryan?"

I didn't have an answer, so we just sat there. A few minutes later, I had another thought that made me feel even worse—which I hadn't thought was possible at that point. "How am I going to tell my mother?"

I couldn't eat. I didn't sleep, but I wasn't awake either. I lay down and got up eight hours later feeling exactly the same. Everything was a haze, and I felt like a caged animal. I didn't end up leaving that room for two days.

The next day, Andy and his lawyers—along with John and other Phonak management—came to help me, and to figure out what the team should do. That was when the news officially broke. The UCI announced that an unnamed rider at the Tour had tested positive. An Italian website reported that the UCI president, Pat McQuaid, said the positive test was "the worst scenario possible." Who else besides me would be the worst scenario? It didn't really matter that McQuaid was dropping such obvious hints, because by that time, John was getting calls from journalists who had inside sources. "Look, we know it's Floyd," they said. "Can you please just confirm it?"

"Floyd, we have no choice," Andy said. "I'd love to stand behind you, but we have to make an announcement saying it's you." He had to think about saving the team, since the UCI can suspend an entire team if it fails to suspend a rider under investigation for doping.

If it had been my decision to make, I would have done it too. To deny that we knew anything about it would be lying, and to stay quiet would make me look guilty. But also, these were my teammates, and I wouldn't jeopardize their jobs or the rest of their racing season. As it was, Andy would have enough of a challenge just trying to save the team.

I knew I had to deal with the problem on my own. So the team announced that the positive test belonged to me, and that they had suspended me.

I spent all afternoon with the Spanish lawyer. In between meetings, I was on the phone with my friends trying to figure out what to do next. I heard from every one of my teammates, my training advisers, old friends, and even old teammates, such as George Hincapie. The text messages and phone calls contained varying degrees of outrage and questioning—how a mistake like this could happen?—but essentially they were all saying the same thing: I'm on your side. Let me know if I can do anything to help.

The support felt good, just like it had after Stage 16, but still I had no plan. No one I knew had the right experience to advise me on an issue like this. I had no lawyers to protect me, and no staff of "people" to handle my public image. I had never in my life thought about my public image. I still managed my own schedule and answered my own phone.

By early evening in Paris, my sister Priscilla in Farmersville sent a text message to Amber. She'd been trying to reach me for hours. "What's going on? We need to know," it said.

Amber called her for me, and Priscilla explained that there were TV vans with satellite dishes parked up and down both sides of the street outside of my parents' house. My mother had been getting constant phone calls from the press, so she had escaped in the car and was a few miles away at a friend's house pulling weeds in the garden and praying, trying to make sense of the news.

I realized it was too late to tell my mom. She already knew. But I needed to talk to her right away, to apologize for what was happening to her. My parents choose to live a simple life, and they deserve to be left alone to do so. Now, as a consequence of the public way of life I had chosen, they were being harassed.

Priscilla drove to where my mom was and told her to go home so I could call her. There were a dozen people with microphones in the driveway waiting to interview her, so she passed her house and continued down the road. She pulled into a neighbor's driveway and snuck back home through the fields and went in the back door. The reporters saw her and walked right up to the house, peering in the windows at her.

I called, and she picked up right away. "Floyd," she said, "what's wrong?"

"Mom," I said, "I don't know what's going on." Up until then, I had kept it together, but when I heard her voice, I started to cry.

"You just tell me," she said. "If you did something, why don't you just confess it and get it out of the way. Great, great men have made mistakes, so if you did it, just say you're sorry and go on with your life. You're my son and I love you no matter what, so it doesn't make any difference to me. Just tell me."

I needed her to know that I won honestly. I could barely get the words out. "Mom, it's nothing like that," I said. "I didn't do it. It's a mistake. And I'm so confused—I don't know how to fix it."

"Floyd, you're going to be okay," she said. "So many people are praying for you. You have no idea how many people you've encouraged over the last two weeks. You have blessed so many. I haven't shed a tear over it and I'm not going to. You'll be fine."

"Mom, I'm sorry," I said. "You shouldn't have to go through this."

"Don't worry about us," she said. "We can handle what's going on here."

My parents are tough, strong people. When we hung up, my mom walked straight out the front door, where reporters swarmed her with stupid questions like, "What do you think of your son now?" The TV cameras rolled, and my mother made a short statement, saying that she believed in me and that when the truth came out, people would think so much more of me. "Now, if you'll excuse me," she said, "I'm going to pull weeds." She marched back to the neighbors' driveway, got in her car, and drove off.

Back in Paris, I couldn't stand the idea that my mother was being harassed.

"That's it," I said to Amber. "I'm going to talk. It's me

they're after." I knew it would be better to wait until I knew more about my test and how I was going to defend myself, but I felt like I didn't have a choice. I needed to give the media something else to focus on so they'd leave my family alone.

I had followed cycling—and sports in general, for that matter—for more than a decade. Doping stories are in the press all the time. The pattern is the same: The scientific test shows a doping positive. The athlete says, "I have never doped," and expresses confusion about the situation. It's science versus a person's word, and the person is assumed to be guilty from the very beginning.

The only way I knew to try to break the pattern was to ask for understanding. "All I ask is that everyone takes a step back," I said to start my first conference call with the media from my Paris hotel room. "I wouldn't blame you if you were skeptical because of what cycling has been through in the past and the way that other cases have gone. But I ask that I be given a chance to prove that I'm innocent."

From there, things went downhill. It was obvious that all the reporters had been cramming, trying to learn everything they could about the testosterone test and what can cause spikes in testosterone levels. How does the test work? What was your T/E ratio from the positive test? Did the lab do the special follow-up test, the carbon-isotope test, to check for synthetic testosterone in your system? I didn't have any of the answers.

A couple of scientific studies floating around on the Internet suggested that extreme alcohol consumption can raise your testosterone. Reporters had read that I had a beer after Stage 16. "Was it just one beer?" they asked. So I told them the truth, that it was a couple of beers, and some Jack Daniel's. Someone actually asked me, "Can Jack Daniel's cause a positive test?" And I said I had no idea, but that I didn't want to speculate. They asked about a condition with my thyroid that Brent had diagnosed a few years ago. "Are you on any medication?" I said, yes, that I had been for a year, but that I had cleared it with the team, and it wasn't a performance-enhancing drug. "What about the cortisone?" I didn't know if it was possible for the cortisone to affect the test, but I explained that I had filed for a medical exemption before the race, and noted it on every anti-doping form. Something was causing the positive, but I didn't know what.

The next day, the U.S. newspapers ran stories saying I was grasping at straws, giving multiple excuses for the positive test.

Looking back, I regret trying to answer every question I was asked. It was naive. They brought up all the potential excuses, and I responded with a lot of "I suppose it's possible, but I don't know," answers.

I had never really been in the press, period, much less in a negative way. I think people assumed I'd be more prepared, like Lance. But he had so many advisers and so many years of experience at being the center of attention. The extent of my big media exposure was at the Tour, where the interviews were easy because I was the expert. "Bike racing this, bike racing that," I would say. "It was hard today, but we won't give up." The questions I was now getting were about something I had absolutely no experience with.

Friday morning, my head was two-feet high on every paper in France, and Amber and I were in Charles DeGaulle International airport trying to fly to Madrid to meet my lawyers. I had my hat pulled down to my chin, and Amber was leading me. We finally made it to our gate and were waiting in the corner to board. Everyone around us had newspapers open, and everywhere I looked, I was staring at myself. I was so sick of hiding, so I said, "Forget it. If anyone has something to say, they can say it to my face." I sat up and turned my cap around backward, just like I had worn it on the podium during the Tour. It felt good to stand up for myself.

"Baby, no," Amber said, and she started crying. "Stop it. I can't do it. I can't take it if somebody says something mean to you right now."

I couldn't help it. I started to laugh a little. "Well, that's not really the reaction I was looking for," I said. "I was hoping for more of a, 'Yeah, fuck 'em.'" But I turned my hat back around and slumped down, for her.

Once we got to Madrid, Perdi picked us up at the airport. "Don't worry about it, man," he said. "We'll figure it out."

My Spanish lawyers advised me to deal with the press

first, so I agreed to an interview, one-on-one with a TV camera in a room. The lawyers prepared a statement for me to read, and about five minutes before I was supposed to go downstairs to be on camera, one of them was reading it aloud to me in Spanish while I was reading a bad Google translation in English on paper. I speak Spanish, so I was fixing the statement as he was reading, and he was getting mad at me for changing things. But I'd say, "Look, this doesn't even make any sense this way," and I'd rewrite it so that it sounded like they intended it to sound.

The statement was three pages long, and I didn't have time to finish editing. I was only halfway through when they told me it was time to go downstairs. I just figured I'd fix the rest as I went along.

It's easy for me to say now that I should have stopped right then and fixed the rest while the camera waited. For that matter, I should have realized that the statement was a bad idea in the first place—I should have kept my mouth shut until I knew more about my test results and had the right lawyers. But I could only see what was in front of me at the moment, and not the big picture.

And I had no idea that downstairs there was a ballroom full of reporters who would mob me as I walked in the door.

The bright lights and whirring cameras and pushing were out of control. Nobody did anything to help shield me from it. Finally, I made my way behind a big podium and sat down. I started reading, but I was flushed and the adrenaline was pumping because I felt like I had just been attacked. I got through the first part of the statement all right, but then I got to the second part I hadn't fixed yet, so I more or less started to improvise. I came off sounding like a complete dumbass. At one point, I said that once my legal team was given the chance to analyze my test results, we would prove that the testosterone in my system was "absolutely natural and produced by my own organism."

The entire thing ran live on CNN.

So, now the whole world thought I was an idiot—an idiot who looked red-faced . . . and guilty.

Later that night, at 3 a.m. Spain time, I did the *Larry King Live* show. In the middle, Lance came on to defend me. We had talked earlier. "Just tell them the truth," he had said.

"I know," I said, "I'm just trying to explain."

"Look, keep it simple, so they don't get confused," he had said. "I've been through it. You'll be all right. Just stick with the truth."

When Lance had been accused of doping by the media, I had always just let it fly because it didn't involve me. It looked irritating, but I had no idea how violating and overwhelming the experience was. Now, I appreciated his support.

Brent was on the show too, to explain some things about the T/E test. Everyone in the media had written that I had high testosterone, but Brent pointed out that the test was a ratio, not an indication of high testosterone. He also made it clear that the testing process wasn't complete—the B sample still needed to be tested—and urged people not to rush to judgment.

After *Larry King*, I said, that's it. I was done. I had to go home and try to rest—and come up with a plan for how to get myself out of the situation. When you finish the Tour and you don't sleep for three days, you don't think clearly.

I regret a lot of things I said those first few days, but I don't see how I could have changed my response. There was no way to know what was really happening except to go through it. In a span of two days I went from champion to national disgrace. The press convicted me. And at the time, I had no idea that I was being convicted.

CHAPTER 11

Presumed Guilty

I can't recall the first time I figured out what doping even was. It was probably the first time I had to give a urine sample for a drug test. Once I became a pro, I did hear other riders gossip and speculate about who uses performance-enhancing substances. Hanging out after races or in a hotel where teams were staying, I'd overhear, "Oh, he's on EPO," or, "It's the testosterone." Others would suggest that a rider must be blood doping.

Because of all the talk, I knew it must happen, but, as unbelievable as it may sound, I don't actually know how many cyclists are doping. Why would I? The dopers, whomever they may be, certainly don't go around talking about it. What I do know is that those who claim that "everyone's doing it" are wrong. It's a smaller number than they think, and it is possible to win clean. I know because I did it.

When the doping topic came up among riders, I never engaged in the conversation. To me it was boring. The riders who talk about it are the ones who complain because they're not winning. Instead of taking action by training harder or using better strategy, they blame others for cheating. "I came in forty-eighth, but there's no way I can keep up because they're all juiced," I'd hear. That kind of whining is one of the things I find most annoying about professional cycling. I have always believed that my best chance to succeed comes when I focus on my own performance, not on what the other guys are doing. If I lost, I never wasted my time coming up with any kind of excuse. Instead, I always figured, "Okay, I need to work harder." And then I got on my bike and pedaled.

I've heard people say that in professional cycling the stakes are so high that there's pressure for the athletes to dope. I disagree. The only one putting pressure on a rider is the rider himself. If someone feels like they need to cheat to win, then it's a question of character and not of outside influence. There are a thousand or so riders in the pro peloton, and in terms of what's right and what's wrong, some people draw the line at different places than others. There are cheaters in cycling, just like there are in the rest of the world. Personally, I never felt that I needed to win so badly that it was worth getting involved in anything that had to do with doping.

I did not use performance-enhancing drugs in the 2006

Tour de France or any other time in my career. All I ever did was train. I put training first, even before my family. When you want to win, you eat, drink, sleep, and breathe cycling. Knowing it's not forever is what makes it doable. So I made the sacrifices I had to make, and I did so honestly.

After I got home from Europe, it was crushing to have my greatest win—not to mention my reputation—taken away from me because the media managed to convince the public to believe something that, in reality, was a mistake. It was worse than anything I ever could have imagined. I thought that I knew what humiliation was after Stage 16, but I had no idea. This was one hundred times worse. The attitude of virtually the entire mainstream media was: Well, Stage 17 seemed too good to be true, and it turns out it was—big surprise. Some blamed me for single-handedly ruining cycling and the Tour de France.

Everyone had a slant. Critics blindly grasped for ways to blame me. Instead of pin the tail on the donkey, it was pin the tail on me. Some sports columnists and bloggers claimed that my initial floundering in the press was a clear indication that I was trying to hide guilt. Others said that I seemed possessed or filled with rage during Stage 17, and that my pumping my fists in the air at the end was evidence of artificial aggression.

Nothing about what I had accomplished seemed to matter anymore. The doping scandal was far bigger news than my winning the race. "Every day during the Tour, I had to search on TV or in the newspaper just to find out how you did," my brother-in-law Max told me. "But after this, you were all over the place. Shit, even I was on the front page." When the A sample results were revealed, reporters had come to our house early that morning and taken a picture of Max on the balcony with bedhead, looking out and wondering who all the people were in the yard. The photo had gone to all the news wires. Reporters canvassed my private neighborhood and questioned my neighbors about me. It was nonsense.

But the hounding of my family and neighbors wasn't even the worst part. The worst part was that my trial by media was not over. It was just heating up, thanks to the UCI's disclosing more about my tests. In addition to learning and reporting that my T/E ratio was measured at eleven to one, the *New York Times* printed a story saying that my urine sample had undergone a carbon-isotope test, a newer and more complex test that detects whether any of the testosterone in a person's system is from an external source, as opposed to being naturally produced. The *Times* cited a source "with knowledge of the results" who was "in the cycling union's anti-doping department" who said that my test "showed that some of the testosterone in his body had come from an external source." It also paraphrased Dr. Gary Wadler, a member of WADA and a medical school professor, who stated that the test was so reliable that it "needs to be done only once, on either an A or on a B sample." In other words, this WADA affiliate was saying that it wasn't even necessary to follow WADA's own rules and do a B sample test to confirm the A sample—I was already guilty.

The fact that the B sample testing hadn't even been done yet didn't seem to matter to the UCI or WADA or the press. They were all drawing conclusions in the case, way ahead of the legal process.

There was no peace in my house. My home number was listed in the phone book, so the phone rang constantly and felt like a reminder of what had happened to me. I didn't have anyone to answer it for me, so I just let it ring and ring. Usually, if things are spinning out of control around me, I can ignore the external distractions and focus on my goal. I'm good when things are bad—as long as there's something I can do to work toward my objective. The problem was that there was nothing I could do to help myself. The only thing to do was to wait for things to happen, which to me is the absolute worst.

I sat on my couch and deleted all the voicemails clogging my cell phone, without even listening to them. I hoped it would feel like progress.

A couple of minutes later, the phone rang. It was Will Geoghegan, my old mountain biking teammate and training buddy. "Floyd, what the fuck," he said. He'd been trying to reach me for days. "Man, seriously, what the *fuck*? I'm coming over."

Will drove from his house in Orange County and didn't leave for a week. "This has snowballed into a huge disaster," he said. "You need help." On the spot, Will became my manager and called the software company where he worked to tell them he was quitting. We stayed up almost all night strategizing, and still we hadn't even begun to control the chaos.

The next morning at 7 a.m. doping control rang the doorbell forcefully. When we hear the bell ring like that, we always know who it is. There were two collectors this time. "Oh, you need backup now," Amber said to them when she answered the door. They explained to me that now I was required to take my shirt off in addition to pulling my pants down in front of them. So the three of us went into my bathroom and I got naked and peed in the cup.

After that it was back to work to coordinating the team that would help me with my defense. Before I had even returned from Europe I had hired a new lawyer, Howard Jacobs, who had represented about twenty-five athletes in doping cases, and knew the process cold. From the outset, he let me know it would be a long fight. "You're looking at six months for the process to play out," he said. "At least."

Very basically, here's how a doping case works: WADA has national agencies and accredited labs around the world. For cycling events, the UCI collects blood and urine samples and has anti-doping tests done at a WADA lab close to the event. For the Tour, sample analysis was done at a lab in Paris. If there's a suspicious sample, the UCI notifies the rider's team, and then the rider has the right to request that the B sample be tested. If it confirms the A sample, then the test is considered positive, and the matter is referred to the national agency of the accused athlete, which in my case is the United States Anti-Doping Agency (USADA). From there, the athlete waits for an official document packet that details the entire testing process and results for each sample, which is compiled by the organized lab and certified by USADA. The athlete has ten days to submit reasons the case should be dropped to a USADA-chosen review board. If the review board denies the submission, there is a period of "discovery," when both sides can ask for any further information needed in the prosecution or the defense. Finally, there is a hearing in front of a panel of three arbitrators. Only after the hearing is an athlete determined to be innocent or guilty. After that, either side has the option of a final appeal to the Court of Arbitration for Sport.

It would be weeks before I could see any of the actual evidence against me in the document packet—at that point, Phonak had only received two single-page faxes listing simple results, with nothing to back them up. A hearing would be months away. But because of leaks and all the negative media exposure, Howard was worried about my getting a fair shake.

I needed to start fighting back in the media to help the public understand what was going on. Michael Henson, an amateur bike racer who had done PR for the Tour of California and other cycling events, became my media coordinator and spokesman. Henson started taking all the media calls, so things at home began to quiet down. We talked about how to turn things around.

"First things first," Henson said. "People don't feel like

they've heard your denials. You need to let your outrage show." Until that point the media had focused only on excuses, not on my anger at being falsely accused.

"Oh, I was angry," I explained to him. "But I was also confused. This caught me so off guard." The problem was that if the UCI had been fair and kept my test results confidential until the B sample could be tested, I would have had time to understand what was happening and prepare.

The UCI president, Pat McQuaid, was quoted in a news report as saying that the organization had released the news because "the French laboratory has a close connection with [the newspaper] *L'Equipe*," and the UCI did not want the information to come through the press. McQuaid said the UCI was sure the paper would have leaked the information.

To give some background, the French lab that analyzed my sample was the same one that, one month after Lance's seventh Tour victory in 2005, leaked to the French newspaper *L'Equipe* that practice testing on old B samples from the 1999 Tour found indications of the use of the endurance hormone EPO. Through different leaks, *L'Equipe* linked several of those samples to Armstrong and caused a big controversy. Lance called it a witch hunt, and in a way it was: Nothing about the testing was official. It was only for WADA research purposes, done on six-year-old urine. In the end, nothing came of it except bad publicity for Lance.

In my case, though, what we had was the head of the UCI, the body that is supposed to ensure fairness in cycling, acknowledging a serious procedural problem with the lab it uses. And rather than taking steps to fix the problem by insisting on sanctions against the lab, he tried to preempt it by throwing me under the bus.

I was so frustrated. Ever since the problems I had getting paid by Mercury years ago, I haven't understood why the UCI is so adversarial with its riders. The UCI cannibalizes the sport of cycling by going after its own at every turn. I didn't expect McQuaid to take my side. All I expected was for him to be neutral and to use his authority to demand fairness from the lab and prevent unfair disclosures from UCI's own anti-doping department.

I explained all this to Henson. "You're exactly right," he said. "The UCI has shown a disregard for its own rules. That's your message."

The B sample results were to be announced August fifth, at 11 a.m. Paris time, 2 a.m. San Diego time. Howard had told me that the B sample almost always confirms the A sample. If the lab made the mistake once, they're bound to make it again. I couldn't bear to hope for a negative. I went to bed.

The UCI's rules state that an accused athlete will be notified of the results directly before it makes a public announcement, but we weren't. Amber was on the phone with Henson, who was back in New York hitting the "refresh" button on his web browser. Shortly after the Paris deadline, he found a news story that my B sample confirmed the A. He found a second news report a couple of minutes later. The UCI had posted it on its website. "Well, the Internet says that it's positive," he told Amber. Nearly two days would pass before we received the official fax notification from the UCI.

Amber came up to the bedroom and shook me awake. "It's positive," she said. I rolled over and went back to sleep.

The next morning my neighborhood was crawling with reporters again. We had undercover police offers on the street trying to help keep things under control. Still, someone lurked around our backyard fence and tried to take pictures through our bedroom window.

Back in Farmersville, dozens of TV-station vans pulled up outside my family's house in the same senseless way they had done before. My mom and dad had a vacation planned, and they didn't see the B sample announcement as any reason to stick around. Not wanting to put anyone to the trouble of waiting around all weekend for a comment, my dad posted a handmade sign in the front yard: GOD BLESS, WENT CAMPING. The television cameras rolled even though nobody was home, and then the crews packed up and left. The next day, in the thick woods of the church campground, a few of my cousins happened to run into my parents. "We thought we might see you here this weekend," one said. "We saw on TV that you went camping."

I decided to go on all the morning shows to state my position. I sat with Amber and we appeared together on NBC's *Today* show, CBS's *The Early Show*, ABC's *Good Morning America*, and CNN. I told every one of them straight up that I hadn't done what I was accused of doing, and that I would fight the allegation to the end. Then I explained that if the UCI hadn't prematurely announced information about my A sample, I would have had time to prepare my thoughts and wouldn't have sounded so confused before. My sport's governing body had forced me into the situation.

Within a couple of hours after I took off the microphone, Pat McQuaid called to try and get me to shut up. "I'm not saying you're a bad guy," he said. "I'm sure you weren't doing anything that everyone else wasn't doing. You're just the unlucky one who got caught." McQuaid suggested I quit trying to defend myself. "You should change your tactics," he said, "and accept a suspension because there's no way you can win."

Maybe McQuaid was trying to explain something that I didn't understand, but the way I interpreted his comments, although he seems to have denied this interpretation in the press, the head of the UCI believes that the whole peloton is doped, and he assumed I was guilty from the beginning. In addition, he seemed certain that I didn't stand a chance of proving myself innocent within the anti-doping judicial process.

"I'm not going to change my tactics," I told him. "I didn't do it."

"You'll end up penniless," he said.

"I don't care about that," I said, disgusted once again by the kind of "support" that cyclists get from their own organizing union.

Following UCI rules about riders who test positive,

Phonak fired me. A day or two later, Amber was talking on the phone and said something to a friend about my being let go. Ryan overheard her. We had been putting off telling Ryan about the whole situation because we didn't know quite what to say. She thought all the publicity had been happening because I won the race. When Amber hung up, she started in with, "What? Dad got fired?" It made no sense to her: Dad had won the biggest bike race in the world, and now they didn't want him on the team anymore? Amber tried to tell her to wait until the three of us could talk about it together, but she demanded to know what was going on right then.

Amber put things as simply as she could. "Daddy's been accused of cheating," she explained. "And of course he didn't do it, so he's going to fight it and he's going to win."

In Ryan's mind, it was a done deal. "When it comes to my dad and bike racing, nobody tells him no," she said. School was starting soon, and Amber warned her that kids might be talking about it, and that if anyone said anything mean to her, it was because they didn't understand. "Mom, I'm not worried about that," she said, sounding like me in a way that made me proud when Amber told me about it. Then she asked, "Can I wear my T-shirt the first day of school?" Someone gave her a yellow T-shirt in Paris that says, "My Dad Won the Tour de France," and she'd worn it on the plane home.

Meanwhile, my case also seemed to be a done deal to the rest of the world. After the results of my B sample were announced, there was no more news to report, because we hadn't yet received the document packet. Media attention faded quickly, and most people probably assumed that my case was over—they thought that I was guilty, and that's it.

Howard Jacobs was sitting in his Los Angeles law office when the telephone rang. It was Travis Tygart, the head lawyer for USADA. Howard had dealt with Tygart for years while representing other accused athletes, and now they were both working on my case. This phone call was unusual, though: Terry Madden, the CEO of USADA, was also on the line. Howard knew Madden, but rarely communicated with him. "From everything we've read about Floyd, he's a straightforward, no-BS guy," Tygart began. "We think he can help us clean up the sport and get to the bigger names in cycling."

I had just won the Tour de France. Who was a bigger name in cycling than me? . . . The only person who would be bigger than me is someone who had won the race more times than I had—say, seven times. It was easy to figure out what he meant. USADA wanted me to give information that would show that Lance Armstrong used performance-enhancing drugs during his racing career.

"If he's willing to do that, we can make him a great deal," Tygart said. Howard asked what Madden and Tygart had in mind, and they ended up offering a suspension of less than a year, so that I would be cleared and able to race the 2007 Tour de France. A suspension that short would be unprecedented. The only things I had to do in order to end the mess relatively quickly and get my life back were to give them information on "bigger names" and to accept the suspension.

"That's completely out of the question," I told Howard when he presented the deal to me. "In fact, I find everything about it offensive." First of all, they were assuming that I was guilty even before we received the full test results. Why would I negotiate for a suspension when I'm innocent? They were trying to use me as a pawn to get to Lance. They didn't really care whether I was a cheater. If they could find an even bigger case than mine, they'd practically let me go, without regard to whether or not I had done what they were alleging.

What didn't make sense to me was why they were going after Lance in the first place. By then, Lance had been retired for more than a year. USADA is supposed to protect the integrity of athletic competition by fighting against doping. It gets about 60 percent of its funding from your tax dollars, and the U.S. Olympic Committee funds the rest. Why would they actively pursue someone who didn't even compete anymore?

"It's how they operate," Howard said. "They're after high-profile cases, because those are like ammunition for them to go beg for more money." Howard explained that USADA is a young organization, founded in 2000, that is trying to prove itself. After BALCO, the 2003 Bay Area doping scandal, USADA made an appeal to Congress that doping permeated all levels of big-time sports, and that more money was needed to combat dopers. Its federal funding had been doubled, and now they needed to show results.

But I didn't have any evidence to give them about Lance, anyway. If Lance had been doping, he sure didn't tell me about it. He would have been a fool to do so. Ever since his first Tour win in 1999, the press and all sorts of different authorities had suspected Lance of doping. The year I joined Postal, in 2002, the team was under doping investigation by French officials, though the case was dropped for lack of evidence. Books have been written with allegations, and people who once worked for him have made claims—but nothing has ever held up in court. All I know is that I never saw anything to indicate that Lance used performance-enhancing drugs, that his blood and urine were tested more than anyone else's, and that he never returned a positive test.

Later, with Will, I couldn't shake my anger about the offer. "If USADA is so sure Lance was a doper, then why didn't their supposedly bulletproof scientific drug tests catch him?" I said. "At this point, whether or not he was doping isn't really even the point." To me the point was: They didn't catch him. They had all those years, and they didn't catch him. They needed to *let it go*. It was over. To focus on Lance was a complete waste of time, and even downright negligent, considering USADA's mission. No possible good could come from rooting up the past. Instead, they should be using all their resources on the problems of the present—like how their tests had snagged someone who didn't use testosterone.

"What a bunch of backward-looking idiots," Will said. "They have no regard for the truth."

◆ ◆ ◆

Everyone's phones started to ring at once. Ms. Rose called Amber, but she was driving and didn't pick up. Our home phone line rang, but I was on the other line, so I didn't answer it. Max's phone rang, and I overheard him say, "What? What's going on?" It was his father on the phone, Ms. Rose's ex-husband. I overheard Max's voice start to crack. "What's happening?" he said. "No. No. No."

"Max, what is it?" I asked.

"David," he said. "David did something. No, he didn't. No, he didn't."

I became very calm and got off the phone. "Max, come here," I said. "Sit down. You have to tell me what happened." That morning, David had parked his car in a garage near the restaurant, put a pistol up to his head, and pulled the trigger. He was dead.

No one had even told me that David had become severely depressed over the summer. The new restaurant was costing him more than he expected, and he and Ms. Rose were running out of money. They had planned to come to France for all three weeks of the Tour instead of just the final weekend, but ended up canceling because of the restaurant. At first, Ms. Rose thought that David was putting in too many hours and burning out. He went back on antidepressant medication, but it didn't seem to help. David stopped riding his bike, and then he didn't even bother to watch the Tour on TV.

I felt so bad for Ms. Rose, but I was also mad. "Why didn't you tell me?" I asked her. "I could have helped." David was like my West Coast dad, and as far as I was concerned, any money that I had also belonged to him. I could have at least eased the monetary stress for him, and I felt like I had been cheated out of the opportunity.

"You needed to focus on getting to the Tour," she said. No one would allow my focus to be disrupted. Even Amber was in on it. "You know, winning the Tour wasn't just your dream," Mrs. Rose said. "It was ours, too." I knew that. David had been so proud in Paris that I think my winning the Tour meant more to him than it did to me. Ms. Rose told me about how they sat in the bleachers, watching as my Phonak team rode our victory lap on the Champs. "He was so tired, but he said, 'Look at that. He always said he'd do it.' His face was like a little boy's."

What she said only made me feel worse. If my winning the Tour had been David's dream too, then this doping scandal had ruined his dream as surely as it had ruined mine. On top of his own problems, he took on mine too. In my head I knew that I wasn't responsible for David's suicide, but in my heart I felt like my situation pushed him over the edge.

Ms. Rose came home with us to Murrieta, and that whole first day, every time someone came through the front door, we all expected it to be David. None of us wanted to accept that he was gone, and there was nothing any of us could do to make things better. It was just a sad situation.

Two days after David died, the doorbell rang briskly at 6:50 a.m.

Amber threw the door wide open, and there was the

doping control agent. "What are you doing here?" she asked him. "Seriously, *what* are you *doing* here? I am *not* letting you in my house. Not now."

I saw that it was the guy who I've gotten to know over the years, the one doping agent who is actually a nice guy. He had a dilemma. He wasn't supposed to let me out of his sight once he'd seen me, but I could tell that he really wanted to leave. He was almost crying. "I don't even know what to say," he told Amber. "I'm so sorry for your loss. USADA told me to come the same day your stepfather committed suicide, and I told them I wouldn't do it."

Again Amber refused to let him in the house, and then she began to sob uncontrollably. She felt like the root cause of David's death was intruding into our home, and she couldn't take it anymore.

I couldn't watch my wife have a nervous breakdown like that. It hurt too much. But at the same time I knew we couldn't slam the door on him, or I'd be tagged with a missed test. I had to do something, fast. "You're not coming in," I said to him, and I walked out the front door. "Let's go." I told Amber that I'd be back, and she needed to try to calm down, and I closed the door behind me. The agent and I walked to the garage, got in my car, and drove to Starbucks. We had coffee, and he apologized the whole time. Then we went back to my house, where things had calmed down, and I took off my shirt, pulled down my pants, and urinated for him.

There was no reason for it. Sometimes after an athlete has

been accused, USADA will collect additional urine samples to create a profile of T/E ratios over time, but by their own rules it's not necessary if a carbon-isotope test had been done, as was the case in my Stage 17 sample. Besides, again by their rules, a profile can be completed with three tests. They had two more of mine from the Tour, from Stages 19 and 20, and they had already been to my house once after the Tour. This was sample number four. As for the timing, David's suicide was nationwide news, so they knew about it. It felt like harassment, and it just wasn't necessary.

After the guy left, I called USADA and asked to speak directly to Terry Madden. He made me wait until he had Travis Tygart in the room. "Floyd," Madden began. "We can't talk to you because you don't have your lawyer on the call."

"Fine," I said. "You don't have to talk, but you're definitely going to listen." I explained that they were way out of line sending a doping-control agent to my house that day. "Do you realize the stress you caused my wife?" I asked them. "Do you understand what has happened to my family?" I asked them to have some semblance of decency and leave us alone.

They haven't been back since.

I needed a break from it all. I put on my cycling shorts and jersey with the plan of going in search of just a couple hours of feeling good. Getting dressed was an automatic response, but then I found it difficult to get out the door.

I lingered in the kitchen, leaning against the counter

and reading the newspaper. "What are you doing, hon?" Amber asked.

"Nothing," I said. "I'm going for a ride." I kept reading.

"You never used to do this," she said. "You couldn't wait to go." She was right. If it was a nice day and I couldn't ride, I'd practically bounce around the room in frustration. I loved to ride my bike. Nothing made me happier.

"I don't feel right," I said. "I don't like it." This had been happening since the scandal broke. For the first couple of weeks, things had been so hectic that I couldn't ride. Now, I didn't want to.

Finally, I left. For the first fifteen minutes, I spun easy to warm up and tried to focus. I said to myself, "Okay, when I get to the hills, I'm going to train hard, like I used to." But when I got to the hills, all I could think about was what it used to feel like, about how much I used to care—and about how little I cared now. So much had happened to take my motivation away. There was no joy left in it. Each time I rode I would try to pretend that things were getting better, but it never worked.

That night Amber and I were home alone together. "It's not just that riding doesn't make me feel good," I explained. "It's that it makes me think about the Tour and what happened afterward, and I feel worse when I get home than when I left."

"That's so sad," she said.

"It's the truth."

"I know it is," she said. "It's just so sad."

"I'm a bike racer," I continued. Amber had started crying quietly, and I could feel tears about to form in my eyes too. "I mean, what else can I do? I suppose I could work in a hardware store. But after this, I don't think people are going to want to talk about nails."

She laughed, but knew that on some level I was completely serious. Which I was. I could probably be anything that required a logical mind—but I wanted to race my bike. That's what I loved. Now, I felt like everything was ruined.

I couldn't hold it in anymore. "The worst thing that ever happened to me in my life was winning the Tour de France," I said. Honestly, that is how I felt. "If I had any idea that things could have possibly happened this way, I wouldn't even have tried. It wasn't worth it. If I could go back and change things to avoid this mess, I would. I'd go back and change it so I never won."

David's funeral was held in the theater next to Hawthorn's. Arnie gave a short eulogy, and put it best: "People with depression and other mental health problems aren't really any different from those with physical problems," he said. Sometimes they just don't get through it, the same way that someone who has a heart attack or stroke doesn't get through it. That really is the heart of the matter. There was nothing that I or anyone else could have done to stop David.

It may sound crass, but to me, if David couldn't take it anymore, then it's much better that his suicide was successful. He was the best friend I had. I believe, though, that what he was going through was worse than our having to deal with the fact that he's not with us anymore.

After the service, everyone went to Hawthorn's for drinks, and I caught up with Arnie. "How are you doing?" he asked.

"I miss him," I said. "I keep forgetting and I accidentally try to call him." Arnie missed him too. He had known David even longer than I had.

Eventually our conversation turned to my doping test. "I'm going crazy because there's nothing for me to do," I told him. "The document packet still isn't here."

"When you get it, I'll take a look if you'd like," he said. "I don't know much about how those tests work, but in a sense the documents are like a medical record." As a physician, Arnie analyzed charts and test results all the time, and for more than a decade had done quality assurance reviews for his medical group and had been an expert reviewer for the Medical Board of California. Even though he had retired from his practice, he devoured all sorts of technical and scientific papers about training.

"I'd appreciate that," I said. Howard and his experts would be closely studying the document packet, but in my opinion it never hurts to have another intelligent person take a look. "I need to know what's in there," I told Arnie. Even though I had been studying all the WADA rules and testing procedures, I felt like I knew nothing. There was some reason the lab called my sample positive, and still I had no idea what it was.

CHAPTER 12

The System Is Broken

When I was in high school chemistry class, we took litmus paper and dipped it in different solutions. If the solution was an acid, it turned red. If it was a base, it turned blue. I'm sure there are people who think an anti-doping test is as simple as that: If it's red, he did it. If it's blue, he didn't. But it's so much more complicated than that, more complicated even than the drug-screening tests that many U.S. employers require before giving someone a job.

As soon as I was informed of my Stage 17 test results, I dove into all of the science and legal aspects of my case to learn everything I could about where I stood.

Because the T/E test screens for an excess of a hormone naturally produced by the body, it is more complex than a test that looks for chemicals you don't produce, like those found in marijuana and cocaine. In a lab, the T/E test is done as part of a screening for anabolic steroids. Labs typically charge about a hundred dollars to perform the test, and it takes the technicians four to six hours to analyze a sample.

If a T/E test is found to be above the legal limit, it is flagged as suspicious. The lab then performs the much more involved carbon-isotope ratio test (CIR test), which attempts to distinguish between naturally occurring testosterone and synthetic testosterone. Of all the anti-doping tests, the CIR test and the one for EPO are often called a blend between science and art, because they require many steps of analysis by the lab technicians, as opposed to being automated. The results aren't just simple numbers spit out of a machine; they consist of a bunch of wavy lines that the lab then interprets. The entire test takes two technicians two days to complete.

All of that is just for an A sample. If the B sample is also tested, then the entire procedure happens again.

I explain this only to inform people of the process, and not to make any claim that these tests, when executed properly, aren't reliable. I believe that just about everything in life can be explained by physics, science, and logic. I trust these ways of thinking, and the accuracy of the answers they give, which is why early on in this fight I wondered if I'd even have anything to argue against.

We received the document packet on August 31, 2006, more than a month after news broke about my Stage 17 urine test.

It was 370 pages long. All in French. And the pages were stamped as if they were in some sort of order, but they weren't.

Howard scanned it at his law office and put it up on a secure website. I asked Arnie and everyone else I knew with a science or medical background to take a look at it: Brent Kay, Allen Lim, and Denise from Phonak, who had all of my team anti-doping test results.

We had ten days to develop arguments and submit them to the preliminary review board chosen by USADA.

Will and I printed out the packet and started going through it in my living room. The stack of official papers was intimidating. It looked as though there had to be some damning evidence in there merely because of how long and technical the document was. We searched and searched, and twenty hours later, when we finally went to sleep, we hadn't found any evidence of anything. "This thing is a total fuck job," Will said, and it was easy to agree with him.

Arnie headed straight to Office Depot and bought a dozen white three-ring binders on sale for $1.99 each, to help him organize the packet and his findings. It took him almost a week even to get the pages in proper order, but after only a day or so he called me. "Um, the sample numbers aren't the same throughout," he said. Each test sample is given an anonymous ID number. Mine from the Stage 17 sample was 995474. "I see three or four numbers that are one digit off from yours," he told me. My doctor friends agreed that this was a big deal. If this were a lab analyzing someone's test to see if they had cancer, and a labeling error resulted in an incorrect diagnosis, it could be a matter of life and death. "I called Brent, and he's so shocked, he thinks we should have a press conference," Arnie said.

I asked Arnie if he thought we should go public. "Let's wait a while," he said. "See what else we find." And Arnie went back to work. The next day, he sent me an e-mail detailing another laboratory error. The day after that, he sent me an e-mail with three more. Among the puzzling things Arnie found early on: My A sample was tested three times for a T/E ratio, and the results were 4.9 to 1, 5 to 1, and then 11.4 to 1—so why was the 11 to 1 figure the one that was released to the media?

Howard was the only one of us with experience looking at a document packet. He hired a carbon-isotope ratio test expert who had once worked for the company that builds the machine used in the test. We couldn't seek the opinion of any scientists who actually perform the tests at WADA-accredited anti-doping labs, because that's against the rules.

WADA sees the sports league, in this case the International Cycling Union, as a "client," and performs the drug test analyses on behalf of their client. So the agency made a rule that no one involved in the WADA system can give expert testimony against a client. The effect of this keep-the-customer-happy rule is that the athletes are prohibited from seeking help from 90 percent or so of the best anti-doping experts in the world, because they all work for the system.

Still, almost immediately, Howard and his expert found problems with my carbon-isotope ratio test, the one that had been portrayed in the media as foolproof. "There are surprising things in here," he said when he called me. "These results are not clear. I think we have some good arguments to make that the lab screwed up."

The WADA rule of what constitutes a positive carbon-isotope ratio is vague, but Howard had a scientific paper that explained the criteria for a positive test at the WADA lab in Lausanne, Switzerland, and my result didn't meet the criteria. In Switzerland, my test would have been negative.

He also found scientific research showing that, of the several measurements taken in a test, mine was clearly negative for the one measurement that is the best indication of the presence of synthetic testosterone in a person's system.

There were things we could fight, and finally I started to feel some relief. It was as if, slowly, we could lift the veil of mystery that had been cast over my case since the beginning. With some of the defense on paper, we had a goal and were developing a plan to reach it. My motivation was coming back.

Howard sent the submission to USADA. One week later, we received a letter. The review board denied the submission. We were headed for a hearing.

Brent, Will, and I went to Los Angeles to visit Howard's law office, and on the way home we stopped by the velodrome at the Home Depot Center so I could present some awards at the national track cycling championships. As the racers sped around the track, cycling fans came up to me to shake my hand, congratulate me on winning the Tour, and wish me good luck in my case.

Allen Lim was there working as a power coach for the domestic team Slipstream. The team was unique because it had recently instituted an unprecedented internal drug-testing program: Instead of having a team representative, who theoretically might be biased toward clearing a rider, do the drug testing, Slipstream had hired the newly created Agency for Cycling Ethics (ACE), an independent organization, to do it. Allen introduced me to ACE co-founder Paul Scott.

After some cycling conversation, Paul said, "We ought to talk." In addition to starting ACE, Scott was then the director of clients—the number-two position—at the WADA-accredited anti-doping laboratory at UCLA. Allen had showed him parts of my document packet. "You need to get someone who is really good at science to advise you," he said. "Because you're not really looking at a positive test here." He didn't want to say much more at that point, out of respect for the WADA rule about lab employees taking the side of the athlete.

"Will you help me?" I asked him. His credibility as a director at UCLA, widely considered to be the top anti-doping lab in the world, would be huge for my arguing my side of the case. He indicated that it wouldn't be possible if he were still at UCLA.

"Quit your job," Will said. Paul indicated that he was open to that idea but didn't have the money.

"Look, at least come over to my house," I said, not wanting to lose the opportunity. "You can go for a ride, and we'll have a barbecue in the backyard. If nothing else, it will be a nice afternoon."

He agreed, and the next week, Paul came to Murrieta and rode with Will and Brent in the foothills of my old training ground. By the time they coasted into my driveway, Will said, "It's done. He's out of there next week." They had figured out a way to get Paul what he needed to be able to resign. He became my science advisor and expert witness for my defense.

"If there's something I can do to keep this from happening to you, then I would like to do it," Paul said. "Now I feel like I'm working for the right side." He also said that at the UCLA lab, they would not have considered my results a positive test. "I know this," Paul said, "because I was the one at the lab who made the final decision on cases like this."

So, if the Tour de France had been in Switzerland or America, my test would have been negative. Apparently the French lab had different criteria for a positive test since it was flagged as positive in France.

Beyond that, Paul completely tore apart the science of my case. "The best way for me to describe it is that it's not merely that the results don't look like a positive test," he said. "They are nothing I'd ever expect to see, whether someone was doping or not. They don't make sense scientifically." In other words, someone screwed up.

"Well, how did that get past the review board?" I asked him.

"Oddly, they didn't seek UCLA's opinion," Paul said. Typically, if USADA is going to prosecute a case involving a complicated test, like the carbon-isotope ratio test, then they will seek advice from the head of the UCLA lab, anti-doping pioneer Don Catlin, to be sure their case is strong. "They'd call Dr. Catlin, who would get his experts together, and we'd hash it out," Paul told me. Often, when a review board voted to toss out a case for lack of evidence, he said, it was due to the fact that UCLA had advised that the case wasn't strong. "But while I still worked there I never saw anything about your case," Paul continued. "That feels wrong."

"What do you mean?" I asked. "Did they not even read our submission?"

"The conclusion I draw is that USADA reviewed it only in a perfunctory manner," he said. "They must have looked at the lab package, taken the results as fact, and pressed on with the case."

"So go tell them now that it's not a positive," I said. It seemed so simple. Here was someone with the right expertise who believed it was a mistake. All he needed to do was go to the right people to clear it up. If USADA was focused on finding the truth, then when they realized it was an error, they'd drop the case and feel good about having done their job, and this whole mess would be over.

"It doesn't work that way," he said. "They'll press on with the case anyway."

"Why?" I asked. That made absolutely no sense to me.

"Because these litigations are not fair," said Paul, who in addition to being a scientist was also a former attorney. "They're designed to be cheap and fast and push cases through, with the athlete receiving minimal information." Paul's advice was for me to find the best, most high-powered lawyer I could find, someone from a big firm with lots of resources who could fight USADA on every point, because there was no way USADA would back down. I felt like the agency didn't care one bit about the truth. It just wanted to win my case.

The international anti-doping system is broken. It's messed up on every level and in so many ways, you could write an entire book about it. But there's no need to expose every element of injustice, because only seeing a few major ones paints the picture well enough.

Start with the ridiculously unfair USADA legal process: USADA wrote its own rules, it enforces them, it acts as prosecutor in legal cases, and it picks which judges hear each case. The agency claims that the arbitrators are "independent," but in reality the athlete is only allowed to choose an arbitrator from a preselected list of candidates approved by USADA.

As I sank deeper into the process, this became my question: Most of USADA's funding comes from Congress, so why is it allowed to have a system of justice in which it is the lawmaker, the police, the prosecution, and the jury? It bears no resemblance to the U.S. judicial system. The worst serial murderer in this country has more basic rights in a trial than I—or any other athlete—have in a USADA doping case.

For example, in the USADA system, there's no free lawyer appointed if you can't afford one. I won the Tour de France, and just a couple of months into my case I realized that defending myself would almost certainly bankrupt me. How are swimmers or gymnasts who have to hold a job just to make ends meet while they train supposed to defend themselves? They're screwed from the start.

Also, as Paul had indicated to me, there is no full disclosure of evidence, as there is in a U.S. hearing. USADA's rules state that the lab is not required to give any information to the athlete beyond the initial document packet. Essentially this means you're not given access to any documents that in a standard criminal or civil case would be considered critical to the defense, such as any information about how the lab may have come up with the results it found. The system is set up so that you can't challenge the science of the test.

Despite the fact that the athlete isn't entitled to any additional information, USADA gathers information "by any reliable means," as its rule states, to serve as additional evidence in the prosecution. At one point in preparation for my hearing, USADA requested nine B samples from previous negative A sample tests of mine so they could test them, including all of my 2006 Tour samples. They were just grasping for any shred of evidence against me, even though anything they thought they might find would violate the rule that a positive test needs to have both an A sample and B sample. (The A samples had all been destroyed in previous testing.) Ultimately, the arbitrators in my case would allow the additional tests, because there was no specific USADA rule against it.

It was a great double standard. As an athlete, I was held to the specifics of the rules very strictly, while USADA justified any action they wanted by essentially saying, "Well, there's no specific rule against it."

Given all of this, it should come as no surprise that in the 165 doping cases that USADA has brought against athletes since it began prosecuting cases in 2001, the athlete has never won. Not one single time. If your record is 165 and zero, why bother with a hearing at all?

There's no point, because they have no interest in hearing what an athlete has to say. Even in cases where it's crystal clear that the athlete wasn't trying to enhance performance, the agency applies its rule of "strict liability," which holds athletes accountable for even purely accidental or insignificant infractions. In previous years, I had watched the rule wreck the lives of other athletes for no good reason.

My friend Scott Moninger and I raced on the Mercury team together. In 2002, after I left to go to U.S. Postal, he tested positive for a steroid. He had never used performance-enhancing drugs. The only variation in his routine had been that, when he ran out of his usual vitamin and amino-acid supplement, he went to a health food store and bought another brand with a similar mix of ingredients. He figured the supplement must have been tainted, but he wanted to know for sure, so he went back to the store and bought four more bottles of the supplement with the same lot and serial numbers, and shipped them off to a lab for independent testing. The supplements were tainted. When he received his USADA document packet, he confirmed that the amount of steroid measured in his urine was consistent with a tainted supplement, but nowhere near enough to give him a performance boost. Despite going to USADA with his independently gathered evidence of his mistake and explaining the misunderstanding, he received a one-year suspension from racing.

Then there's the case of Zach Lund, a skeleton racer from Salt Lake City. He was competing at a World Cup sledding event in Calgary, Alberta, in 2005, when he gave a urine sample that the lab said was positive for finasteride, a chemical WADA had added to the banned list that year as a possible masking agent for steroids despite the fact that there is no consensus in the scientific community that it is. The chemical was an ingredient in the antibaldness medication Lund had used for over five years. Every time Lund competed, he noted on his anti-doping form that he was using it, but that year he failed to check the banned list to see that finasteride had been added. Ultimately, Lund was suspended for one year. The arbitrators handed down the decision less than two weeks before Lund's race in the Turin Olympics. Instead of realizing his Olympic dream, Lund was sent home as a cheater. The arbitrators didn't want to ban him, but they were forced to by the "strict liability" rule. They even wrote in a statement that they "had the feeling that Mr. Lund was not well-served by the anti-doping organizations."

To me, the way anti-doping agencies apply this policy of strict liability is similar to the way my church applied the words of the Bible when I was growing up in Lancaster County. If you do something wrong—even if you don't know you are doing something wrong and "wrong" isn't hurting anyone—what you've done is an absolute sin. You're guilty. End of story.

How did the system get this way? In the beginning, WADA wrote its own rules without independent oversight, and USADA, when it was created a short time later, did the same thing, using WADA's legal practices as a blueprint.

The assumption that an athlete is guilty until proven innocent and the adversarial attitude that pervades every aspect of the system comes from one man: Dick Pound.

Dick Pound is the head of WADA, the man at the absolute pinnacle of the global anti-doping effort. The position has so much potential to improve the world of sports and foster a positive attitude of clean competition. But instead, Dick Pound acts like a fundamentalist crusader in a very public way that ends up undermining the entire system.

WADA rules state that agency members must not comment on active cases in order to ensure a fair hearing for the athlete. It's a good rule, and similar to the one in the American legal system that says the prosecution can't talk about criminal cases. But Dick Pound blabs to the media about athletes accused of doping with complete disregard for his own rule. In every case, he tries to create a public perception that his organization is always right, and that the athlete is always guilty. He sometimes invents absurdly damning ideas and presents them as fact. It's despicable. There is no other word for it.

From the time my test results were announced in late July and into the fall, Pound said many things about me that were inappropriate, to say the least.

First, Pound told the Associated Press that "the winner of this year's event is busted," and that it was a shame for cycling. "You build up and create a new hero, and he gets slapped down," said Pound. "It's a serious blow."

A couple of weeks later, in an editorial in the *Ottawa Citizen*, which Pound wrote himself, he said that I seemed "to have taken a morning-after pill to recover from the previous failure." He continued, "Let us resign ourselves to the customary flow of denials of any drug use, notwithstanding the scientific results of the test, performed by expert, World Anti-Doping Agency–accredited laboratories," and mockingly suggested that one of my excuses for my test result could be that I was "ambushed by a roving squad of Nazi frogmen and injected" with testosterone.

"He was eleven minutes behind or something, and all of a sudden there's this Herculean effort, where he's going up mountains like he's on a goddamn Harley," Pound said in a *New York Times Magazine* story. "It's a great story," Pound said. "Wonderful. But if it seems too good to be true, it probably is."

The writer of the story, Michael Sokolove, asked Pound about all different sports. Pound had once claimed that one-third of the players in the National Hockey League were using performance-enhancing drugs, and Sokolove asked him how he knew that. "It was pick a number," Pound said. "So it's twenty percent, twenty-five percent. Call me a liar."

Dick Pound is a liar. Think about that. The man who is the face and voice of the agency trying to rid the sports world of cheaters and liars is himself an ethical hypocrite.

"I mean, it was eleven to one!" Pound also said in the *New York Times Magazine* story, referring to my reported T/E ratio. "You'd think he'd be violating every virgin within 100 miles. How does he even get on his bicycle?"

Dick Pound is also pathetically uneducated, considering his position. Using the T/E ratio to imply that my testosterone level was high shows not only that Pound never bothered to look at my test, but also that he doesn't even have a clue about how testosterone testing works. As Brent had been saying since the beginning, the testosterone/epitestosterone test determines a ratio of two hormones. It is not a measure of high testosterone. In fact, Arnie found in the document packet that I didn't have high testosterone. The level of testosterone in the sample fell in the low to normal range. The epitestosterone, however, was extraordinarily low, which caused the ratio to spike.

For subsequent interviews, Pound didn't bother to learn

more about my test. He told the *New York Daily News*, "He has to find some way to overcome the fact that there is an A and B sample that is up to its eyeballs in testosterone."

Then, in *Wired* magazine, Pound claimed, "His nickname on the circuit was 'Roid Floyd.' But I repeat it as hearsay only." Hearsay, because it's made up. The only way I can interpret these comments is that they are a deliberate attack on my character.

Dick Pound single-handedly makes his agency—and by extension the entire WADA community—look uncredible. It baffles me that no one with the authority to fire him has realized that it would be a good idea to do so.

He oversees an unchecked bureaucracy that allows lives of innocent athletes to be ruined. Mainstream American sports leagues like the NFL, NBA, and MLB are working to develop their own drug-testing programs and have indicated that they don't want anything to do with the screwed-up WADA system. Referring to my case, NBA commissioner David Stern told the Associated Press that WADA "is actually getting harder to take seriously." Also speaking about my "controversial" case, NFL Players Association executive director Gene Upshaw told the *Charlotte Observer*, "I have my doubts about WADA and their history."

Even though no halfway intelligent person believes what comes out of Pound's mouth, he still has sway with his words. There's no getting around it. Sometimes people just want to believe the man in charge, because they're used to thinking that he's there for a good reason.

One day my phone rang when I was between conference calls with lawyers and advisors. "Why is the head lawyer for USADA calling me to ask me if I've ever heard the name 'Roid Floyd'?" asked Jonathan Vaughters on the other end of the line. He and I had spoken a few times since he sent me that text message after Stage 16 in the Tour, mostly so I could get his advice on my situation. First as a rider and then as the director of Team Slipstream, the team doing independent drug testing with the Agency for Cycling Ethics, Vaughters has always been outspoken about wanting to clean up cycling and its reputation.

"You're kidding me," I said. "He did not."

"He did," Vaughters said. The lawyer, Travis Tygart, had started with some ambiguous questions. Vaughters's impression was that Tygart wanted information he could use in my case. "At one point, he said, 'It would be the right thing to do,'" Vaughters said. Then Tygart asked about the nickname, which of course he had never heard. "Frankly, I don't see what relevance I have in this anyway," he said.

"Look, tell him everything you know about me for all I care," I said. "But if I can ask one thing, just please don't lie." I didn't need more untrue rumors on top of the ones that were already out there. Vaughters said of course he wouldn't lie, and that he had already told the truth—he didn't know anything. I thanked him and said good-bye.

Will was over at my house, and we tried to figure out exactly why Tygart would want to dig up dirt on me if the USADA case against me was so strong that my review board denied my submission to drop the case. It didn't make any sense. "To them it's just a contest," Will said, "not someone's life and livelihood."

"Well, I'm good at contests," I said. "I'm not sure if they understand who they're dealing with. I'll make their lives hell." I began to look at my case in the same way I viewed training for the Tour. All of my energy would go toward defending myself against what were now clearly ridiculous allegations. I would bring the same focus and intensity to my defense that I had brought to my training.

The only problem was that no athlete had ever prevailed against USADA. I was in the process of being steamrolled by the system, and we had to figure out a way to fight back.

CHAPTER 13

Whole Again

Replacing my worn-out hip should have been the single most stressful point of my life. I struggled so much with the decision initially, and there were times on rides with Brent when we'd be talking about the pain and I'd confess that sometimes I wished the joint would fail and that I'd be forced to have it replaced. I knew it would probably end my career, but the pain had eaten away at my resolve almost to the point that I didn't care. The gray area and the waiting and the decisions used to drive me crazy. If the joint just collapsed, at least I wouldn't have another choice to make.

But after the Tour I wasn't worried anymore. Part of the reason was because all of my mental energy was going into fighting the doping allegations, but also I was confident that we had found a procedure that would give me the best chance of being the same kind of racer I was before—and maybe even better.

Right from the time that Brent told me I had avascular necrosis in my hip, I had started researching hip replacement possibilities. In my typical obsessive way, I spent three days straight on the Internet, skimming over FAQ pages, reading comparisons of different high-tech materials—plastics, ceramics, metals—and reading each company's pitch for why their hip is the best one in the universe. For me to sift through all those ads and be able to find one that was better than the other would be like someone who had never ridden a bicycle trying to determine the best bike out of all the high-tech, carbon race bikes at the Tour.

Dr. Chao and Brent became my eyes and ears to help me pick the best replacement joint. Right away, Dr. Chao mentioned a procedure, called resurfacing, that's less invasive than a full hip replacement. Instead of slicing off your femur at the neck and installing a whole new joint, they shave off the dead bone and put a round cap on top of it. The way Dr. Chao describes it, a hip replacement is like taking all the ice cream out of an ice cream cone and replacing it with solid chocolate, "but resurfacing is like scraping off the melted part until you get to frozen ice cream, and then dipping it in chocolate."

Compared to a traditional hip replacement, resurfacing preserves more original bone and creates a more durable ball-and-socket joint, making it a good option for young, active people. In many traditional hip replacements, the ball is made of metal, but the socket is lined with plastic, which we were pretty sure I'd grind down quickly. But Dr. Chao learned that a metal-on-metal joint, which I'd get with resurfacing, would last longer.

The decision we were leaning toward was confirmed by the flood of letters and e-mails Brent got after we made my hip problems public at the Tour. Making a big scene got us the expert opinions we were looking for, though unfortunately we weren't able to get the Floyd Landis Foundation up and running as quickly as I had hoped because I suddenly had to put all my resources into legal defense. Still, I hope to make some good out of it once this mess is behind me.

In the end, after reading all the opinions, we were confident that we knew the best choice for my new hip: the Smith & Nephew Birmingham Hip Resurfacing System.

The Birmingham hip device looks like a space-age spinning top. It was developed in Birmingham, England, and had been around for nearly a decade by 2006, so it had the longest track record of success. When I first held the two pieces in my hand, I was surprised by how heavy they were. They're made of this ultra-sturdy high-carbide cobalt chrome—no superlight titanium material here—that is so hard, there's no chance it will wear down.

Then there are the joint surfaces themselves. They're highly polished in a way that goes far beyond shiny. When I took the dome piece and twisted it, it just spun and spun in the socket. A few seconds later, it was still going. Then, a few seconds after that—still going. It seemed like the kind of surface that could stand up to three weeks of intensive racing in July.

One of the codevelopers of the resurfacing procedure, Dr. Ronan Treacy, had performed nearly 3,500 of them in England, but the Birmingham hip didn't receive approval from the Food and Drug Administration until May 2006, making it the only resurfacing device approved in the U.S. The timing was perfect. I'd have the surgery done at Oasis in San Diego by Dr. Chao, with Dr. Treacy flying in from England to be sure it was done right.

By the day of surgery in late September, I couldn't wait to get it over with.

It turns out that Dr. Treacy spends his winters in the French Alps, and in 2005 he had rented a helicopter for two days to watch the Tour wind its way through the mountains. "Ah, Courchevel," he said. "Courchevel is absolutely stunning." Courchevel is an old ski village that served as a mountain-top finish one of the days Treacy was watching from above. It is a beautiful place, with mountain views in all directions, and I had memories of doing well in that stage. So, I'm told that when the anesthesiologist was putting me under, I caused a bit of a scene. I was lying there in that stupid blue surgical hairnet that looks like a shower cap, and for what-ever reason I started flailing my arms, saying, "Oh, I wish I was in Courchevel! Courchevel!" They had to strap me down after that.

Brent was in the operating room to watch and take pictures. To hear him tell what happened during the surgery is like hearing someone talk about seeing an absurd, gory movie.

Hip-replacement surgeons typically go in through the front of the hip, because it creates a smaller scar and it's easier to access the joint that way. But Dr. Chao said that going through the front would create scar tissue on my hip flexor, which is used very heavily in cycling. Instead, the surgeons made a huge incision, about ten inches long, down the edge of my butt, basically filleting my Tour de France–winning ass. That was fine with me, since I was worried about how well I'd pedal, not what I'd look like in a bikini. As they went, they were careful to preserve my muscles where they could, or, as Dr. Treacy put it to me beforehand, "The idea is to part the curtains, rather than cut through them."

Then they had to twist my leg to dislocate my hip and gain access to the joint. As I lay on my left side, they bent my right leg at the knee and pulled it forward, like the motion of pulling off a chicken wing, so that the outside of my ankle was facing the floor. "It's not delicate work," Brent said in his understated way. "It's like carpentry on the body."

When Dr. Treacy first saw my rotting femur, he said, "Wow, it's worse than it looked on the X-rays." Typically, surgeons need a hammer and chisel to break off pieces of dead bone, but after just a few snips of scar tissue, a piece of bone the size of a quarter just fell off. It had been sitting there like a loose tile.

After studying my case, Dr. Treacy had been surprised that I could even walk, much less win the Tour de France. "If you showed me these films blind," he said, "I'd say no way this patient could play nine holes of golf." But once the surgeons removed the obvious dead parts, Dr. Treacy said, "Oh, this is very good." The surface was completely trashed, but underneath there was plenty of healthy bone for them to work with.

My hip socket had become rough from the misshapen ball part grinding on it. To smooth it out, the surgeons used a drill pretty much like you'd find at a hardware store with a big, circular bit the size of the socket. Once the socket was buffed smooth, they placed the cobalt-chrome cup piece in position and slammed it four times with a giant metal mallet to press it in. There's no glue or pin or anything to hold it in place—only the hammer swings to set it and then the pressure of the ball part against it. Over time, bone would grow against the backside of the cup to fuse it all together.

Then they shaved the rest of the dead bone from my femur to make a nice platform and drilled a small hole in the bone for the centering peg of the dome. By being extra careful to take off as little bone as possible and position the cup precisely, they were able to lengthen my right leg to make it as long as my left again.

Next, the dome piece went on with a little surgical

cement, and then the same metal mallet slammed it into place with four strong swings. *Whack. Whack. Whack. Whack.*

They twisted my leg back into place, and that was it. It was just one hour later. I had a new hip.

I woke up in my room feeling good and wanting to go home, but they made me stay overnight. By the next day, I was lying in the bed moving my leg around, saying, "Hey, look, I couldn't do this before." Already, I had more mobility in certain directions—and I was ready to go. I wanted out so bad. Suddenly I was filled with an energy I hadn't felt since the Tour.

So while the physical therapist brought in my crutches and was giving Amber my discharge instructions, I hopped up. "That's it, I'm outta here," I said, and crutched my way down the hall. I stole a wheelchair and did some hot laps around the surgery center. I was *ready*, and I'm sure people were annoyed, entertained, or both.

Immediately I noticed that the all-day ache was gone. And I was sleeping like a baby. Six days after surgery I pedaled for ten minutes on a stationary bike at just 100 watts, barely even turning the cranks. It was the weirdest feeling, like I had never done the motion before in my entire life.

As the weeks went by, I pedaled a little more, and then a little more. My hip would ache a little sometimes, but not the same as before. It was a more of a healing soreness than a deep-down pain. When I finally got off the crutches, it felt like I was walking on a hill because I wasn't used to my legs being the same length.

The nice thing was, I was ready to take my time with rehabilitation. Before, I was stressed about missing out on training in Europe or making a Tour team. But I had won the Tour, and this was my chance to fix the problem, not just find a way to make do. There was no rush.

CHAPTER 14

The Wiki Defense

In early October, Will, Arnie, and I were driving to another legal meeting with Howard Jacobs in Los Angeles. Arnie was scheduled to give one of his monthly talks at a San Diego bike shop the following week. "It's supposed to be on nutrition, but would you mind if I talked about some of my findings instead?" he asked. "I could make a slideshow."

Arnie had studied the document packet every single day since it had arrived, and every single day he found more errors. He was devoting forty hours per week to tearing it apart and had developed so many different arguments for the inaccuracy of my supposedly positive test results that he had to go back to Office Depot to buy more three-ring binders to keep everything organized.

"I don't see why not," I said. "What do we gain by keeping their mistakes a secret?" I couldn't think of any reason not to share the information. In fact, presenting some of what Arnie found would help people understand what was happening to me. Not much about my case had been in the news since the B sample results were released two months before.

"They're going to be absolutely blown away," Will said. "As long as you're making a slideshow, you might as well put it online, so anyone can download it."

From there, the ideas snowballed. I had already requested that my hearing be open to the public and the media. USADA has a little-known rule that an accused athlete can request a public hearing, and although no other athlete had ever done so before, I couldn't think of a better way to tell my side of the story. People needed to witness the truth.

"Well, if the arbitration is going to be open, and the slideshow is online," Arnie said, "why not put the entire 370-page document packet online? It would be full transparency." Arnie had been talking a lot about my case with Brian Rafferty, a masters bike racer he coached who lived in New York City and whom I had met several times over the years. Brian specialized in public relations for big international financial transactions. "If you're on the side of the good guys," Brian had told Arnie, "then total transparency can be a huge strategic advantage." If that logic was good enough for Brian and his multi-billion-dollar corporate deals, then it was good enough for me.

We got to Howard's and presented him with the idea.

"You want to do *what*?" he asked, the pitch of his voice rising on the last word. As is typical of lawyers, Howard didn't like the idea of revealing anything. Not only was he concerned that once we released the information, we'd have no control over it anymore, but also that if Arnie posted his analysis, we would be revealing key points of our defense to USADA ahead of time.

"Well, I'd only reveal four or five arguments that are easy for the average person to understand," Arnie said. By now, there was no shortage of arguments—he had dozens—so we wouldn't be showing all of our hand. "Besides, it's also possible that someone could find things that would help us. It could be like a Wikipedia entry, with experts adding to our information when they found something new."

By that point, I was fired up. "I refuse to hide," I said. "Let's go apeshit. I want to put up a fight like USADA has never seen." After the way I had been treated by every association every step of the way, I wanted to make this as public as possible. "They're the ones picking on the poor crazy guy with nothing to lose," I said.

"Apparently, USADA has never heard the rule, 'Don't poke the crazy guy,'" Will said. He loved the idea too, and after a while even Howard got used to it.

When Arnie presented his slideshow, "What's Fair Is Clear,"* at the bike shop, the audience liked it much better than the proposed lecture on what to eat on a bicycle ride. A

---

* For an explanation of several key flaws that Dr. Arnie Baker found in the document packet, see the Appendix, "What's Fair Is Clear," page 287.

short time later, we posted the presentation on my website, along with the complete document packet and the motion we submitted to the USADA review board. Arnie named the project the Wiki defense.

Now anyone, including the media, who wanted to bother to understand the facts of my case had every bit of information that we did, and they could objectively form their own opinions.

A month after my hip surgery, in late October, I was able to ride my bicycle two or three hours per day. And a surprising thing began to happen to me: I wanted to ride again. In fact, I couldn't wait. I love to ride more than anything, and I had missed it. I don't feel right when I don't ride. But, feeling the sun on my face and the sweat pouring out as I climbed the desert foothills, pedaling was like medicine, and I felt healthy again.

On one ride, I felt so good that I stood up in the saddle and sprinted like I was trying to win a stage. My PowerTap showed 900 watts. It felt amazing. My hip was a little sore afterward, though, and instead of just ignoring it and pressing on, I backed off. It was a new experience for me after so many years of pushing through hip pain. Now, I waited for the hip to come to me.

And it worked. A few weeks later, Brent and I did a 60-mile ride with 4,500 feet of climbing. I averaged 250 watts, and maintained 380 watts on the big climb, which was not too far off from where I should have been for Tour training. My hip felt great, better than it had in all the time since I first broke it. I even did a one-legged strength test that showed that my right leg could produce more power than my left. My bad side was stronger than my good side. I was back. I turned to Brent as we pedaled along. "Man, I should have done this a long time ago."

"Ah, hindsight is always twenty-twenty," he said. "It was a big unknown, and we did the best we could with what we had." He was happy that I seemed to have the fire back. "Besides, look at you now."

The irony was that, now that I was finally ready to ride, I didn't have time for the training I would need in order to be in shape for something like the Tour. I absolutely had to win my case, and it took up almost all day, every day. It was my only objective, because without being exonerated, there would be no racing. As much as it hurt me, I decided to write off the entire 2007 racing season to focus on my defense strategy. I had to be sure it was done right.

Even though USADA isn't required to give defendants additional documents besides the original lab packet, there was nothing stopping us from at least asking for a few things that would help us make points in my defense. Early on, we had an indication that USADA would be cooperative. We had asked for my past drug testing results for comparison, and Travis Tygart wrote to us, "Once we receive all of the data, we intend to bates label it and provide you a copy."

In the meantime, we submitted our official request for all the documents we believed were necessary to mount my defense. We had so many questions about how the French lab arrived at its wrong answer that our request was ten pages long and asked for seventy-nine items. Some of the items were complicated, scientific pieces of evidence that my experts wanted in order to challenge the science. But others were for very basic information, such as the list of steps the lab goes through when performing a test, how the lab's testing machines were calibrated, and what criteria the lab used to determine whether a test was positive.

A couple of weeks later, we got a rejection letter. We would be receiving no such documents. Not even the ones Tygart had said he would provide.

"After extensive review by us of your voluminous requests," wrote Tygart. "I am writing to inform you that we will not be providing any documents or other information in response to your requests. As you should know, the rules applicable to this proceeding establish the set of documents that are provided by the laboratories when a sample tests positive. After studying your requests and those rules, every request you make appears to seek documents or information not called for by the rules."

My guess is that once Tygart saw the extent to which I intended to fight, he freaked out. "Not called for by the rules" meant to me that because the rules didn't specifically require him to send the documents, he didn't have to if he didn't feel like it. So he didn't.

To me it was more evidence that USADA was interested in winning, not finding out the truth about what really happened with my test. If I didn't have any additional evidence, then I'd have trouble calling the lab's scientific methods into question. If the lab procedures appeared perfect every time, then USADA would win the case every time.

We put our "voluminous" request and the rejection letter up on the Internet.

In mid-November, the French lab made a claim that someone had broken into its computer network and stolen data. The media picked up this "hacker" story and ran with it. Whether it was a hacker or a lab insider, whoever did it had a sense of humor, because while they were in there they posed as a lab employee and sent fake letters to the International Olympic Committee and WADA-accredited labs around the world, saying that the French lab specialized in making errors and wasn't reliable at all.

This supposed hacker also took letters from the lab from the past two years that chronicled at least four instances in which the lab had to retract so-called positive tests because of errors. Three of the letters detailed simple numbering errors, such as an incorrect date or sample labeling, just like the ones in my case. Another referred to a test done on a swimmer's urine sample in which the lab admitted it had accidentally contaminated the urine sample with an anabolic steroid from another athlete's sample, and so the swimmer had been falsely accused. The botched test occurred in July 2006, during the same time the lab was analyzing Tour de France samples.

Copies of these documents mysteriously appeared in the mailboxes of various members of the media—as well as in Arnie's. The documents were damning. Were they real? No one has been able to prove that they are because the lab hasn't confirmed it, and none of the athletes referred to in the letters has come forward. At the same time, neither the lab nor WADA has claimed that they're fake.

As far as I could tell, the only problem with all of the information released was this one: *L'Equipe* claimed to have a French police source who had reason to believe that the hacker was a "close associate" of mine.

Speculation spread like wildfire about the identity of this person who was out to discredit the French lab. In Tucson, Arizona, where Arnie was giving his "What's Fair Is Clear" presentation at a bike event, a French journalist approached him carrying a French newspaper. He pointed to a hacker story in the paper and said, "They say it's you."

This sent Arnie into a tailspin. He called me after the event in a serious state of distress. "This is surreal," he said. "I have no idea what's going to happen." He felt accused for absolutely no reason, and it confused him. In a way, he sounded like I did right after the Tour when my sample results were publicized. I had sympathy for the guy, but I didn't really know what to tell him. There was a time when I would have told him not to worry, because the truth would come out. But I didn't trust that idea anymore.

I also had to laugh a little bit. Arnie's imagination had

gone wild. "What if the CIA or the FBI comes to take my computer?" he asked.

The good thing was that Arnie didn't stay on the hook for long. The idea that my defense team was somehow involved was short-lived. A few more stories came out speculating who the hacker might be. The best was in the French paper *Le Monde*, which suggested that it might have been Lance.

It was actually getting funny.

The very day after the hacker story broke, perhaps to distract the media from the fact that they had lax security and were being publicly embarrassed, the French lab announced that it had made a single "typing error" in my document packet. The slip-up "has no significance whatsoever on the findings in the samples," said the head of the French lab in media interviews. "These little mistakes happen. They are corrected, and noted."

Will was at my house when we read that. "This is a total joke," he said. He waved his hands to the side, like he was trying to shoo something away. "Don't look over here at all these documents that show how incompetent we are." Then he pointed in the other direction, shaking his finger and nodding. "Yep, look over here instead. Oops, we got one number wrong. We admit it."

What could we do at that point besides make fun of it? Lance is the hacker. There's only one mistake in my document packet. These ideas were so far-fetched that, finally, after months of having my life turned upside down with false accusations, character assassinations, and bullying by USADA, I was starting to be able to laugh again.

The jokes began flying. "How's it going?" Will asked when he called me one morning.

"Well, here we are, just another day of trying to win the Tour," I said. "Stage 129. Damn, this thing is long!"

With the document packet online, the media began reporting on more than just Dick Pound's preposterous comments. Stories started coming out about the science of my case and mistakes in procedure that the French lab made.

Daily Peloton, a large online cycling forum, exploded with scientific debate about my tests, with experts debating the finer points of page after page. Various blogs pondered new elements of my case every day—and people read them. One blog, Trust But Verify, which was started by an architect in northern California, began listing a daily compilation of every mention of me on the Internet, and site traffic jumped twelvefold during the early Wiki days. Finally, instead of the masses assuming that I was guilty without looking at the facts, people were realizing the truth. It was gratifying to see the shift in public perception.

The Wiki defense helped with our scientific arguments, too. Arnie began hearing from hundreds of people telling him where to look in the document packet for more mistakes. "Today I got a call from a NASA scientist," Arnie said during an update call. The scientist was an expert in mass spectrometry, the method of analysis used in the carbon-isotope ratio test, and he wanted to point out flaws in the French lab's analysis. "He said, 'I bet you never thought you'd hear from a NASA scientist.' But he's the fourth NASA scientist I've heard from."

Arnie also received calls, e-mails, and paper documents from doctors, chemists, and even anonymous sources within the anti-doping community—all of them either pointing out errors or helping him learn where to look for them. One source gave him nonpublic minutes from a meeting of the World Association of Anti-doping Scientists, and another informed him of the Australian WADA lab's criteria for a positive carbon-isotope ratio test—turns out my test would have been negative there, too.

With all of the new information coming in, Arnie had to buy even more white binders to house his compilation of all the errors—the master blueprint of the defense team.

Our Wiki was in full swing.

My defense team began meeting at my house regularly. There would be six of us sitting at the marble kitchen countertop, all staring into our laptops, working away—me, Will, Arnie, Howard, Michael Henson, and Paul Scott.

I could tell that Paul enjoyed the freedom of being away from UCLA. "It's really refreshing the way you're doing this," he said. He loved the idea of making everything public, because so much in the anti-doping world is done behind closed doors.

"Why wouldn't I do it this way?" I asked him.

"Well, you're the first athlete who ever has," he said.

Typically, athletes wouldn't want to publicize their document packets because they would be damning. "I used to see all of the cases that came through the lab. The science is usually obvious. Most of them are guilty."

Paul kept working to tear apart the science of my test. He came up with several theories of how the French lab had messed up, and ultimately developed a favorite. "There are signs of some sort of bacterial contamination," he said. He believed that unknown bacteria were metabolizing epitestosterone, which was why the level in my sample was so low. "There certainly are other conceivable possibilities," he said. "But I think that's the most likely one."

The frustrating thing was that studying my document packet was like looking at a crime scene. We only had the outcome. We could try to reconstruct scenarios of how that outcome was reached, but there was no way to know for sure what had happened. "It would be nice if I had some of the urine so I could do a culture on it," Paul said. But every sample gets completely used up in testing.

Despite all the progress we had made in mounting my defense, nothing seemed to be happening in the USADA process to move my case forward. Four months after the Tour, we had no hearing date set, and no idea when we'd get one. Something was delaying the process.

I wasn't the only one frustrated by the delays. All the riders and teams were pissed off because no one had been awarded prize money for the Tour yet—not for first place or ninety-ninth place. The Tour officials had decided that they wouldn't hand out a single euro until my case was settled.

Andy had decided to fold the Phonak team, and my teammates had to find other teams to race for in 2007. I didn't talk to them much because I felt so bad about what had happened. I wanted my guys to get paid. They deserved their prize money and bonus money for helping me win the Tour.

It was clear that the fact that there was no end of my case in sight was a national embarrassment for France. The Tour is France's most prestigious sporting event, and still there was no 2006 winner. In a couple of months, it would become clear that the 2007 race would happen before a 2006 result was declared. Someone in France had had enough.

I received a notification by registered mail in December 2006 that the French anti-doping agency, the Agence Française de Lutte contre le Dopage (AFLD), had decided to take matters into its own hands and file its own suit against me, with a hearing in France on January 25, 2007—whether I showed up or not. Basically, I was going to be tried twice for the same thing. The French were kind enough to send me a list of approved people I was allowed to use as counsel—all French experts, and no one else, certainly not anyone I would choose. I'm no lawyer, but I figured my chances in that hearing probably weren't so good.

There was no legal precedent for this course of action, and it was never clearly explained on what grounds the French agency was allowed to initiate a parallel hearing. My guess is that the French were doing it because they wanted resolution for the Tour de France, and were sick of waiting. They had seen the Wiki defense on the Internet and wanted to put the matter to rest to avoid further damage to the French lab's reputation.

The way the WADA system is supposed to work, athletes are referred to their home country for the processing of a doping case. This parallel legal action wasn't detailed anywhere in WADA rules, and was clearly unjust. WADA asked the AFLD to halt the case, but the AFLD said no, and WADA claimed it didn't have the authority to intervene. I'm not sure why WADA wasn't able to stop it, but if the way anti-doping agencies tend to interpret the rules is any guide, then the justification would probably be something like, "Well, there's no specific rule against it."

Now we had a second battle to fight, and we were overwhelmed.

For the parallel French case, we received a separate copy of my document packet. It was stamped "certified original," but Arnie quickly noticed that it was different from the one USADA had provided for the American hearing. In the new French document packet, one of the pages with a sample number error had been corrected, and another page with a sample number error had been omitted altogether from the package. The page had simply disappeared. "You know, in medical practice, that's not just a mistake," said Arnie. "That's malfeasance." After a week of review, we found that several things had changed in the packet, all addressing issues that we had found and published online.

We couldn't know for sure that the changed document packet was an attempt at a cover-up. Whether it was or it wasn't, it was clearly another case of gross incompetence. I had been asked early on in my case whether I thought my being falsely accused of using testosterone was some sort of French conspiracy. Frankly, I don't think it was a setup because if I were going to set someone up, I'd do a much better job than the French lab did. Their errors were too obvious and too frequent to be some sort of plot. I had no evidence that there was any sort of conspiracy—by the French or anyone else—and my defense team and I viewed it as a waste of time to speculate. Instead, we focused on winning my case, because if my hearing was fair at all, we believed we had strong enough arguments that there was no way we could lose.

With two hearings to fight, I needed more legal help. It was time to pull out all the stops. I knew that hiring a high-powered law firm would effectively quadruple the cost of my defense, but this was my life and reputation. I decided that I was willing to spend every penny I had ever made to fight this fight. I'd pump gas to feed my family if I had to, but I would not quit. Ever.

After extensive research I hired Maurice Suh, a partner in the international firm Gibson, Dunn & Crutcher. Maurice used to be a public corruption prosecutor, had done complex commercial litigation, and was the former Los Angeles Deputy Mayor of Homeland Security and Public Safety.

I liked Maurice's attitude from the beginning. "This

system has been in place for six years," Maurice said at the outset. "And USADA has bullied athletes the entire time. Not anymore." He was going to fight the agency on every point, which they weren't used to because athletes typically don't have the resources to challenge them so thoroughly. Typically, athletes will run out of money and roll over because they have no other choice.

My case became like a game of chicken, with USADA dragging it out and hoping I'd run out of money, and me spending money and making them look bad as I exposed the system.

USADA's annual budget is a matter of public record. It's about $12 million, with roughly a quarter of that going toward processing doping results, investigations, and legal actions. We had already estimated that my defense was going to cost $2 million, which I didn't have at the time. If the case was also going to cost USADA $2 million, then, looking at the numbers, it seemed like USADA might not have the money either.

This whole thing has been a colossal waste of money. There has been so much money spent on *nothing*. When Paul brought me some astounding news from his contacts inside the anti-doping community, I realized that the waste might be having serious consequences aside from my going broke. Paul told me that he had heard of two strong cases of doping violations by American athletes in the fall of 2006 that USADA declined to pursue.

He and his source had discussed possible reasons the cases might have been dropped—mistakes in procedure, errors in the lab packet—but there were none. Then they realized that in both cases the athletes had enough money to afford good lawyers, so they would likely mount strong defenses. With my case overwhelming USADA already, Paul suspected that the agency couldn't afford to fight more.

"My opinion is that USADA thinks those athletes are smaller fish than you," Paul said. "And they're not willing to spend the money to litigate those."

One of the athletes was a cyclist and the other was a track-and-field athlete. Both were cases of alleged EPO use. The cyclist's document packet was one of the last ones that Paul personally supervised before he left the UCLA lab. "To me, that's a rock-solid case," Paul said. "Indefensible by the athlete." For the other, Paul had been shown the document packet, and the case appeared to be very strong.

"Who the fuck is in charge here?" I asked him. "Why is no one paying attention to this?" I thought I couldn't be shocked anymore, but I was when I heard about this. To me, it was corruption. USADA was using all of its legal resources to try to convict an innocent athlete, and now here was the possibility that cheaters were being allowed to go free because of it. I felt like USADA could say and do whatever it wanted without having to answer to anyone. They needed to be held accountable.

Of course, by USADA's rule of not commenting about ongoing cases, there was no way to find out from the agency what the real impact of my case was—not that they'd be likely to admit to what Paul was suggesting.

"I don't know the answer," Paul said. "For all the problems in the anti-doping system—and there are many—I've never seen anything like this."

"This is unacceptable," I said. Just winning my case was no longer good enough for me. If I won, the system would keep rolling along as it always had. "Things have to change." My mind was made up. Not only would I find a way to make sure that no innocent person ever had to go through what I was going through, but I'd also push for major reform of the anti-doping system in order to clean up this mess. Nothing less would be good enough.

It was a great idea, but I was running out of money, fast. There was no way I could take on the system if I couldn't even pay for my case.

At this rate, though, despite not paying Arnie a cent, I'd be bankrupt in only a couple of more months. "You need a legal defense fund," Will told me. Henson and Paul told me the same thing, and so did Arnie's masters racer, Brian Rafferty, who had been helping us pro bono for about a month.

I didn't even want to think about it because I absolutely despised the idea of asking people for money. But they all kept telling me and telling me that I needed help. They were right, and I was ashamed of the fact that I needed financial help.

◆ ◆ ◆

Arnie put on a weeklong training camp for the cyclists he coaches in Borrego Springs, California, a tiny desert town east of San Diego. I went along to get in some miles on my new hip, and Brian Rafferty went too.

Every day during camp, Brian and I rode together and talked for hours about how screwed up the anti-doping system was, and how my situation had the potential to make people realize that things needed to change.

"When your case first came up," Brian said as we spun along the first day, "my basic assumption was that the anti-doping guys were the good guys, and the people they caught were the bad guys. But that's not always the case."

I had told him about people like Scott Moninger from Mercury, and other athletes I knew of who hadn't been treated fairly. "Cycling deserves better, and my friends who are racing deserve better," I said. "I'm going to do something about it, too, but I'll have to wait until my case is over." Until then, I didn't have the time or money to focus on it.

We pedaled for a while longer, past mile after mile of sweeping views of rock, cactus, palm trees, and blue sky. Then Brian spoke.

"That's not necessarily true," he said. "There are two things you need right now: money, and a platform to deliver your message that the system should be made fair. You can have both at once. In fact, that's best that way."

A standard defense fund would pass the hat and raise money to try and beat the false accusations against me. But by using some of the fund money to build a team to help me take on the system, we would be forward-looking. "People already know about your case and want to help you fight the larger fight," Brian said. "Let them help you."

I liked the strategy. "That's how I won races," I said to Brian. "The moment you adopt an offense, instead of just reacting to what happens, you become much more powerful."

He said that we should try not only to get more public support, but also to speak to the people who could actually make a difference: the members of Congress who controlled USADA funding. "Let's explain to them what's going on," he said. "Maybe they'll listen."

That night at dinner, Brian had an idea for a name for my defense fund: The Floyd Fairness Fund. "You're a first-name kind of guy," he said. "And this isn't about a 'defense,' it's about fundamental fairness for all athletes."

We skipped out of the last day of camp to attend a dinner in La Jolla hosted by wealthy Southern California business-men. Brian was right. They wanted to hear what I had to say about the system, and they wanted to help me.

The next day Brian and I went for one last ride together. I talked about how I wanted to make my fight bigger than just my case. I was worried that, given the way the USADA rules are set up, I might not end up with a fair hearing. "It certainly hasn't been fair up to this point," I said.

"No matter what the legal outcome," Brian said, "the fund is the way to get your message out about the system." We fin-ished the ride and sat on a bench. "You be the leader of the team," Brian said. "And your team will handle the rest."

"Okay," I said. "Let's do it." Brian became chairman of the Floyd Fairness Fund, and Henson became the executive director.

In just a few months I had assembled a team of lawyers, PR people, and scientists to help me. I never in my life thought I would have "people." And while on one hand I wished my life could be simple again, on the other, I had absolute confidence in my new team and in our mission.

CHAPTER 15

Making It Right

Amber and I went to Macy's, where she helped me pick out a business suit and necktie. I have never owned fancy clothes or liked dressing up. If given the choice, I'd hang out all day in a T-shirt and jeans. But I was taking my case very seriously, and I decided that if I wanted to be taken seriously by other people, I needed to send a message with how I looked. The business suit was going to be like my new backward baseball cap. "Look out," it would say to the so-called authorities, "I'm on your turf now and no one is going to stop me." I would wear it anytime I appeared at a public event, and everyone on my defense team would do the same.

A few weeks after we established the Floyd Fairness Fund, on January 4, 2007, I flew to Washington, D.C., to meet with some of the members of Congress who determine funding for the White House Office of National Drug Control Policy, which is in charge of allocating funds to USADA. Will, Henson, and I went to different House and Senate office buildings, the kinds of places where your dress shoes click against the hard floors and echo through the old marble hallways, the kinds of places that just feel important.

Our meetings were short. I specifically avoided talking about my case. It wouldn't have been appropriate to ask anyone to take a position on my innocence or guilt. Besides, the science is way too complicated, and the members of Congress have better things to do with their time than consider my situation. But I did explain to them that the USADA system doesn't offer athletes the same basic rights that defendants are given in the American judicial system. In America, the government is charged with doing the right thing in a court case, not with trying to win every case. But USADA sets out to convict without attempting to get to the truth. It has all the resources, and the athlete has none. I explained that, as an innocent athlete, I didn't stand anywhere near a fair chance because I was denied the evidence I needed to defend myself properly.

That struck a chord with the lawmakers.

Most of them weren't aware of the USADA rules, or the extent to which the hierarchy is riddled with the potential for conflict of interest since the same people make, enforce, and prosecute the rules, as well as pick the pool of judges. The main experience the lawmakers had with USADA was when the agency came to them asking for more money to catch more cheaters. Of course Congress would want to help, because no one wants cheaters to go free. But Congress had never had occasion to pause and look at USADA's legal process, because no one had ever brought it to their attention. They were shocked by the injustice that innocent athletes who slip into the punitive system could face.

In addition to informing Congress, I wanted to speak directly to the people. Since we started the Wiki defense, we had seen that a lot of cycling fans appreciated having the information to form their own opinions, but they hadn't heard from me directly. Through the Floyd Fairness Fund, we began hosting a series of town hall meetings, more than a dozen across the country. Anyone who was interested in hearing more about what had been happening to me since the end of the Tour—the real story—could come and speak to me directly. Part of our objective was to raise money for the fund, so we charged admission to the events, a fact that I was never completely comfortable with. Even though I'm very proud of the fund and its goals, I'll never get used to the idea of people having to pay to see me, or give money to help me afford the high costs of this fight.

Arnie often came along to present "What's Fair Is Clear," and to take questions people had about the science of the case. Henson explained the strategy of the fund, and we explained to people how they could help the cause for fairness by contacting their congressional representatives.

The nice part about the town hall meetings was that fans

also wanted to hear about cycling. Finally, I had the opportunity to explain what really happened during the 2006 Tour, how I had bonked during Stage 16, how my team had used smart tactics to help me escape on my solo breakaway the next day, and how I used my power meter to pace myself as if I had been on a hard training ride. It was a nice change to be able to talk like a bike racer again instead of like a lawyer, which I had begun to do more and more.

We also had fun, auctioning off items like autographed jerseys, Jack Daniel's boxes, and a book of quotations by Dick Pound, which he compiled to use for inspiration when he spoke to the media. I would personally dedicate Pound's book to whoever bought it, just for the paradox.

In February, I went to the Tour of California, the race where I had my first victory of 2006. I thought that I would be fine going back into the cycling world for the first time since the Tour, but I was wrong. I felt as if I was existing in some sort of parallel universe, on the outside watching a version of my life go on without me.

Still, I wasn't going to disappear. I wanted to show my face as much as possible to serve as a reminder to everyone what a mess the sport of cycling is in, and how screwed up the anti-doping system is.

One remarkable thing happened in San Francisco at the pre-race press conference: three riders spoke out in support of me. Privately, my friends in the peloton have all continued to support me—none of them is happy with the extraordinary level of control the UCI has over their lives or the way that cycling deals with anti-doping issues. But because cycling teams are funded by corporate sponsors, the cyclists are very careful about what they state publicly, to avoid taking a political position that makes the sponsor angry. I understand that. Like it or not, that's the way the cycling world works. That's why I was surprised and proud when, one right after the other, top American riders answered the question honestly when asked what they thought about my situation.

"Floyd is a friend of mine," said Discovery's George Hincapie. "I hope he can clear his name. I hope he is able to get all the help that he needs."

Levi Leipheimer, now on Discovery, said that the cause of athletes' rights "is something that everyone here would support one hundred percent. There are definitely some issues that need to be resolved." One of them, he said, was the fact that it was going to be more than a year before there was any outcome in my case, which reflected poorly on the process.

And Bobby Julich of CSC said, "I think the recurring theme is that the testing procedures are being questioned." In response to Operación Puerto and other doping scandals of 2006, his team had developed its own internal anti-doping testing program. In it, riders would undergo at least a dozen team tests, in addition to the many in- and out-of-competition ones required by the UCI. "I have signed up for twelve to sixteen more opportunities for these tests to be flawed," Julich said, "so I think that Floyd Landis fighting for the rights of the riders is very important."

I appreciated their willingness to speak their minds, and I hope that in the future other riders do the same.

My defense team's mission at the race was to host three town halls to reach as many cycling fans as possible so I could tell them about my fight for fairness, and also to be in the finish town of each stage of the race so I could hang out at the expo booth of Smith & Nephew and talk about my new hip. Five months after surgery, it was wonderful to be able to ride as well as I could. But given what my life had become—lawyer meetings and airplane flights, mostly—I was even more surprised by and grateful for how well I could sleep, sit, and even break into a little run rushing through airports. My hip was perfect, like nothing ever happened.

I also wanted to show support for the other sponsors that had stuck with me despite all the bad press after the Tour: Speedplay pedals, Giro helmets, and, of course, CycleOps, makers of my PowerTap meter.

The week was like one long road trip, driving from finish town to finish town blasting our theme song for the week, "The Unforgiven" by Metallica. It was an obvious choice, but we found it very motivating, especially when we cranked up the volume and sang along: *You labeled me, I'll label you. So I dub thee unforgiven.*

The morning of Stage 2, which finished in Sacramento, Will, Henson, and I were sitting in the lobby of a Holiday

Inn wearing our suits. A fan came up and asked me, "What's with the suit?"

I had been getting that question a lot lately. "When someone's wrecking your life by accusing you of something you didn't do, you don't show up in sweatpants," I said. I felt like the suit had been working for me, though I still wasn't very good at tying neckties—Will or Henson usually helped me.

That day at the Smith & Nephew booth, we had by far the longest line in the whole expo area, just like we would for the entire week. Sometimes when people got up to the front they were surprised to see me. They had joined the line without knowing what it was for, just because it looked like something exciting was happening. Once they reached me, they were full of questions about cycling, my hip, and my case.

After a few hours of signing autographs, we started to hear the noise level of the crowd rise slowly. We knew it wouldn't be long before the race arrived.

"Let's go see the finish," I said to Will and Henson. I began walking from the booth to the finish-line area with Will and Henson flanking me. Because three men in business suits and ties marching around the finish of a bike race is pretty unusual, everyone's heads turned to watch us. The crowds parted to let us through, and people yelled out words of encouragement to me the entire way. "I think I'll go do some announcing," I said to Will. "Just for fun."

There were three guarded gates between me and the

announcer's stage. At each gate, I walked up and opened it like I was supposed to be there, and the police let all three of us through every time. I took the stage, and the announcer said, "And now, here's the 2006 Tour de France champion, Floyd Landis!" He handed a microphone to me without my even asking, and people cheered as if I was on a winner's podium again.

I thanked everyone and then answered some questions from the announcer about my case. When we were done, the crowd cheered again.

"You're a man on a mission," Henson said when I stepped off the stage. "It's like they'll let you go anywhere as long as you're wearing that suit."

"Yeah," I said. "Maybe it would be a good idea for me to have more than one."

That day, Henson received a phone call from the office of a senator we had visited in Washington the month before. The senator's chief of staff mentioned that the senator had made a phone call to USADA to inquire about its judicial process. We were making progress already.

That night, the three of us went shopping, and I bought four more suits.

By late February, Arnie had filled more than thirty white binders documenting errors in my lab packet. He had spent nearly fifteen hundred hours analyzing it, and he kept a running tally of all the mistakes in an electronic document that was now a hundred and fifty pages long.

He had downloaded the operating manual of the carbon-isotope ratio test machine from the Internet, read it cover to cover, and learned that the lab was not only operating the machine out of the recommended range of calibration, but that it was also using ten-year-old software that was obviously out-of-date and not designed for use with the machine.

Every day Arnie read, he continued to find more problems, some of them utterly ridiculous. "Now they've found something that doesn't exist!" Arnie said one day on an update call. In T/E testing, the lab adds a chemical before analysis for comparison purposes. "They were supposed to add deuterated androsterone, but they omitted it, and then when they analyzed the sample, they found the standard amount as if they had added it."

"Thanks, Arnie," I said. "Keep reading." My hearing date had been scheduled for May 14. Arnie still had a few months to go, and I knew he'd continue to find more errors.

With the assistance of the Paris office of his law firm, Maurice Suh was able to work with French authorities to delay the France's parallel hearing until after my USADA hearing, but only after I agreed not to race in France in 2007. It turns out that, lab packets aside, the French anti-doping authorities were forthcoming, helpful, and decent people, especially compared to everyone we had encountered in the USADA process.

Once the panel of three arbitrators for my U.S. hearing was selected in February, Maurice and Howard began a full-court press to discover more documents that would enable us to better challenge the French lab's results. They filed a new briefing listing of all the documents and justifications we needed, and this time instead of being just ten pages long, it was four inches thick.

The arbitrators ruled in a preliminary hearing that we were entitled to some of the key discovery documents we were after, and told USADA they had to either provide them to us or explain why they weren't able to get them.

Finally, I felt like a fair-minded decision had been made. Since December, when Maurice first began working on my case, USADA had done nothing but stonewall our efforts with stunts that revealed their clear desire to win, regardless of the truth. When Maurice and Howard were trying to stop USADA's plan to illegally re-test my Tour samples at the French lab, which it wanted to do just one week after first notifying us, Maurice sent a letter to Travis Tygart demanding that USADA cease and desist, and he directed the French lab to do the same.

The next day, Maurice received a letter from Tygart which, among other things, declared, "You are not authorized to send communications to persons or entities of which you are aware will be witnesses in this matter, including the French laboratory."

When Maurice showed this to me, he was baffled. To go from big-time litigation to dealing with USADA's antics was a shock to him. "What kind of a lawyer says things like that?" Maurice wondered. "I mean, you're going to be a witness,

Floyd, does that mean I'm not authorized to talk to you?" At every turn, when my legal team pushed the USADA system in a way it wasn't used to, we were met with attempts to shut down the flow of information and to close the system as much as possible, using tactics that lawyers in the American judicial system would find odd, even unethical.

In another incident, my lawyers wanted to step up efforts to get the electronic data files of the test machines at the French lab as part of our discovery, something we had been asking for since the beginning. With that information in hand, we'd be able to test the data file on a machine that was properly calibrated and that used up-to-date software, to see if the result was different from the one the French lab came up with. USADA refused to allow us the files, reasoning that my lawyers would be likely to direct the lab techs to tamper with the files in order to change the outcome of the test.

Maurice was offended. "I've been a public corruption prosecutor and done all sorts of complicated litigation, but I've never seen anything like this," he said when we were hanging out after the hearing. "They accuse the lawyers of wanting to cheat?" I wondered about their logic. If the data is so easy to manipulate, then how hard would it have been for the French lab to change it? Howard asked that question of USADA, and they had no response.

In one of the preliminary hearings I attended, USADA complained about how public I had been regarding every aspect of my defense, and the fact that I was allowed to comment in the press and they weren't. They actually suggested that it was too one-way and unfair. Maurice became aggravated but remained patient—the way an adult reacts to a misbehaving four-year-old. "Well," he said to the USADA representatives and the arbitrators, "let me explain. All across the country in the U.S. judicial system, prosecutors are not allowed to talk about the facts of their case except to the jury. And in all those cases, the defendant does have the right to talk to the press, and often does so."

Still, the arbitrators issued a protective order saying that the rest of the arbitration process had to be closed. I couldn't post any more discovery documents or correspondence on the Internet, and couldn't talk to the press about any further rulings made by the arbitrators until after the hearing. The Wiki was being idled. And I was pissed.

Depending on the day or on the rulings we received from the arbitrators, as my hearing date approached, I swung from feeling excited that my defense was gaining traction to feeling demoralized that the case wasn't being heard fairly.

One day in his law office Maurice had a thought: Why not ask to meet with the head of the French anti-doping agency, Pierre Bordry, who had recently been given oversight of the French lab, just to sit down like gentlemen and discuss my case? There was no reason not to try. Bordry agreed to the request, and so Maurice flew to Paris.

"He was unaware of what was going on," Maurice said when he returned. "So I explained that our defense was essentially to take down the French lab in an embarrassing way." Bordry told Maurice that he had never met with an athlete's lawyer before. "I asked him why," Maurice said. "And Bordry just shrugged and said, 'Eh, no one ever asked before.'" Maurice asked Bordry to consider an acceptable resolution that would prevent a hearing. And Bordry, being a reasonable man, said he would take what Maurice had said into consideration.

The whole meeting made me wonder: How much aggravation and bashing in the press and monetary expense could have been avoided in this entire thing if everyone had sat down together in the very beginning and had a conversation about how to solve this problem like adults?

Later, I realized that given the current system, this would be impossible. In early April, USADA took its antics to a new level. The agency's law firm sent a request to Maurice for discovery documents from me to help them learn what my hearing defense strategies would be. It included some truly ridiculous items that had no relation to the substance of my case, such as the name of every person who had given more than two hundred and fifty dollars to my defense fund, all correspondence between my team and the French anti-doping agency, and all correspondence between my team and the UCI. This was the best, though: They wanted copies of any documents from my team "to any government official in connection with Mr. Landis [sic] efforts to influence, pressure or coerce governmental officials to instigate investigations of USADA or otherwise interfere in this adjudication process."

Again, Maurice couldn't believe the level of absurdity in his dealings with USADA. "This has been a case of firsts for me," he said. My feeling was, well, if they're mad enough to think I'm trying to coerce anyone into anything, then finally they must be feeling the pressure of scrutiny on the system.

It was time for me to go back to Farmersville. My original plan after the Tour was to visit my family and have a giant homecoming where the town could celebrate my victory with me. But the plan was derailed, all my energy went into defending myself, and it took me much longer than I wanted for me to get there.

When I started doing town halls, Mike Farrington of Green Mountain Cyclery called me. "Hey, you gotta come back," he said. "People here really want to show you how much they're behind you." He and his wife, Jen, offered to organize the whole thing, a massive town hall in late March at the Performing Arts Center in nearby Ephrata. Less than three days after Mike and Jen started selling tickets, they sold out. So we added a second night.

My defense team was into it. "I'd really like for your parents to see my slideshow," Arnie said. "I'd like to show them the evidence." Of course my parents hadn't been on the Internet to download the presentation, and they didn't know much about the details of my case beyond what I had explained to them and what was in the newspaper. They had absolute faith in me—but Arnie wanted to show them the science, too.

And so in late March we brought our business suits to Farmersville, and my team had a traditional Mennonite dinner with my parents, siblings, cousins, neighbors, and family friends. My old riding buddy Eric Gebhard was there too, and at night we hung out at Mike and Jen's and goofed around like in the old days.

I used to think that nothing ever changes in Farmersville. In the long term, it's true. I go back and it seems like everything is exactly the same way it was the day I left when I was nineteen. But the weekend of the town hall, I heard stories that surprised me. It turns out that when I won the Tour, Farmersville did change, for a couple of days at least. I had just never heard about it.

The afternoon of the Stage 20 time trial, when I reclaimed the yellow jersey for good, our neighbors, Neil and Tammy Martin, hosted a party in their yard. That morning my dad and Mr. Martin spray painted a big message in the middle of Farmersville Road: 2006 TOUR DE FRANCE CHAMPION FLOYD LANDIS. They took turns, one painting while the other scouted for traffic, as if they were a couple of neighborhood kids up to no good.

Throughout the course of the day, nearly a thousand people stopped by the Martins' to have food and lemonade, and to join in the party. There were local people, but also cycling fans who had driven in from other towns, and even total strangers from foreign countries. The Farmersville fire engine did a lap around the block with its sirens blaring.

One by one, hundreds of people walked across the yard to my parents to congratulate them. One woman went to my mother with tears in her eyes. "She said that she and her husband had lost their son in Iraq seven months before," Mom said. "She told me, 'My husband has never gotten over it, but he rides a bicycle and he watched every single stage. He's a different person now since your son won. It was like healing to him.' I just felt so blessed that you were able to inspire someone while doing something that you love," Mom told me. I never rode my bike in order to have an effect on anyone else, but I understand that people are influenced by what they see. When my mom told me this story, I was really touched that I had helped someone.

The night of the second Floyd Fairness Fund town hall, the entire town showed up to see me, or at least that's what it felt like. The line snaked down the sidewalk and halfway into the parking lot. When we opened the doors, people filed in politely and took their seats. My mom and dad sat front and center, Mom in her dress and head covering, and Dad in his Phonak baseball cap.

"Usually when I start one of these town halls, I thank my team for all their help," I said, turning to all the people in suits behind me. "But tonight is different. You all have been with me since the very beginning. You are all my team, so thank you."

During the question-and-answer period, Eric Gebhard walked up to the microphone to ask a question. "So, yeah, you have this big fight now," he began. "But for twelve years all you talked about was winning the Tour. And you did it, man. So, can't you, you know, take just a minute and enjoy it?" The crowd went nuts, and I put my microphone down and smiled. For a moment, everything was as it should have been. I was back in Farmersville with my buddy Eric, both of us proud that I fulfilled what had been my dream for more than a decade.

The sport of cycling is sick and in need of major reform. The UCI has way too much control over athletes' lives. We riders need to form a true union to protect ourselves. Without us, there is no race. But as it is, the UCI profits from our efforts, and then fails miserably to protect us from injustice.

By organizing, riders could have more power in salary negotiations with teams and more collective force in fighting unjust anti-doping policies that lead to terrible consequences and do nothing but kill fans' enthusiasm for cycling.

My case should never have happened.

The Operación Puerto scandal should not have impacted the sport the way it did. Officials should have had enough proof to convict before they forced teams to kick riders out of the 2006 Tour.

The problem is that the way the UCI rules are set up, all it takes is a suspicion to halt a rider's career and put his reputation in doubt. What's to stop me from starting a rumor right now and wrecking someone's life? It's way too easy to presume guilt. There needs to be accountability for cases where there is harmful presumption without solid proof.

Some of the riders allegedly linked to Operación Puerto chose to retire from cycling rather than deal with the hassle, while others were cleared by their national federations to race in 2007. The Spanish criminal court hearing the case threw it out in early 2007, because sports doping wasn't illegal in Spain at the time Dr. Fuentes was arrested. But the UCI has been granted jurisdiction over the Puerto investigation and says it will ultimately prosecute any riders it finds evidence against. Nobody knows when Puerto will rear its head again, if ever, or if it will ever keep riders out of the Tour de France again the way it did in 2006.

Riders need to have more of a say in their fates, rather than having them determined behind closed doors by men in suits. I know it's difficult for pro cyclists to organize, because we have absolutely no time. Days are consumed by training, eating, and sleeping—there is nothing else. But I hope that more of us can start to speak out for athletes' rights. Just as in racing, a team is always stronger than an individual.

Unquestionably, there also needs to be positive, meaningful change to the WADA and USADA systems. The agencies are young, and they have never been truly challenged. It's time for athletes and sports fans around the world to speak out for major reform.

Recently, there have been a few hopeful signs of change. In 2006, Dick Pound announced that he will retire as WADA president in November 2007. I hope that whoever replaces him has a sense of decency and respects the WADA rules enough to refrain from public comment while an athlete's case is in progress, and has the vision to set a more positive and less antagonistic tone for the entire anti-doping movement.

Perhaps this is mere coincidence, but once our political

efforts ramped up, USADA held a board meeting, and afterward USADA head Terry Madden announced that he will step down in the fall of 2007. Travis Tygart was named to replace him, so there is unlikely to be a substantive shift in tone within the organization without a long overdue public call for action.

Also, the WADA code is undergoing its first revision since it was implemented in early 2004, with the new version to be completed in late 2007. In a rare act of transparency, the agency released comments from various national sports officials about what changes should be made. Many called for arbitrators to have the leeway to issue a warning, instead of a suspension, to athletes who commit accidental or benign offenses that clearly do not enhance performance. Several officials also mentioned that WADA's recent reduction in the T/E ratio legal limit from six to one down to four to one was essentially arbitrary, and not based on peer-reviewed scientific consensus. It did nothing but cost these national sports agencies more money, because the lower limit flagged more samples, which then needed to undergo complicated and expensive carbon-isotope ratio follow-up tests, none of which led to finding any more doping violations. If the ratio hadn't been lowered, my initial T/E screening may not have raised any flags, and I might never have gone through this whole ordeal.

Many of the proposed changes in the WADA code are good ones, but the system needs more than a few tweaks. It needs a major overhaul, and the current proposed changes don't go nearly far enough to protect the rights of athletes in the testing, analyzing, or adjudication phases of the process. One major problem is that athletes are not directly involved in the process. All of these key decisions are being made about athletes' lives—and the athletes don't have a voice in the matter.

The other day, I was home in Murrieta on the phone— another conference call with my lawyers—when Amber said, "Hon, when are you going to be off?"

I rolled my eyes. "Eh, probably not for another four months," I said.

Deep down, I am a bicycle racer. I am supposed to be outside getting funny tan lines and pushing the limits of what the physical body can do. Never in my life did I want to be a person who wears a business suit or sits all day long in meetings. But this is who I have become—for now.

Sometimes I still pause from focusing on my case and wonder how a mess this big could possibly have gotten made. Everyone has a theory. My guess is that the lab made mistakes, and for some reason it pushed my test results through the system anyway. The UCI jumped on the supposed positive, blindly trusting the science and making a public announcement so quickly that there was no going back. Someone, somewhere must have noticed that my test results were completely bogus, but by then it was too late. They weren't going to say, "Oops, sorry, we accused the winner of the biggest cycling race in the world of being a doper, but never mind. We were wrong!" There was too much at stake by then.

Given the way the rules of the USADA judicial process are set up, someone must have figured that the agency could still win the case even though the scientific evidence didn't show that my test was a positive. It's not hard to figure out who would stand to benefit from such a decision: For USADA to have a positive test against me or any other high-profile professional athlete would give them leverage to go to Congress to ask for more money.

Or perhaps I'm giving people in the anti-doping agencies too much credit. Maybe no one noticed all the mistakes because no one bothered to look carefully, and once the lab called it a positive, everyone assumed that the rest of the process was mere formality.

We won't know USADA's evidence against me or its justifications for the flaws in my test until my hearing in May. We may never know the truth.

Regardless, the damage is done now—to everyone. As Arnie says, in this case there are no winners, only losers and bigger losers. The UCI, USADA, and WADA look bad. And no matter what happens in the future, my career has been derailed and my reputation tarnished.

My life will never again be what it was. Sometimes that brings me down. The situation just plain sucks, and it's been hard on me—and especially hard on my family, because they want more than anything to help me but feel powerless to do so. However, my frustration about this whole thing is outweighed by the opportunity to make sure this never happens to anyone else, and to make things better for cycling. Long after my case is settled, the Floyd Fairness Fund will continue to push for fair treatment of accused athletes.

And I will continue the fight, for everyone. I'm proud of myself for winning the 2006 Tour de France and proud of the way I did it. If something is worth fighting for, then I'm going to fight, no matter what. Give me a week of bad days like Stage 16—a month of them—and I will not give up. Once I put my mind to something, I see it through to the end, no matter how hard things get and no matter how long it takes. I am not going to quit, and I am not going away.

APPENDIX

What's Fair Is Clear: Debunking Floyd Landis's Allegedly Positive Doping Test

Prepared by Arnie Baker, MD[*]

We all depend upon laboratories. When medical or doping laboratories perform an analysis, they must be held to the highest standards. Whether the conclusion is high cholesterol, cancer, or doping, our health—and indeed our lives—may depend upon the correct diagnosis. In the case of Floyd Landis, the Laboratoire National de Dépistage du Dopage (LNDD) and World Anti-Doping Agency (WADA) have failed.

This presentation contains four key arguments for the dismissal of the allegation that Floyd Landis's urine sample constitutes a positive doping test. I have developed sixty such arguments in the hundreds of hours I have spent analyzing the

[*] Baker is a retired San Diego physician. While in active medical practice, Baker had more than a decade's experience in medical peer review and quality assurance. Baker has written about bicycling medicine for the public, the International Olympic Committee, and the medical community.

370-page document packet provided by the United States Anti-Doping Agency (USADA); these are a few of the most important and easily understood basic problems. By WADA's own rules, each of these four items on its own shows sufficient reason to dismiss the case. Taken together, and when considered along with the numerous additional flaws I've found, they are evidence of a system in dire need of improvement to ensure the fairness and accuracy of drug testing programs for all athletes.

1. Mislabeled Sample/Lab Errors

One of the most easily visible examples of lab error involves sample identification or labeling. Each sample identification number consists of two parts: a lab ID number and the athlete's sample ID number.

When Floyd gives a urine specimen, he urinates into a container and the contents are split into two sample bottles, an A sample and B sample, both of which have a bar code with his sample ID on them. Floyd's Stage 17 sample ID is 995474. In the page of the USADA packet that summarizes the testosterone and epitestosterone (T/E) results from the A sample, the athlete's identification number is 994474—off by one digit. The lab ID number on the page is incorrect as well. The correct lab ID number is 178/07, and the lab identification number listed is 478/07. Using the numbers given in the official evidence packet, there is no clear way to determine if the sample is even Floyd's urine. Off-by-one numbers are one of the most common types of medical errors—just as they are one of the most common reasons for misdialed telephone numbers.

Many of us who work in the healthcare field or with legal documents have it drilled into us: If you want to make a change to a document, you need make a single line through the error, write the new text and put your initials and the date. WADA's own rule states, "Any forensic corrections that need to be made to the comment should be done with a single line through and the change should be initialed and dated by the individual making the change. No white out [sic] or erasure that obliterates the original entry is acceptable."* Yet on a handwritten page summarizing the results of the A sample, the sample identification number has been overwritten, and it appears on the photocopy we received that Wite-Out has been used.

Another questionable sample number appears on the specimen transport record. Each sample collected during a stage of the Tour de France is included on a transport record sheet to account for who is in custody of the samples as they travel from the end of the stage to the lab. On the handwritten record, it appears that the sample number is listed as 99547$\underline{6}$. Again, the correct sample number for Floyd is 99547$\underline{4}$.

In yet another example of mislabeling, the summary sheet of the lab's record of abnormalities in three different samples (from three different riders tested) collected after Stage 17 identifies Floyd's sample with the handwritten number is 99547$\underline{5}$. Interestingly, this is a sample number associated with another athlete's urine that was analyzed in the lab at the same time.

* WADA Laboratory International Chain of Custody, TD2003LCOC, 2003.

The LNDD has clearly botched the routine process of tracking numbers. Everywhere in our lives, from FedEx and UPS packages to the checkout counter at any store, we encounter bar codes used successfully to track things. The process is not complicated. So the question arises: If a lab is so obviously sloppy with keeping track of a sample and/or its number, how can we have confidence that the lab can keep track of the many analytic steps required to accurately conduct a doping test?

2. Specimen Contaminated

WADA recognizes that contaminated or degraded specimens cannot be fairly examined and should be discarded. Degradation can result from many factors, including bacterial contamination, improper storage, biological or other chemical contaminants (such as blood), and adulteration. The WADA contamination rule is clear: "The concentration of free testosterone and/or epitestosterone in the specimen is not to exceed 5% of the respective glucuroconjugates."[*] Simply put, if contamination or degradation levels of either of the free (unbound) hormones testosterone or epitestosterone are greater than 5% of the total (bound to glucuroconjurates), then the sample is contaminated and should not be analyzed. Just like food with mold or maggots, it has deteriorated beyond use and should be thrown out. From levels clearly stated in the analysis of the B sample (for reasons unknown to us, there is no evidence in the document packet that the A sample was tested for contamination), here is the simple math:

[*] WADA Technical Document TD2004EAAS

	Epitestosterone	Reference Document
Free (Unbound)	0.44	USADA0283
Conjugates (Bound)	5.7	USADA0288
Concentration Ratio	7.7%	

According to WADA protocol, since the degraded epitestosterone level of 7.7% exceeds 5%, the specimen should never have been analyzed further. The process should have stopped here.

3. Unreliable Testing

No lab test is perfect. It's quite common to analyze a specimen several times and get a different measurement each time. This is similar to when you weigh yourself and then step off the scale and back on again —the weight may not be exactly the same each time. According to the LNDD's standards, the acceptable variance level of testosterone levels in repeated testing is within 20%, and for epitestosterone the acceptable level is within 30%.

	Testosterone	Epitestosterone	Reference Document
Analysis #1	61.37	5.2	USADA0092
Analysis #2	172.23	17.59	USADA0212
% error	181% error	238% error	

In the table above, results are shown from two separate analyses of the testosterone and epitestosterone levels of the A sample. Both analyses use the same urine sample and were performed by the same method, yet the results are substantially different. These gross variations cast doubt on the lab's ability to repeatedly and accurately test a sample for specific substances. Using the scale analogy, it would be as if I weighed myself once at 61 pounds and then weighed myself again at 172 pounds. By the lab's own standards, the percentage of error is far too high for the lab tests to be acceptable.

Similarly, there is extreme variation in the results when the sample was screened for the T/E ratio. When the sample was initially screened, the ratio was 4.9 to 1. When the sample was tested again to confirm the ratio, it was found to be 11.4 to 1. The lab rules state the ratio has to be within 30%; clearly it is not, because 4.9 differs from the average of these ratios by 60%.

In 2005, WADA lowered the legal limit for a T/E ratio from 6 to 1 down to 4 to 1. But a T/E screening ratio between 4 and 6 should not create the presumption of doping. In 2005, twenty-five out of thirty-three WADA-accredited labs reported their T/E ratio test results. A total of 955 T/E ratio tests results were between 4 and 6. Of those, just two tests were deemed doping positives when a carbon-isotope ratio test was performed for confirmation. By these findings, a T/E screening value between 4 and 6 could be interpreted as a 99.5+% proof of innocence. It is only when T/E ratios are above 15 that more tests than not are confirmed positive.

4. Carbon Isotope Ratio Test:
Positivity Criteria Not Met

The carbon isotope ratio test (CIR) for synthetic, or exogenous, testosterone has been played up in the media as the foolproof gold standard, so accurate that it simply cannot be challenged. But no test is infallible, and the CIR test does have problems—in this case, one problem is the interpretation of the results by the lab. In fact, according to published scientific studies and WADA's own protocols, the test wasn't even positive.

In the CIR test, four testosterone breakdown products, called metabolites, are examined. According to WADA's 2006 World Anti-Doping Code, the concentration of all four of these metabolites must exceed the range of normal for a test to be considered positive: "Where an anabolic androgenic steroid is capable of being produced endogenously, a Sample will be deemed to contain such Prohibited Substance where the concentration of such Prohibited Substance or its *metabolites* or markers . . . in the Athlete's Sample so deviates from the range of values normally found in humans that it is unlikely to be consistent with normal endogenous production" (italics added).

Considering WADA's criteria for an abnormal metabolite (3.0 units) and the lab's stated accuracy (±0.8), the isotope absolute values must be higher than 3.8 for the test to be considered positive by the lab's own standard. Here is the CIR analysis of the B sample, from USADA documents 0351-0352:

Metabolite	Isotope Absolute Values
Etiocholanolone - 11Ketoetio	2.02
Androsterone - 11Ketoetio	3.51
5ßAdiol - 5ßPdiol	2.65
5αAdiol - 5ßPdiol	6.39

Only one of the four breakdown products examined in the sample even arguably meets the criteria to determine a positive result (arguably, because there are many other contested technical issues with the accuracy of the test, which are not discussed here).

In order for the LNDD to have considered this a positive, we must assume that the lab interpreted WADA's rule to mean that the CIR test is positive if *any* of the metabolites are abnormal. However, we don't know for sure how the rule was interpreted because the lab has not supplied us with its standard operating procedures, and USADA has refused to provide the information.

However, if we look at the body of peer-reviewed scientific studies that have been published on the subject, every study clearly supports the idea that *all* metabolites must be abnormal in order to reliably determine the presence of synthetic testosterone. In eight separate studies—four of which come from the WADA-accredited lab at the University of California, Los Angeles, by far the largest anti-doping lab in the world—there is not a single example of a positive test with only one abnormal metabolite. Single metabolite abnormalities are uncommon, and such results raise suspicion for a lab error.

One troubling aspect of using inconsistent criteria to determine a positive test is that this is directly at odds with WADA's fundamental mission. As set forth in the WADA Code, the core document that provides the framework for anti-doping policies, rules, and regulations within sport organizations and among public authorities, the primary purposes of the World Anti-Doping Program are:

• To protect the Athletes' fundamental right to participate in doping-free sport and thus promote health, fairness, and equality for Athletes worldwide.

• To ensure harmonized, coordinated, and effective anti-doping programs at the international and national level with respect to detection, deterrence, and prevention of doping.

Although WADA is charged with the task of unifying labs, the CIR test–positivity criteria differ from lab to lab. The rules are not universal, which results in a failure on WADA's part to provide fairness and equality and ensure a harmonized program.

For example, Australia's WADA-accredited lab criteria were published in a 2004 scientific paper that clearly states that *all* of the values of the metabolites must exceed the limit for a sample to be called positive. Further, the Australian lab uses a positivity threshold of 4.0, instead of 3.0, in order to reduce the likelihood of a false-positive result. By Australia's lab criteria, Floyd's test is negative.

Similarly, the U.S. WADA-accredited lab at UCLA uses criteria that specify that *all* metabolites must be positive, and establishes positivity criteria higher than 3.0. By UCLA's lab criteria, Floyd's test is negative.

By WADA's 2006 published guidelines, Floyd's test is negative because only one of his metabolites is beyond the threshold, and the rule states "metabolites," plural. Clearly, practices vary widely from lab to lab. That the same results would be called a positive in one lab and negative in another is disquieting, and a failure of WADA to achieve its primary purposes.

Some sources have suggested that an abnormality over 3.0 (not taking into account a margin of error, which for the LNDD is ±0.8) in *any one* metabolite is sufficient to cause a positive test. However, such a standard is absurd. In the seminal carbon isotope study done at UCLA, the lab established its positivity criteria based on seventy-three control, or "normal," subjects. The control subjects were medical students whose natural body chemistry was measured—they were not using synthetic testosterone. The highest values among some of these medical students exceeded 3.0 for two metabolites (the highest value for 5αAdiol - 5ßPdiol was 3.72, and highest value for 5ßAdiol - 5ßPdiol was 3.17). In other words, if the LNDD assumes that *any* value over 3.0 constitutes a positive test, then it would have labeled some of these negative/normal medical students taking part in the study as dopers.

5. Other Considerations

Many other problems show substandard laboratory practices that at times appear to be more science fiction than science. The lab was using obsolete computer software that could have altered results. There were errors in analysis, such as the documentation of the reference solutions they used, incomplete processing, and the questionable identification of the substances they were monitoring.

The laboratory operated its carbon isotope machine incorrectly, as I learned after downloading the machine's operating manual from the Internet and finding that the lab's machine was out of range of the recommended calibration. Perhaps this was because, as the lab has since admitted, it had no operating manual.

Scientific misconduct was suggested when, for the parallel anti-doping investigation in France, the lab submitted documents stamped as "original" that differed from the document packet delivered by USADA. In the altered packet, original errors pointed out by Floyd's original Wiki defense had been corrected.

Conclusions

The official document packet provided by USADA is riddled with errors.

WADA's own rules specify that laboratories must be accountable and held to standards. Failure to maintain reliability and accuracy of tests and the reporting of results is grounds for revocation of WADA accreditation. According to the WADA International Standard for Laboratories, lab accreditation may be revoked "for any . . . cause that materially affects the ability of the Laboratory to ensure the full reliability and accuracy of drug tests and the accurate reporting of results." Furthermore, referring specifically to proficiency testing, "No false positive drug identification is acceptable for any drug . . ." By these rules, because the French lab has demonstrated unreliability and inaccuracy, WADA should sanction the LNDD instead of Floyd.

Drug testing is important. Floyd's case illustrates the need for improving the testing process to ensure fairness and accuracy of drug-testing programs. For my complete analysis of the flaws of Floyd's test, see my book *The Wiki Defense*, available at www.arniebakercycling.com. To learn how you can help make the anti-doping process more fair for athletes, visit www.FloydFairnessFund.org.

EPILOGUE

After nearly ten months and well over a million dollars spent, my arbitration hearing started at the Pepperdine University School of Law in Malibu, California, on May 14, 2007. It was open to the press and the public, as I had requested, and I couldn't wait for the world to see the system for what it is—biased against the athlete and bent on achieving a guilty verdict to make their system seem legitimate, no matter what it takes.

Just about everyone from my support crew attended the hearing. Behind my legal and advisory team of Maurice Suh, Howard Jacobs, and Paul Scott at the defense table was a row of chairs filled by Amber, my parents, Brent Kay, Michael Henson, Will Geoghegan, and Arnie Baker. Amber's brother Max, Ms. Rose, Allen Lim, RV, Denise from the Phonak team, and other longtime supporters were in the gallery when they could be, as were friends of my parents and Amber. This whole experience has been extremely traumatic for a lot of people in my life, and I appreciated beyond words everyone's presence.

Arbitration is a private dispute resolution process, and not a true court hearing, so the rules are a lot more flexible. Case in point: Because the testimony would be so scientifically technical, the arbitration panel appointed an "independent" expert to assist them in understanding the key issues, even though there's no rule in the guidelines that anticipates such a position. Their pick? Francesco Botrè, who seems like a nice enough guy, but who is the head of the WADA lab in Rome. It's against WADA's rules for any affiliate to go on the record as disagreeing with another WADA lab's results, so from the very beginning I was very concerned about his impartiality and the sway he would have over the arbitrators deciding my fate.

The prosecution went first. On USADA's list of potential witnesses were five heads of WADA labs, seventeen employees of the French lab, three-time Tour de France winner Greg LeMond, and some middling pro racer who testified how much doping helped his own cycling. But much of their testimony was for show.

The WADA directors obviously testified because they had to, not necessarily because they believed in USADA's case. When asked about the rule prohibiting WADA affiliates from testifying against WADA labs, Don Catlin, who recently retired as director of the UCLA lab, said, "It's very clear it is not permitted to testify against other labs." He said "no question doping was going on," but he admitted that my test wouldn't have been positive at UCLA. When asked about the poor quality of the French lab's work in cross-examination, Catlin said that when he reviewed the graphs, "I didn't look for the bad ones, I looked for the good ones." Christiane Ayotte of the WADA lab in Montreal, Canada, and Wilhelm Schänzer of the WADA lab in Cologne, Germany, also testified, saying the French lab's results were perfectly fine with them, though they all admitted that if they saw this standard of work in their own labs, they would have concerns about the quality.

The lab technicians who actually handled my sample also testified. They had erased data in some cases and performed manual manipulations, without documenting why they did what they did, explaining only that they were trained to perform the tests that way. It may shock some to know a few details about their experience and training. The technician who handled my A sample from Stage 17 was hired as a lab intern in 2003 and trained by the lab tech before her, with no machine operator's manual or software manual to refer to. She was promoted to supervisor after three years, and exclusively trained the technician who handled my Stage 17 B sample. At the time, that B sample technician had only been authorized to use the machine for five months, and she also admitted that she knew the urine sample belonged to me when she performed the analysis. So much for anonymous, unbiased testing.

The supposed smoking gun for USADA's case was that ultimately they were allowed to retest my B samples from seven other stages of the Tour (the A samples had all tested negative) before the hearing. Four of those samples, they claimed, showed traces of synthetic testosterone—based on tests performed by the same lab technicians on the same machines at the French lab. We had so much reason to call the lab's reliability into question that I had requested my samples to be retested at another WADA lab, but was flatly denied.

USADA's house-of-cards theory was that, even though

my A sample screenings were all negative, I had somehow been doping the entire Tour. It was a ridiculous idea, all the more so because my observers at this retesting, Paul Scott and Simon Davis, technical director of Mass Spec Solutions, a company that manufacturers the testing machines, watched most of the retesting (they were barred from observing all of it) and knew the retesting results were suspect.

A few days into the hearing, at a point when my team was confident that there was nothing damaging that USADA could throw my way, Will cracked. He had been angry about the pending testimony of Greg LeMond, who we believed was going to suggest that I admitted that I did it and asked him for advice, neither of which is true. We all had been angry about the way we anticipated LeMond would testify, and the way USADA seemed to want him to appear purely for the purpose of character assassination.

Here's the back story: When news of my test results broke last July, LeMond started speaking about me in the media, implying I was guilty and urging me to "step up and tell the truth." He had done this sort of thing on and off for years with Lance Armstrong. Whenever there was a supposed doping controversy involving an American champion, the media would ask LeMond about it, and he'd open his mouth to get his name in the paper.

After my B sample results were announced, LeMond spoke again urging me to "come clean." I called him that day, not for advice but to explain that I wasn't guilty and to ask him to please stop speaking publicly about me because clearly he didn't understand the facts. In response, he told me that keeping secrets can destroy a person and launched into a long, painful story of how he had been sexually abused as a child. I was floored by the twist in the conversation, and felt terrible for the guy. I can't imagine a more traumatic thing that could happen to a person. The problem was that months after the call, LeMond again spoke about me at a WADA meeting, again suggesting I was guilty and had sought his advice.

So at my hearing, on top of the stress of the past ten months, we now had to deal with the anticipated LeMond sensationalism. I prepared my team by telling them about my LeMond phone calls, including the abuse. The night before his testimony, a bunch of us were sitting in a banquet room in our hotel where we had dinner set up. People filed in, ate, and filed out. At one point, Will and I were alone at the table, him on the phone and me checking my BlackBerry, not paying attention until I heard him talking like he was making a prank phone call about LeMond's childhood abuse. It instantly caught my attention. Trash-talking LeMond generally is one thing, but making fun of his abuse was *not* okay with me.

Brent walked in to hear the end of Will's outburst, which lasted only a few seconds, and I asked, "What the hell are you doing?" as Will hung up. His phone rang. "Greg LeMond is calling me back," he said. "Should I answer it?" I didn't believe what I was hearing. Will had Greg LeMond on the line when he said those awful things. This was bad.

Will is one of my oldest friends, so I was utterly shocked

at the way he not only crossed the line but ran right over it and dove off a cliff. He realized what he had done and left the table. I went to my room and considered calling LeMond right then to apologize, but after our past I didn't trust him on a phone call. The only thing I knew right away was that Will needed to go. I went to his room and helped him pack his things.

The next day LeMond's testimony was like a bomb exploding. He made the claims we had anticipated, and then told the story of receiving Will's call and filing a police report afterward. When Howard tried to ask questions about the things Armstrong had supposedly told him in conversations (which Armstrong flatly denied), LeMond said, "I'm not going to answer anything about Lance Armstrong." LeMond's personal lawyer, who he had brought with him, said LeMond wouldn't answer those questions, though he would not provide a legal basis for cutting off the testimony about Armstrong. We were unable to do a full cross-examination, so the arbitrators quickly terminated LeMond's testimony and told him to leave the stand. We publicly fired Will, and he left the hearing for good.

LeMond's testimony made a mockery of the hearing, and nobody—USADA, LeMond, Will, me—came out of it looking good. I understand that some people's belief in my integrity was shaken by Will's awful action. It was a terrible, regrettable situation. But Will owned up to his mistake, apologized to LeMond and everyone else, and at Brent's suggestion immediately sought counseling to address his stress and anger issues. The way I was raised, when people sin but they're sorry and try to take every action in their power to make things right, they deserve forgiveness. Will is still my friend. I forgive him, and I hope LeMond forgives him and moves on with his life in peace. I also hope that people don't base their belief that I did or didn't cheat on a gut feeling, but rather on the scientific facts of my case.

For the rest of the hearing, my expert witnesses blasted the French lab's results. The initial T/E ratio testing is unreliable, they said, because there's nothing in the lab packet to show how the lab got the result it claims. They explained how the lab technicians performing the carbon-isotope test weren't necessarily even identifying the right substance to measure.

Then there was the testimony of Simon Davis, who had been working with Howard since the beginning of my case. He showed exactly how he had seen the machines being misused when he'd visited the lab to observe the retestings, and how those mistakes affected the results. In one instance, Davis had to help the lab technician load software onto the machine because she didn't know how to do it.

When it comes to the competence of the French lab in performing accurate carbon-isotope tests, Davis noticed something about the lab's newer machine, used to retest my B samples, that pretty much sums it up. Because the instrument is so heavy, it comes with large metal lifting rings attached—we called them Dumbo Ears—which need to be removed before the machine is used. When Davis saw the instrument at the Paris lab, he was astonished to find the Dumbo Ears still attached to the machine, years after delivery. These machines have two massive magnets that are highly sensitive and key to the accuracy of test results. Think of how an iron object placed near a compass distorts the magnet, inhibiting its ability to reliably point north. The Dumbo Ears could have a similar effect on this machine, Davis said. In other words, not only are my B sample retesting results suspect, but *every* test *ever* done on this unit may be unreliable, and no one at the lab ever noticed it before.

To complete the picture, Simon teed up a demonstration on an ancient carbon-isotope testing machine, identical to the one used to test my Stage 17 samples, complete with 1980s-era floppy disks, to show the bogus results you get when you perform the test the way the French lab technicians did.

To me, and to anyone who paid attention to the science in the hearing, there was no question. The French lab and USADA had no basis to say my urine sample was positive for anything. The sad thing is that, even after all the decisions and appeals are made in my case, if I am vindicated, the WADA/USADA system is still in place. It needs to change so that athletes get a fair shake, and I'm going to keep fighting until it does. This is not over yet.